CONTEMPORARY APPROACHES TO GEOGRAPHY VOLUME 2: PHYSICAL GEOGRAPHY

Series editor: Charles Rawding

Chris Kington Publishing

A catalogue record for this book is available from the British Library.

Written by:
Steve Suggitt

Edited by:
Giles Flitney

Design by:
Character Design
& Tom Kington

Printed in China by:
1010 Printing International Ltd

Published by Optimus Education: a division of Optimus Professional Publishing Limited
Registered office: 33-41 Dallington Street, London EC1V 0BB
Registered number: 05791519
Tel: 0845 450 6407 Fax: 0845 450 6410

www.optimuseducation.com

ISBN 978-1-899857-97-5

Foreword

Contemporary Approaches to Geography is a series of texts for geography teachers designed to introduce the latest ideas from geography in higher education to the secondary geography teacher, while at the same time demonstrating how these ideas can be used in the delivery of examination specifications for 14 to 18 year olds. In recent years there have been significant innovations in teaching the subject at Key Stage 3 as a freeing up of the National Curriculum has enabled teachers to introduce newer ideas into the subject. However, in many cases the introduction of new ideas has not continued into the examination years, largely as a result of constraints, real or imagined, relating to examination specifications. At a time when new examination specifications are being introduced across both GCSE and A Level, it seems timely to offer new approaches that can be effectively incorporated into the classroom ensuring the relevance and topicality of geography and cementing its place as a central component of the curriculum.

The structure of the books has been guided by the headings of the range of examination specifications available across England, Wales and Northern Ireland, and there is cross-reference to these specifications provided in an appendix (see p192). However, these texts have not been designed with a specific specification in mind. Indeed, the authors would argue that the growing tendency for senior examiners to write textbooks designed to 'deliver' their specification is a trend that could result in school geographies being artificially constrained within particular fixed frames of reference. This should be considered of particular concern given the rate at which the subject is changing. These texts argue that what is required is an ability to think geographically, which will enable students to understand and interpret changing geographies as they are encountered. In the context of physical geographies, perhaps it is timely to remind the reader that places should be seen as physical places as well, people move through places, but so do rocks, albeit at a rather slower rate. The entire planet – human, environmental and physical – needs to be viewed as a place in continual motion.

Within the texts, you will find significant elements of the personal geographies of the authors. In this text, for instance, the author has made extensive use of over 30 years fieldwork experience covering a wide range of different environments. Such an approach has been taken deliberately as it reinforces the importance of developing the personal geographies of students to enable them to think geographically. In similar vein, the extensive use of photographs within the texts reflects the beliefs of the authors that students must 'see' the real world in terms of its geographies in order to understand the relevance of the subject.

A central theme of the texts is that geographies (a deliberate plural) can only be understood in the context of modern society and by investigating the linkages between themes. Indeed, it might be argued that it is time to reconsider the prevailing thematic approach within school geography if we are to achieve effective synthesis and explanation. Each chapter attempts to make these linkages explicit by clearly signposting where connections with other chapters can be made; these cross-references have been made across all three books and it is intended that the three books be regarded as an integrated collection.

Embedded within the narrative, there is a range of suggested teaching activities, some of which have been further developed and have been provided in electronic format on the accompanying CD-Rom. Additional teaching resources, including a more extensive collection of photographs, have been provided on the CD-Rom and are signposted in the text. At the end of each chapter there are suggestions for possible website usage and a short selection of possible further reading. A full bibliography is provided at the end of the book.

Contents

Acknowledgements

The author is grateful to a large number of former Edge Hill University Geography PGCE trainees who have provided a range of inputs, particularly in terms of teaching ideas provided. He would especially like to thank Lucy Rushton, Briley Habib, Amy Laurence and Andrew Grant for the materials and advice that they have provided and Paul Weeden of Birmingham University for providing valuable material on flooding. In addition, a number of colleagues have provided much valued support: Graham Lymbery and Michelle Newton from Sefton Metropolitan Borough Council Coastal Defence team, Gerry Lucas and Charles Rawding from Edge Hill University and Sylvia Woodhead, now retired from Edge Hill.

Individual teaching ideas or resources have been acknowledged where appropriate within the text.

Many thanks for the encouragement and perseverance of my family.

Photography

All photographs are by Steve Suggitt unless otherwise indicated.

The author

Steve Suggitt is Physical Geography and Geology Programme Leader, Geological Science Pathway Coordinator and a Senior Lecturer at Edge Hill University. The focus of much of his research and experience is in the field of glacial and Holocene landforms and materials. He has a strong belief in the necessary role of fieldwork and practical study in the geosciences and is a firm believer in the need to view the natural environment as an holistic entity.

Introduction

Thinking geographically

This book is one in a series of three, designed to cover the principal aspects of geography as defined by examination specifications in England, Wales and Northern Ireland. The series has been divided according to recent practice into human, environmental and physical geographies (note: environmental geography is a relatively recent addition to what was previously a dualism within the subject). However, a key theme running through the books is that it is essential that students are assisted in making links between the different areas of geography. Quite simply, if they are to become good geographers, they must be able to synthesise information and draw conclusions across a range of topics – something which has not been aided by the modularisation of the education system. To assist the reader in identifying these links, margin notes under the heading 'Making the links' [☞] have been included, in order to suggest where there are links between chapters in the three books.

Stressing the need for effective synthesis raises the question: what exactly does 'thinking geographically' entail? A section on 'thinking geographically' from Doreen Massey (figure 1) demonstrates what it might mean to think geographically. It is an extremely good starting point for any discussion of what geography is, who geographers are and what purposes they serve in modern society.

Figure 1: Thinking geographically

See accompanying CD-Rom

Thinking geographically.doc

There is an argument – about climate change – that goes like this.

'...the UK's contribution to global emissions of greenhouse gas is only a small percentage.'

'...there's not much point in taking responsibility for our own place when India and China are growing as they are.'

Now I might have found that a comforting argument. But it seems it is a totally inadequate geography.

What that 'small percentage' counts is the greenhouse gas emissions from the United Kingdom directly. In that sense, it treats the UK as an isolated entity.

But it is not.

That calculation, it seems, misses out the effect of all the things we import from elsewhere (many of them, indeed, from China [☞]). We demand those goods, but we do not count as our own the pollution of producing them.

See Volume 1: Human Geography, ch 6, Industrial geographies (p128).

Nor does that 'small percentage' take into account the role of UK companies in production around the world. It has been estimated, for instance, that something like 15% of global carbon emissions derives from companies listed on the London Stock Exchange. Our economy is said to benefit from those companies. So what responsibilities do we, as UK citizens, have towards them?

> I could go on. The point is this. That 'small percentage' is meaningless in an interconnected world. We cannot pretend that because all that greenhouse gas emission doesn't happen here it doesn't happen because of us …that we are in no way implicated.
>
> But surely, might come the reply, we are improving? The UK is on course to meet its Kyoto target.
>
> Indeed it is. But why? Well, largely because:
> - we have allowed our manufacturing to collapse
> - we closed the mines and dashed for gas
> - we opted for an economy based on services and, especially, on finance.
>
> It is not so much that we are behaving better, as that:
> - we have exported our pollution
> - and we have reshaped the UK's role in the global economy.
>
> And that reshaping has also reshaped the geography of the UK itself, as:
> - manufacturing regions have declined
> - the north-south divide has widened
> - our economy revolves more and more around London's financial sector.
>
> Forget that comforting geography of small percentages. These are some of the other geographies that lie behind responsibilities for climate change.

Source: Professor Doreen Massey, *GA Magazine*, Spring 2008, p5.

Teaching idea 1

Present students with a copy of the extract in figure 1 and firstly ask them to highlight those sections they consider to be human/environmental/physical geography. Then ask them to produce a mind map showing the connections between the elements in the passage. How can this exercise help them to think geographically?

See Volume 1: Human Geography, ch 6, Industrial geographies.

See Volume 3: Environmental Geography, ch 1, Ecosystems (p20).

The series of books attempts to demonstrate these links. For instance, chapter 6 of *Volume 1: Human Geography* looks in detail at the development of industry in China; at one level this can be seen as a classic example of industrial development based initially on low-cost labour, government policies, foreign investment and so on. However, it can also be seen as an example of the interdependence of nations, since the UK has come to rely heavily on Chinese imports [☞], while at the same time China has been seen as a major culprit in terms of the emission of greenhouse gases and pollution more generally. However, it is demand from countries such as the UK that has resulted in the growth of Chinese industry, with smoke from Chinese factories and power stations entering the atmosphere, our atmosphere, everyone's atmosphere. The concept of an 'ecological footprint' [☞] can be usefully deployed here to illustrate the global inter-relations of environmental impacts and to reconnect the apparent dislocation between production and consumption.

What do physical geographies encompass?

The images of Earth sent back by the Apollo space missions (1961-1975) provided the context for viewing the Earth as an integrated whole, and a powerful visual stimulus for such an holistic approach. Physical geography has always been seen as an exploration of our world [☞], from the classical topographic descriptions of the Greeks and Romans updated by Arab/Islamic thinkers through to travel and exploration during the European Renaissance of discovery, conquest and colonisation. In the past, physical geographies have been viewed in terms of uniformitarianism (the present is the key to the past, slow change not catastrophism) and in terms of evolution (Darwin's legacy, Davisian cycles of erosion, denudation chronology). The discipline has gone through a quantitative revolution with a switch from description and somewhat taxonomic classification to the start of analysis and explanation. Scientific method has been introduced with the linking of theory to empirical measurement and experimentation and the contrasts between logical positivism (ordering observation and knowledge to produce hypothesis) and critical rationalism (derive hypothesis, try to disprove it, modify it, and retain a new probable hypothesis). The current view taken by this text is that of realism: the blending of general principles with local events, subscribing to the uniqueness of each individual setting in terms of physical and human inputs, and looking at the space or area involved, the timing of events, the thresholds involved in the changes in process intensity, and the frequency of the processes involved.

See accompanying CD-Rom

Thinking geographically.doc

Throughout the book we will be using examples from specific places and considering timescales, thresholds, and the uniqueness of locations. Concepts of how and what processes are operating at or near the Earth's surface, and how these fit into a hierarchy of scale, along with a consideration of their frequency of operation, provide us with the concept of magnitude and frequency of occurrence. When we consider the nature of the materials and landforms these processes are operating on, this introduces

PHOTOS: CHARLES RAWDING

Figure 2: Physical geographies

See accompanying CD-Rom

Thinking geographically.ppt

the concept of polycyclicity in landscape development. It is essential we consider the importance of past heritage and view the landscape as a continually evolving palimpsest within which we interact and live.

Teaching idea 2

Ask students to investigate their local area in terms of its geology and landforms to provide some background knowledge of where they live. Move on to include general climate and vegetation/land use and then get them to consider the uses people have put their physical environment to, both now and in the past. Have there been changes through time that can be seen? Where and in what direction might developments move in the future? Why? In terms of creating scenarios of desirable futures, what would your students wish to see happen?

The book has been structured to provide a range of independent but interlinked themes in physical geography. It does not aim to be comprehensive but to provide a series of relevant topics for you to consider. Chapter 1, Restless Earth, investigates the geological basis of our planet, geological materials, the rock cycle and plate tectonics and the major landforms that these processes and materials produce. Chapters 2 to 5 are thematic and look specifically at river, coast, desert and ice environments but attempt to highlight the main geomorphic principles inherent in any specific location. They focus on the main processes, materials and landforms of these environments while drawing out the importance of the principles of frequency, magnitude and polycyclicity in their evolution. Chapters 6, Geohazards, and 7, Globalisation, move to highlighting the interaction between the materials, landforms and especially processes in the physical world, and their effects on, and attempted control by, humans. This holistic conclusion seeks to emphasise the role of humans as an integral part of the global system.

One of the principal purposes of this book is to demonstrate how the latest thinking in higher education can, where appropriate, be incorporated into the geography classroom in the secondary school. This text does not deliver chunks of knowledge to be imparted to the class – indeed, it argues strongly against such an approach. As geographers, we need to move away from notions of fixed content and skills towards concepts and strategies for addressing complexity, difference and uncertainty and permanently shifting positions. This also involves challenging structured and ordered views of the world and moving towards more complex and multi-faceted perspectives. This book is an attempt to help people, both teachers and students, to think geographically, in order to apply that thinking to whatever situation they need to understand.

Restless Earth

1

Introduction

The Earth's surface, on which we live, is the result of millions of years of interactions between the solid Earth materials that make up the rocky part of our planet and the Earth's atmosphere and oceans. It is easy to realise and appreciate the dynamic nature of the atmosphere – the wind blowing and rain falling – and the dynamism of our oceans – the tides and waves – but we also need to appreciate the active nature of the Earth 's interior and surface crust. Without this activity, we wouldn't have the rocks, sediments and weathered materials that are acted on by surface processes, to carve the landscapes we inhabit, provide us with the physical resources for our everyday needs, and, at the same time, pose threats to us through the natural hazards that occur.

In this first chapter, we aim to investigate the geological model of the Earth, its interior layers, the plate motions of its crust and the geological materials that the 'solid' Earth is made of. We shall look at how these materials circulate through the Earth, as part of the rock cycle concept, which links internal processes to our changing surface landscapes through the means of plate tectonics. We will look at how these processes produce tectonic landscapes at various scales and how they bring about change in relative land and sea levels. We will also discuss the idea of the landscape being in a continuous state of change, with surface processes slowly modifying landforms and materials, while at other times thresholds in how a process operates are breached and higher magnitude, often catastrophic, changes take place. The polycyclic nature of the Earth's surface will be identified, along with the interactions of time, thresholds, climate, materials and surface processes. These processes together produce an ever changing kaleidoscope of natural environments, giving us the physical resources and natural hazards that are part of our daily lives.

We finish this chapter with a consideration of the heritage nature of the landforms and materials discussed. We look at the concept of geodiversity and how this is important to us today. We shall also examine our moral duty to future generations to conserve and pass on our natural heritage.

Earth model

Planet Earth has been in existence for close to 4,600,000,000 years (4,600Ma or 4.6Ba: Ma stands for 'millions of years' and Ba for 'billions of years'). This, our home planet, is the third planet out from the sun, a terrestrial or rocky planet in the inner solar system. The solar system itself is generally accepted as forming as a result of the accretion of a number of bodies from a spinning disc of gases, largely hydrogen and helium, plus a much smaller proportion of dust particles. All this resulted from an earlier supernova explosion of a star in this region of space. The planets have roughly 10% of the mass of the solar system and their rotation around the sun (the primitive solar nebula or PSN) prevented them from contracting into a single planetary object. These early proto-planets later gained further mass from impacts among themselves and with other solar system material. This process continues to the present day, meteorite by meteorite. Over time, the major planetary body we now call Earth gained enough mass and energy from these impacts (and from heat energy released by the decay of internal radioactive isotopes) to raise its temperature and become molten. At this time, differentiation by density of the elements and chemical compounds that made up this early Earth started to occur. Over time this has led to our current status as a differentiated or layered planet that can be modelled as a series of concentric shells based on differences in temperature, pressure and chemical composition (figure 1.1).

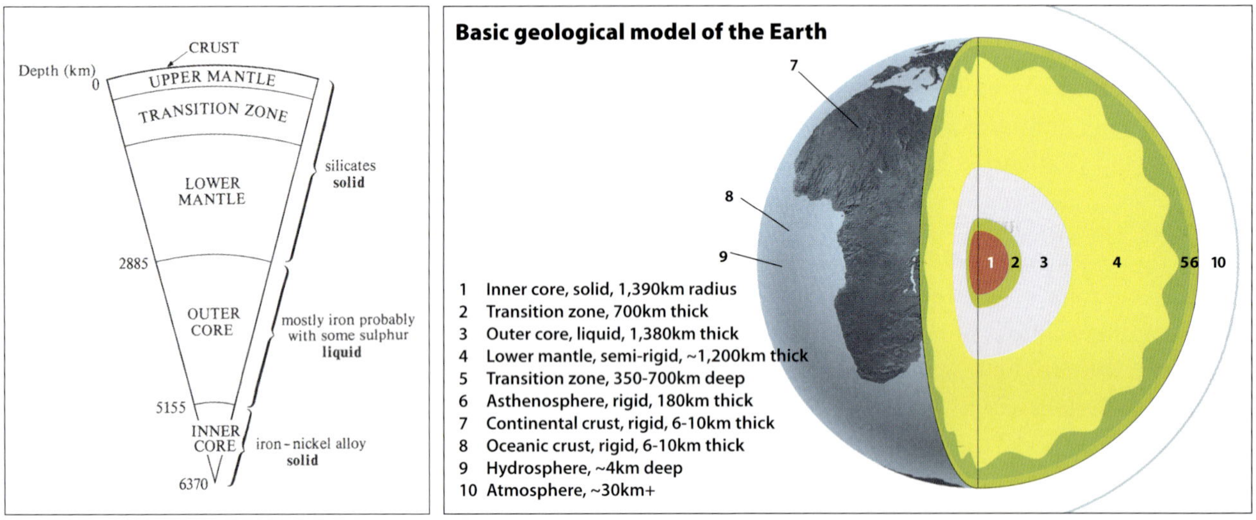

Sources: adapted from Brown and Mussett, 1981, and Holden, 2008.

Figure 1.1: Geological model of the Earth

See accompanying CD-Rom

Earth model.ppt

This model of the Earth has evolved from information provided by seismic waves (earthquake vibrations) that pass through the Earth's interior, and tell us about the physical nature of the internal materials. This is helped by study of the Earth's magnetic field, which is believed to be generated as a self-exciting dynamo within the Earth's interior, thus showing us the probable liquid physical nature and potential iron-rich chemistry of at least part of the Earth's outer core. Surprisingly, additional evidence comes from space. Over a million kilograms of meteorites still impact on the Earth each year. These extraterrestrial rocks are mainly from the asteroid belt between Mars and Jupiter, plus some debris from comets, and possibly from the Moon and Mars themselves. They are the remains of minor planets and smaller bodies of more primitive solar material. They show the nature of the primitive solar system before and during early planetary accretion and, importantly for us, since many come from the break-up of terrestrial minor planets, we can use them as proxies for material inside the Earth that we cannot physically access. Most meteorites are 'stony' ones composed of rock material called peridotite with a small proportion being 'iron' ones composed mainly of iron-nickel (see *Rock types and materials* on p26).

From the corroborative information gained from these three different sources, we now have a model of the Earth's interior in which we have some confidence. The Earth's core is composed of two layers: a solid inner core (from 6,371km to 5,154km) composed of iron with probably a little nickel; and an outer core (from 5,154km to 2,900km) which behaves as a liquid and is iron, with about 10% of oxygen and/or sulphur. Above this the mantle (2,900km to 7-80km), sometimes called the mesosphere, comprises several different sub-layers of rock material of essentially peridotite composition. The lower layers of the mantle are essentially hot and plastic in behaviour, with the upper layers being cooler and more rigid, the upper part being termed the asthenosphere (from the Greek for weak, *asthenia*). The outer part of the asthenosphere and the overlying crust are strong and rigid, and are together termed the lithosphere (from the Greek for rock, *lithos*). The crust comprises 7 to 8km-thick oceanic crust material, and up to 120km-thick continental crust material. The lower boundary of the crust is defined by a marked change in seismic wave velocity, called the Moho (Mohorovičić Discontinuity). Oceanic crust is generally denser than that of the continents, 3g cm^{-3} as opposed to 2.8 to 2.9g cm^{-3}. While this may seem a small difference, it is important in allowing the floating of the continental crust on the mantle. This is the principle of isostacy. The average density of the Earth is 5.52g cm^{-3}.

Thus, it appears that the interior of the Earth must comprise materials of a notably higher density than those we can access in the crust. Usefully, in a few locations, some of that material is brought to the surface, providing us with direct evidence of at least some of the Earth's interior. In some volcanic eruptions fragments of green peridotite can be carried to the surface from within the Earth. This peridotite (figure 1.2) appears similar to that from some meteorites and generally has a density around 3.3g cm^{-3}. The pressure as we move closer to the centre of the Earth rises dramatically, being over a million times that of the surface within the inner core. This suggests that at depth where the interior pressures are rising, the peridotite will become more compressed and alter to higher density versions, but such changes are not enough to account for the average density of the Earth, so there must be even denser material within the lower mantle and core. This provides a fourth independent piece of evidence to corroborate our model of the Earth.

Figure 1.2: Example of peridotite rock

See accompanying CD-Rom

Earth model.ppt

As we can see from the discussion above, the hot dense material that forms the Earth's mantle is the driver for forces that play a big part in the operation of our surface landscapes. These internal forces, brought about by temperature, pressure and material differences, have been operating since the planet became segregated into its current layers, and so it follows that the surface of the Earth has had many different forms prior to the present one. The current oceanic and continental crust and their disposition may be controlled by internal forces, but the surface sculpturing of them is also affected by external solar energy inputs, both directly, in terms of incoming solar radiation, and indirectly via our oceanic and atmospheric environmental systems.

Plate tectonics

The theory of plate tectonics provides an overarching umbrella for the areas of study relating to how the Earth operates. The development of this theory has revolutionised the geosciences, geology and physical geography, and made it possible to formulate links between hitherto unrelated observations of the Earth, such as the nature and location of earthquake zones, the location of volcanic activity, and why different types of eruption take place in different places. Tectonic theory also explains both why major mountain belts exist as long linear features, and the shape and location of oceans and continents.

Continental drift

The idea that the continents moved around on the surface of the globe has been widely known since the work of the German meteorologist Alfred Wegener in the early 20th century, though the jigsaw-like character of some continental outlines had been commented on since at least 1620, by people like the English philosopher Francis Bacon. In his hypothesis of 'continental drift', Wegener pictured the continents floating on the mantle much as ice floes drift on the oceans. He suggested that all the present continents had once been joined together as a 'supercontinent', which he named Pangaea, and that they had split apart and been drifting on the mantle since roughly 165 million years ago in the Jurassic Period. Wegener based his evidence for continental drift on the way current coastlines of continents on either side of the Atlantic Ocean fit together, an observation clear to see today in an atlas or on a globe. His other main pieces of evidence related to ancient climates and fossil distributions.

See Volume 3: Environmental Geography, chapter 2, Climate and weather.

Essentially, there are four main present-day global climate types [☞], those of hot deserts, tropical/subtropical regions, temperate environments and polar climates. Hot dry deserts are restricted to between 30°N and 30°S of the equator, hot and wet tropical regions between 20°N and 20°S and polar, snow and ice environments to latitudes between 60° to 90°N and 60° to 90°S. Temperate environments occur between 30° and 60°, either side of the equator. Each of these four climate types, and the latitudinal zones in which they are located, generate distinctive, often climate-sensitive, sedimentary rock deposits. A hot, arid desert like the present-day Sahara or the interior of Australia has abundant windblown sand which is occasionally affected by influxes of water from cloudbursts and flash floods that bring iron and other solutes into the area. Evaporation of these waters brings about precipitation of the dissolved iron on the surface of the sand grains, producing red-coloured sandstone, a characteristic of hot desert environments (see figure 1.3 on p9).

Figure 1.3: Isle of Barra beach sand and local Triassic red desert sandstone

See accompanying CD-Rom

Plate tectonics.ppt

By contrast, Amazonian swamps have a hot, wet environment with a high level of decaying vegetation that gets buried and turned into peat and, eventually, coal. At the other extreme, cold polar locations are the site of most of the world's glacier ice. These ice sheets produce distinctive glacial till deposits that will become tillite rocks. These rocks are distinguished by the wide variety of shapes and sizes of fragments, not to mention rock types, of which they are composed. Figure 1.4 shows examples of both coal and glacial till.

Figure 1.4: Examples of coal and glacial till

See accompanying CD-Rom

Plate tectonics.ppt

Moving the continents

Climate is clearly related to the latitude, while rock type can be related to the climate. Thus, the study of rock types changing over time can provide us with a geological record of climate change at a particular location. Similarly, a study of the location of rock types at a specific geological time can be used to show us where the climatic zones of that time were located. If we assume that the climatic zones of the past have mirrored their present global distribution, then any changes of rock type distribution from this standard latitudinal pattern must have involved those rocks being moved to their present position from where they were originally formed. The continents must therefore have moved.

If we were to look at the pattern shown by the rock types discussed above, for part of the Carboniferous Period, 320Ma (figure 1.5), we can readily see that our climate-sensitive rock types do not conform to the global climatic zones based on the present location of the continents. Coal deposits are mainly seen outside the current tropics in North America, Europe, Russia, China, North Africa and South America. Occurrences of glacial till deposits spread from Antarctica to South America, South Africa, Australia and even India, and from the South Pole northwards across the equator, including current tropical locations. Wegener's ideas of continental drift could readily account for this distribution. For example, by moving Europe and North America next to each other (closing the Atlantic Ocean), and moving them both southwards towards the equator, we can neatly position them within the 20°N and 20°S latitudinal belt. In this way, the coal deposits of the Carboniferous can be explained. In a similar manner, moving the southern tips of South America, South Africa and India together and pulling them southwards to fit against Antarctica in more or less its current position, and then pushing south-east Australia similarly southwards against Antarctica, results in all the 320Ma glacial till deposits fitting neatly together between 60° to 90°S. Moving the continents in this manner not only places all the climate-sensitive deposits of 320Ma in their 'right' climate zone but also brings most of the continents together to form Wegener's supercontinent Pangaea.

Figure 1.5: The Carboniferous disposition of the continents

See accompanying CD-Rom

Plate tectonics.ppt

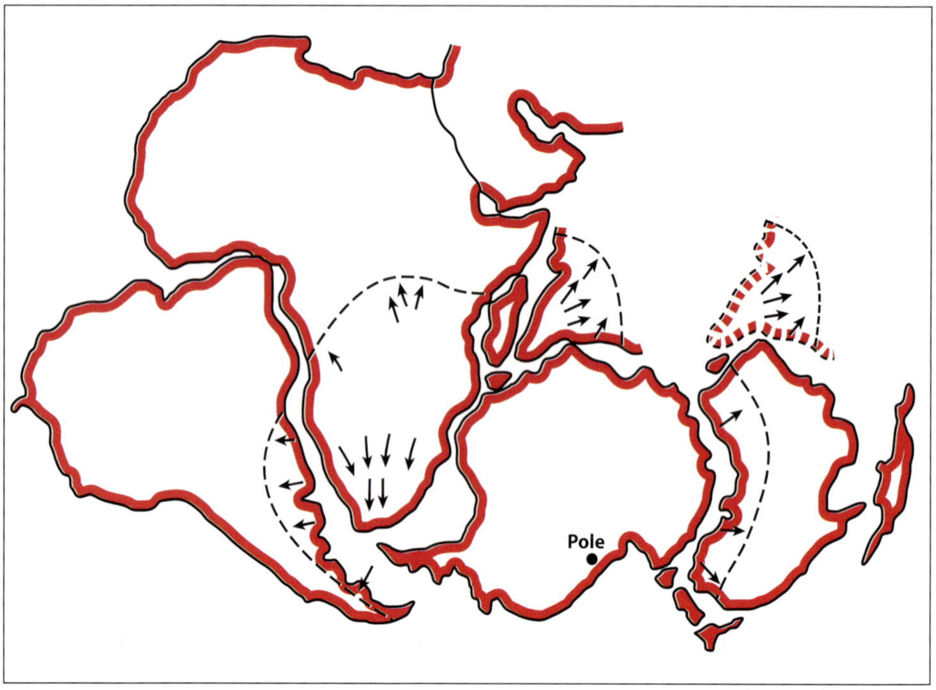

Source: Smith, 1972.

Note: a good set of reconstructions can be found through the Palaeomap Project at: *www.scotese.com*

Teaching idea 1.1

Provide your students with a map of the world and ask them to copy the outlines of the main continents to produce a set of jigsaw pieces. Get the students to move the pieces together to close and open major ocean basins like the Atlantic and the Indian oceans and to open up others like the Mediterranean. They could compare this to the maps from the Palaeomap Project website above.

Teaching idea 1.2

Ask students to map the movement of a chosen landmass from its origins to its current location in the British Isles (see figures 1.6, below, and 1.7, on p12). Such an activity could be used to fire geographical imaginations about the dynamism of the planet. For instance, Skiddaw in the Lake District (figure 1.7), started out in the southern hemisphere 500 million years ago, and only rose out of the sea 10 million years ago. For a more detailed discussion see *Landscape geodiversity* (p37).

Figure 1.6: Geological timescales

See accompanying CD-Rom

Geological timescales.doc and Plate tectonics.ppt

Million years ago	Period	Comment re British Isles
Less than 2.6	Quaternary	
2.6-23	Neogene	
23-65	Palaeogene	Britain and Ireland sit just south of their present position on the edge of the opening North Atlantic ocean.
65-145	Cretaceous	
145-200	Jurassic	Britain and Ireland occupy a tropical position and are below sea level.
200-251	Triassic	
251-299	Permian	Positioned just north of the equator, Britain and Ireland experience desert conditions, while to the south, Antarctica is covered by a vast ice cap.
299-359	Carboniferous	
359-416	Devonian	Britain and Ireland have collided and are located on the flank of a mountain chain on the edge of an arid continent.
416-444	Silurian	
444-488	Ordovician	The northern half of Britain and Ireland occupy a position south of the equator and are separated from the southern half by an ocean.
488-542	Cambrian	
More than 542	Pre-Cambrian	

Source: adapted from *www.bgs.ac.uk/education/climate_change/climate_through_time.html*
Note: A full version of the current geological timescale can be found on the IUGS website: *www.iugs.org*

Fossil evidence

In the cause of good science, it is essential to test our observations on the occurrence of continental drift with a different set of observations, this time using fossil evidence. If we look at the location of terrestrial organisms today, we can see that separate continents can have entirely different types of fauna and flora. Kangaroos (and most marsupials) are almost entirely restricted to Australia, the armadillo to North and South America. The reason for this is because most terrestrial organisms [☞] are restricted to living on the continents they evolved on because they cannot cross the large ocean distances involved in colonising elsewhere. However, if similar organisms occur buried as fossils in sedimentary rocks of the same age on what are now widely separated landmasses, then it is logical to infer that those landmasses were once joined together at a time when those organisms were alive. Fossil remains of a reptile, mesosaurus, have been found in rocks of about 260Ma in South Africa and Argentina. Mesosaurus was a small, brackish water reptile (about one metre long). It probably lived in lagoons, swamps or estuaries in a slightly salty water habitat and so is highly unlikely to have had the ability to cross the thousands of miles of the South Atlantic Ocean. Therefore, the South Atlantic did not exist when mesosaurus was alive.

MAKING THE LINKS

By way of contrast see: Volume 3: Environmental Geography, ch8, Globalisation (p196)

Britain and Ireland sit just south of their present position on the edge of the opening North Atlantic ocean.

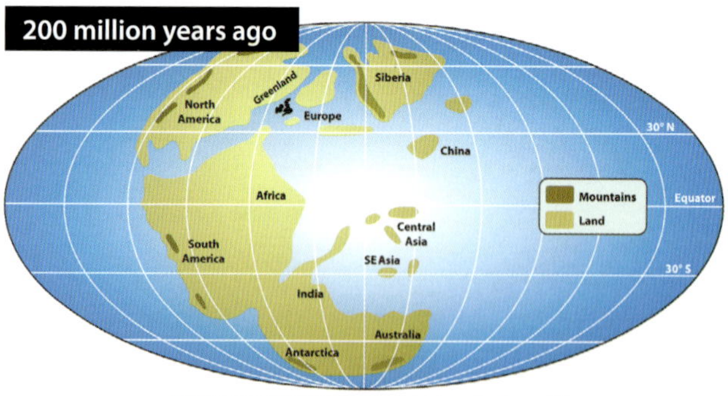

Britain and Ireland occupy a tropical position and are below sea level.

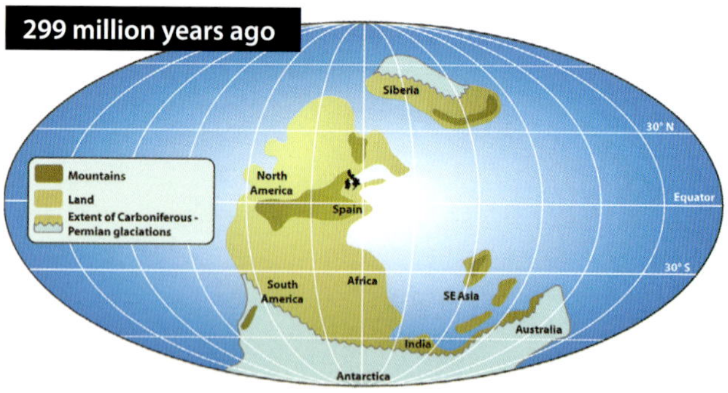

Positioned just north of the equator, Britain and Ireland experience desert conditions, while to the south, Antarctica is covered by a vast ice-cap.

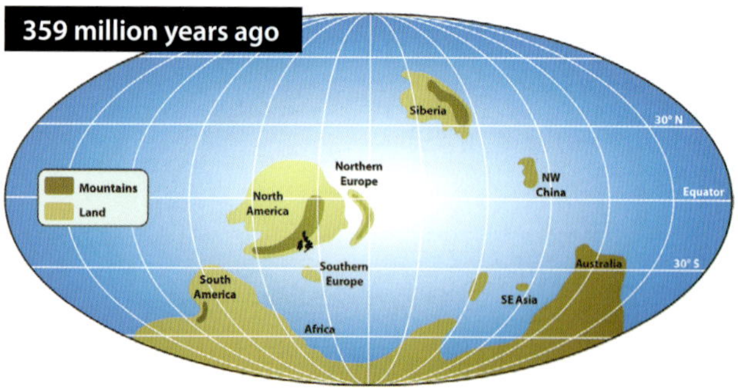

Britain and Ireland have collided and are located on the flank of a mountain chain on the edge of an arid continent.

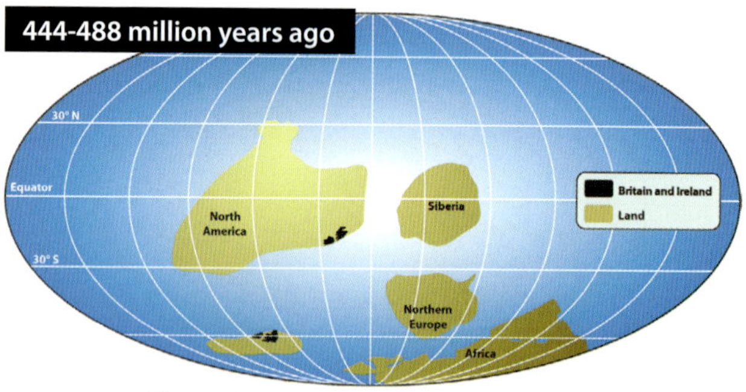

The northern half of Britain and Ireland occupy a position south of the equator and are separated from the southern half by an ocean.

Source: British Geological Survey.

Figure 1.7: Skiddaw

See accompanying CD-Rom

Changing locations of Britain. ppt

We now know that other examples of plants and animals show similar distributions that are impossible to explain unless we move certain continents back together again at different times in geological history.

Although Wegener proposed continental drift based on what we may now feel is rather compelling, almost 'common sense' evidence, his views were seen as radical at the time and, as he was not able to supply a suitable mechanism to have brought about continental drift, the idea tended to drop out of mainstream science. However, scientific developments in the late 1940s and 1950s resulted in more data becoming widely available: information from bathymetric maps on the topography of the ocean basins, and from magnetometers on anomalies in the Earth's magnetic field (as shown by magnetic minerals in rocks on the ocean floor). Many of these scientific breakthroughs were made by the United States for military purposes, as with the more effective mapping of ocean floors in the search for Soviet submarines. These enhanced sources of evidence from bathymetry and palaeomagnetism fed directly into a re-evaluation of Wegener's continental drift hypothesis and, fairly quickly, led to the setting up of the concept of sea floor spreading and then the theory of plate tectonics.

Sea floor spreading

From the construction of bathymetric maps of the deep ocean basins, we can see the presence of a large, almost continuous line of submarine mountains in a central position along many of these basins, as with the mid-ocean ridge along the centre of the Southern Ocean (figure 1.8).

Source: after Heezen and Tharp, 1977. Note: see the USGS (United States Geological Survey) website, This Dynamic Planet section: *http://pubs.usgs.gov/gip/dynamic/dynamic.html*

Figure 1.8: Mid-ocean ridge, Southern Ocean

See accompanying CD-Rom

Plate tectonics.ppt

These submarine mountains have a central rift valley suggesting a mechanism of uplift to produce the mountains, and of tension pulling them apart to form the large rift valley features. Also, it has been found that the deepest parts of the ocean floors are again largely linear features, ocean trenches, which are always located at the edges of ocean basins. At the time of their discovery, no existing theories either predicted or explained such observations.

In the 1960s, Harry Hess of Princeton University suggested that hot currents of molten material made by the Earth's own internal radioactive minerals produced convection cells within the mantle. These convection cells are rather like a pan of boiling milk with upward moving arms, which reach the rigid lithosphere, where they move across its base and start to cool, thus becoming denser and sinking back into the mantle. Where the ascending limb of hot mantle material forces its way through the crust, it produces submarine volcanoes along a mountain range pushed up by the rising hot mantle magma. These volcanoes produce lava which cools and solidifies along the central rift, which has been caused by the same upward force of the magma stretching and thinning the crust until it breaks. This action is aided by the convection cell moving across the base of the lithosphere, causing frictional drag and tension as it forces the crust apart, in opposite directions, between two adjacent convection cells. As the size of the Earth is constant, then we need to be able to remove crust at the same rate at which it is being created at these mid-ocean ridges. The deep ocean trenches, such as those bordering the Pacific, suggest themselves as locations where the convection cells, with cold ocean crust now on their upper surface, move back into the mantle.

Most of the magma and lava that solidifies to make the ocean floor at these mid-ocean ridges contains some minerals of magnetite (Fe_3O_4, an iron oxide), which form as the molten rock cools from temperatures above 1,000°C. As the rock cools below the Curie point, 600°C, the minerals of magnetite, usually very small crystals, become aligned along the direction of the Earth's magnetic field, and so permanently record the direction of this field in the rocks. Once frozen in the rock, any changes in the Earth's magnetic field cannot affect these minerals or the magnetic information they hold. Such information shows that the Earth's magnetic field periodically reverses so that a compass needle pointing north today would point to the south, a period of reversed magnetism. These reversals take somewhere in the region of 20,000 years to occur, a fairly rapid span in geological terms, and they have occurred for at least the last 75Ma, and probably much further into the Pre-Cambrian (see figure 1.6 on p11) beyond 600Ma. When magnetometers were being passed across the sea floor, the generally random swirling pattern of this palaeomagnetic reversal pattern seen on land was replaced surprisingly by a clear and definite pattern of parallel stripes. This was first shown in a map produced from data off the western coast of California in 1961. Vine and Matthews (1963) suggested that these magnetic stripe anomalies show a representation of magnetic reversals fixed into the sea floor, as molten rock solidifies along the linear mid-ocean ridge. If this 'construction' of new oceanic sea floor is taking place, then the patterns shown by these magnetic stripes should be symmetrical. A mirror image should be seen either side of a mid-ocean ridge. Data from the Juan de Fuca ridge off the coast of Alaska was first used to show this to be the case in 1965 by Vine and Wilson.

Vine and Matthews were also able to use the magnetic stripe data and radiometric dating of the source rocks of this data to calculate movement rates and directions for sea floor spreading. Most spread rates vary from between 1 to 10cm yr^{-1}. These calculations are now confirmed, and have been overtaken by direct measurements using accurate laser positioning from orbiting satellites.

Earthquake zones provide a third line of evidence for sea floor spreading. Since the setting up of a global seismic network (to monitor underground nuclear testing), geophysicists have acquired a lot of detailed information about the epicentres (point on Earth's surface directly above the location of the earthquake) of earthquakes, their foci (specific location of movement zone within the Earth's crust) and their direction of movement. Maps of these distributions show that most of the earthquakes around the world are confined to a limited number of narrow belts. Looking at the position and depth of the earthquakes (epicentre), and the movement directions of the rocks involved, Isacks et al (1968) showed that there were a limited number of rigid crustal plates, continually moving next to each other along these major earthquake zones. McKenzie and Parker (1967) placed this information into a global geometrical model, and so the theory of plate tectonics originated.

If you look at the location of volcanic zones around the globe then it is easy to see that they mirror the information from earthquake zones, suggesting that geophysical activity is concentrated along relatively narrow linear belts, and so independently supporting the developing theory of plate tectonics (figure 1.9)[☞]. In support of a theory of sea floor spreading, the global ocean drilling programme (ODP), designed to improve our knowledge about the ocean basins, shows that the sediments deposited on the ocean floor are nowhere older than 200Ma. A definite age structure is shown from mid-ocean ridge to edge of continents, from young to old respectively. This observation clearly provides evidence for the recycling of ocean crust as the topmost part of convection cells (figure 1.10). The crust is being created at mid-ocean ridges, transferred across the ocean basins as ocean crust, picking up increasing sediment cover with time as it moves, and finally passes down (is subducted) back into the mantle

MAKING THE LINKS
See ch 6, Geohazards, figure 6.5.

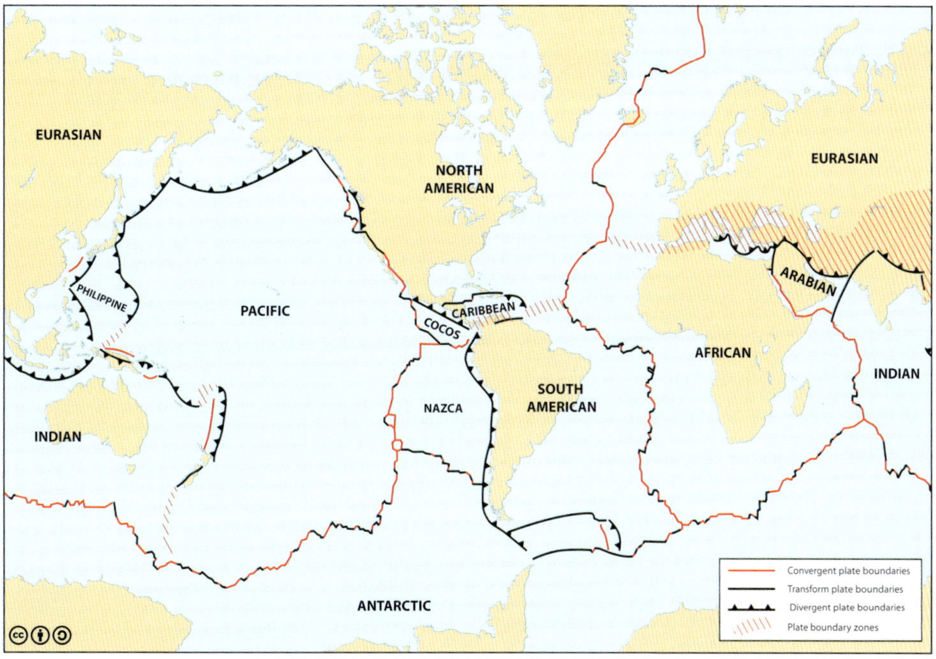

For an electronic version see: the USGS (United States Geological Survey) website, This Dynamic Planet section: *http://pubs-usgs.gov/publications/text/dynamic.html*

Figure 1.9: The main plate boundaries

See accompanying CD-Rom

Plate tectonics.ppt

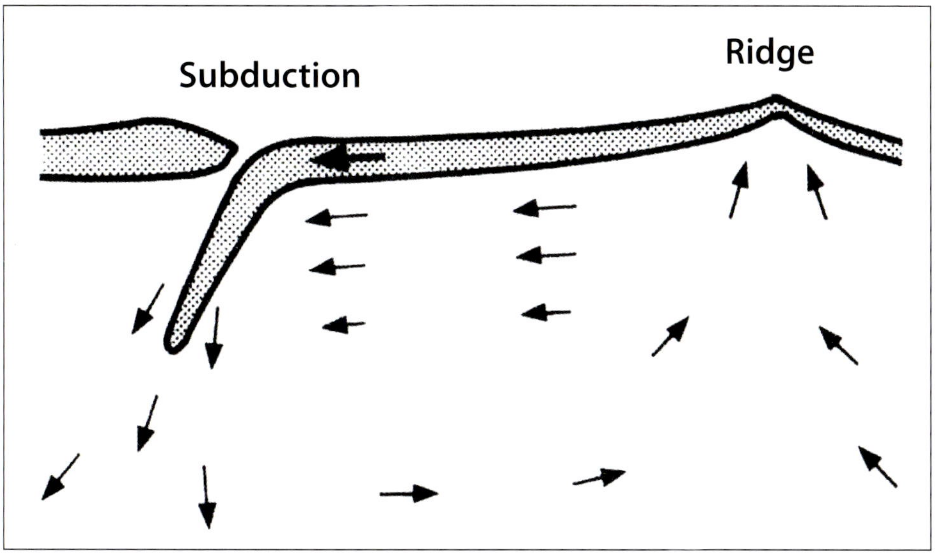

Figure 1.10: Convection cell style

See accompanying CD-Rom

Plate tectonics.ppt

where it melts at deep ocean trenches. As the ocean floor is very young compared to the continents (maximum age c. 3,900Ma), this can be used independently to reinforce the theory of plate tectonics. If the continental crust has existed for a much longer time period than the ocean crust, which is continually being created, forming widening ocean basins (Atlantic) which eventually shrink in size as they are destroyed in ocean trenches (Pacific), then the continental crust must be moved around the surface of the globe to accommodate this ocean basin creation and destruction, either as one piece (Pangaea) or as many (the Americas, Eurasia, Africa, Australia and Antarctica today).

The theory of plate tectonics

All the initial evidence that was put forward to develop the theory of plate tectonics, and the independent lines of evidence that support this theory, have literally caused a revolution in the geosciences. This has led to many re-evaluations, new ideas and greater explanation and understanding in other disciplines. One of the most obvious of these developments is in the explanation for the location and nature of the major mountain belts around the world. We shall visit this later on in this chapter, but for now we need to continue our journey into understanding what our planet is made up of, and how it functions.

Plate tectonic theory states, in its simplest form, that the lithosphere of the Earth is composed of a series of rigid plates that rest, essentially floating, on top of the denser mantle (see figure 1.9 on p15). These plates consist of oceanic and continental crust together and are bounded by the major ocean ridge and ocean trench systems, and the main linear earthquake and volcanic belt sites, such as the Mid-Atlantic Ridge and the Pacific Ring of Fire. Also, they are sometimes bounded purely by major crustal fault sites – transform faults such as much of the boundary between the small Scotia Plate and the Antarctic and South American Plates. There are seven major plates: Eurasian, African, Antarctic, Australian, Pacific, North American and South American, along with 20 or more small minor plates (sometimes called mini-plates or platelets). These include the Arabian, Philippine, Nazca, Cocos, Caribbean and Scotia, along with several even smaller ones in South-east Asia and the Mediterranean. The Anatolian Plate in the Mediterranean is an example of a smaller platelet.

At a plate boundary the relative motion of the two plates is determined by the nature of the geological processes in operation, and this, in turn, helps to determine the geological features found there (see figure 1.11 on p17). Divergent boundaries, or constructive plate boundaries, are sites where new lithosphere is being created from upwelling molten mantle material as it cools and solidifies. These are the mid-ocean ridges which, though they may start life in a mid-ocean position, such as the Mid-Atlantic Ridge in the middle of the Atlantic Ocean, or the Carlsberg Ridge in the Indian Ocean, rarely end their life in the same place. The best example is currently the East Pacific Rise off the coast of South America, and its extension northwards under the North American Plate in the region of Baja, Southern California. Staying in the same part of the world, the San Andreas Fault is probably the best known example of a transform fault boundary where plate boundaries slide past each other, neither creating nor destroying oceanic lithosphere, but producing many earthquakes (see figure 1.9 on p15).

The third type of plate boundary, a convergent or destructive plate boundary, is where plates are pushing towards or against each other. Where purely oceanic lithosphere is involved, the plate with the faster motion generally overrides the slower moving plate, which is forced down into the mantle where the rock is subducted. As it descends, the rock heats up by a combination of friction and conduction, and begins to melt, with magma being produced which rises to create a line of island arc volcanoes, so called because they form an arcuate shape across the surface of the globe. The islands of Japan are an excellent example of this situation.

Alternatively, the oceanic lithosphere may be pushing against continental lithosphere. Here the density differences and relative thicknesses of the crustal materials come into play. The denser oceanic plate material is subducted again, forming a trench, but with the molten magma produced rising into the overlying continental crust, partly melting this crust and so changing the chemical composition of the magma. The eruption of this magma as lava at the surface produces volcanic mountains. The best examples are between the Nazca and South American Plates, forming the Andes Mountains, and between the Pacific and North American Plates, producing the Rocky Mountains and the Cascades Range.

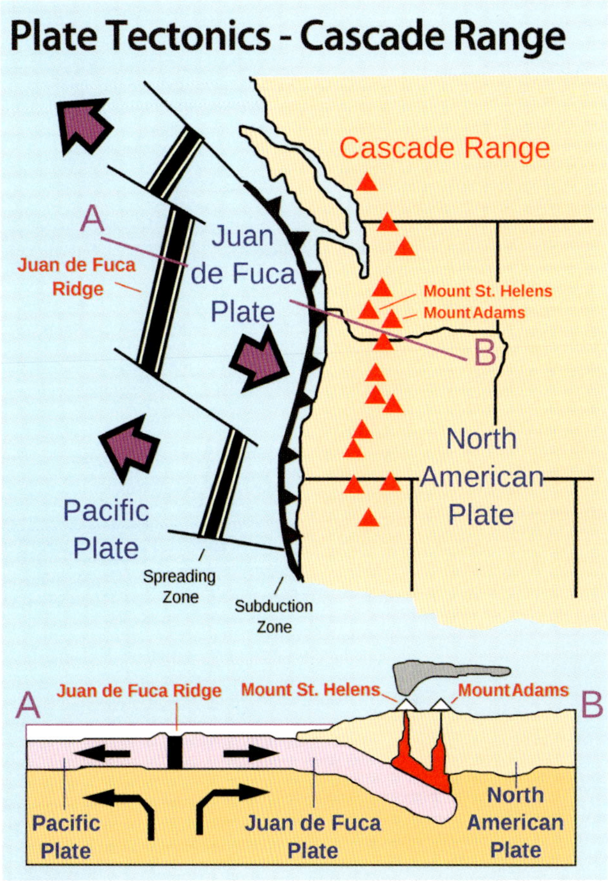

Figure 1.11: Nature of the plate boundary between the Pacific and North American Plates

See accompanying CD-Rom

Plate tectonics.ppt

As stated above, the forces that cause the initial origin and motion of the plates are mantle convection cells, which transfer heat, and therefore energy, from the Earth's interior to its surface. The exact layout of these convection cells is still a matter of scientific investigation and debate. Currently, it is thought that 'whole mantle' convection cells are the initial driving force for lithospheric plates, but that their igneous nature, in terms of producing new oceanic lithosphere, is aided by magma that is produced as a result of the action of more isolated mantle plumes, or hot spots, whose source is located deep within the Earth near to the core-mantle boundary. The volcanic nature shown by the Galapagos Islands in the eastern Pacific is a good example of convection cell volcanicity associated with ocean ridge activity, whereas mantle plumes are equally well described by the activity over the Hawaii hot spot in the centre of the Pacific Plate. Though mantle convection is the initial driving force for plate motions, pushing the plates apart and dragging their lower boundaries along, when we consider the nature of subduction zones, we can clearly see that there is also a role to play for the descending, cool oceanic crust. At this location, furthest from the construction site at the mid-ocean ridge, and now laden with cold ocean floor sediments, the descending oceanic crust starts to act as a drag on the rest of the plate pulling it down into the mantle. This is often termed the 'sinker' effect. We thus have two main groups of forces bringing about the motions of the surface plates and these in turn help us to understand the location of the major surface features of our planet, and how they are formed.

Tectonic and structural landscapes

In this section we are going to look at the major structural landforms of the Earth and show how they can be understood when linked to ideas based on plate tectonic theory. As such, this section will link major plate tectonic processes to their boundary types.

Teaching idea 1.3

Ask students to use relief maps in atlases to investigate the global topography at the main plate boundaries. Can they find similarities and differences between the major landforms at different boundaries? Can they locate hot spot volcanoes within the plates?

Divergent boundary features

There are two plate tectonic settings involved with divergent boundaries: mid-ocean ridges and land-based rift zones. At mid-ocean ridges, magma pushes up the sea floor and produces linear volcanic mountain chains. Here, the rate of spreading can be directly related to the nature of the chain. For example, the faster spreading East Pacific Rise has a spread rate of 16.5cm per year and produces a broad, relatively low, mountain range, whereas the slower spreading Carlsberg Ridge has produced a narrower but steeper mountain zone with a spread rate of 1.7cm yr^{-1}. All ridges have a central rift valley or graben which is the site of the sporadic outpourings of lava, normally by means of a fissure-style eruption. The volcanoes producing these eruptions have the form of long fractures aligned parallel along the central graben, and produce large volumes of liquid basalt lava. These lavas do not flow as far as on land because the cold ocean waters chill the surfaces of the lava flows, producing a crust that covers the lava as it billows out, before the lava breaks through a fracture and produces another lobe (see figure 1.12 on p19). These are pillow lavas and they promote somewhat steeper topographic forms. Examples of these can be seen from the geological record within the British Isles also, showing that this type of activity has taken place here in the geological past – for example, in Pembroke, South Wales.

As these lavas chill rapidly, they shrink, producing a network of veins along which hydrothermal fluids move, issuing onto the sea floor to produce chimney-like features termed 'black smokers'. Over time, the newly formed crust at this hot, active central ridge moves away, cools, sinks and gets buried by ocean sediments to produce a more featureless plain. On land, rift zones occur where upwelling magma causes the continental crust to thin and stretch, leading to parallel fault development and a rift valley or graben forming. The East African Rift Valley is an excellent example of this type of structure, with a deep central rift containing hot spring activity, and adjacent uplifted mountain blocks showing the upward pressure from the magma below. The adjacent Red Sea has gone a stage further; with basaltic lavas and blocks of faulted continental crust lining the central rift, the subsidence is now so great that the Indian Ocean has flooded in. If these processes continue, then a new mid-ocean ridge will form here, the early stages of which will see lava flowing over land surfaces producing fluid lava rivers and lakes, as well as increasing flows from fissures. Such a development would be similar to the current development of Iceland.

SOURCE: COURTESY OF USGS

Figure 1.12: Pillow lavas erupting off the coast of Hawaii and at Strumble Head, Pembroke

See accompanying CD-Rom

Tectonic and structural.ppt

Convergent boundary features

Here again there are two main types of boundary: those with subduction of oceanic crust and those where continent is pushing against continent. Oceanic crust can be subducted either where two oceanic crust plates meet, or where oceanic crust is pushing against continental crust. In the first case, such as in the formation of the Indonesian island arc, the Pacific Plate is being subducted beneath the Philippines Plate (both oceanic crust at this point). As the Pacific Plate descends, the ocean floor is pulled down along the subduction zone and a deep ocean trench forms, the Mariana Trench. This forms the site of extensive earthquake activity (tsunami hazard) and of basalt to andesite volcanic activity. This volcanic activity forms the Indonesian island arc chain, the site of many of the world's major natural disasters. To the north of here, there is a similar situation where the oceanic crust of the Pacific Plate is descending (the northern Mariana-Kuril Trench) beneath the edge of the continental crust of the Eurasian Plate. In this location, some of the ocean floor sediments are scraped off the descending plate and added as the metamorphosed sediments (termed an 'accretionary wedge') to the Eurasian Plate. The rest of the sediment and the basaltic ocean crust descend. The water and other volatile elements within the rock pile cause the basalt to melt at a relatively low temperature. Once molten, the basalt starts to rise and begins to melt the overlying continental crust, producing a thicker, more andesitic magma. This magma is much less fluid than basalt, and so cools closer to the vent, to build up a relatively steep volcano where the andesite lavas are often interspersed with volcanic rock and ash fragments (pyroclastics) from phases of more explosive activity where the vent becomes blocked with congealed lava allowing gas and magma pressure to build up. Mount Fujiyama, Japan, is an excellent example of such a steep-sided andesitic volcano. With continued activity the magmas produced may turn even more rhyolitic and stickier with dissolved gases and water leading to more explosive activity. The production of extremely hot, incandescent clouds of lava droplets flowing from volcanoes across the Earth's surface as ignimbrites are a particular problem associated with such a high degree of explosive activity.

Teaching idea 1.4

Ask students to do a web search for the rock type ignimbrite (see figure 1.18 on p27). What type of volcanic activity is this associated with and what hazards might it pose for people? The USGS or BGS websites are useful starting points:

- United States Geological Survey: *www.usgs.gov*
- British Geological Survey: *www.bgs.ac.uk*

Owing to the location of these subduction zone volcanoes in the sea, a particular problem is caused where the amount of material ejected in a particularly violent eruption is very high. As the magma chamber empties, the crater may partially collapse and seawater gains access, causing an even greater explosion leaving a large caldera as the remains. Santorini in Greece (1628BC) (which effectively ended the Minoan civilisation) and Krakatoa in Indonesia (1883) are both good examples of this process.

Teaching idea 1.5

Ask students to investigate historic eruptions such as Santorini or Krakatoa. What were their main effects? Ask them to use an atlas to locate these and identify patterns of habitation in their vicinity today. Do they think people may be more at risk today or not?

Useful website reference: *http://en.wikipedia.org/wiki/Minoan_eruption* and *http://en.wikipedia.org/wiki/Krakatoa*

Where two continental plates collide, we have a situation where both are composed of crust, which is less dense than the mantle. The plates are therefore both buoyant on the mantle, and neither can be pushed under the other. As the plates squeeze together, the rocks are folded, faulted and highly deformed (see *Metamorphic rocks* on p28). The crustal pile becomes thicker, causing mountains to be uplifted with a corresponding deep root pushing into the mantle below, in order to maintain isostatic equilibrium (see *Earth model* on p5). This process produces linear mountain belts, such as the Alps where Italy has been pushed north to collide with the Eurasian Plate, and, on an even more impressive scale, the Himalayas where the Indian subcontinent has similarly collided with the Eurasian Plate. The Himalayan Mountains first started to form some 45Ma ago, and are still being pushed up by the continuing northward movement of India. Some of the world's more impressive landforms last for a very long time.

Hot spot features

A 'hot spot' is a parcel of magma that has risen from near the core-mantle boundary upwards through the mantle, and has literally burned a hole through the Earth's crustal plate resulting in the formation of a volcano. More than 40 of these features have been identified to date. Hot spots can be located either with divergent plate boundaries, such as Iceland on the Mid-Atlantic Ridge, or separated from other plate tectonic processes lying within the plates themselves. Sites may be either oceanic crust, for example the Hawaiian chain in the Pacific Plate, or continental crust, for example Yellowstone National Park in the North American Plate. The next section considers the different landforms produced in each setting.

Iceland is part of an ocean-spreading centre and so plates diverge away from it. The island itself can be regarded as being stationary in terms of the movements of plates across the Earth's surface. This being the case, then the large volumes of magma and lava produced can build significant volcanic islands centred on the same geographical surface location. The result here is the island of Iceland. The whole of Iceland is made up of igneous rocks, and indicates the volumes of material that can be produced over time.

If we move on to consider Hawaii, then a view of an atlas will show us a chain of islands over 500km long, rather than a single large one such as Iceland. The reason for the different appearance relates to the movement of the Pacific Plate across the globe. If we look at the age of the volcanic rocks on each of the islands in the Hawaiian chain, they show clear movement of the Pacific Plate across a hot spot. The most western island of Kauai is the oldest, and is now extinct, as are the next in line, Oahu, Molokai and Maui (figure 1.13), while Hawaii is still active. Current activity is centred on the Mauna Loa volcano shown in figure 1.14 on p22.

PHOTO: GERRY LUCAS

Figure 1.13: Volcanic activity on Maui, Hawaii

See accompanying CD-Rom

Tectonic and structural.ppt

Figure 1.14:
View of Mauna Loa on the island of Hawaii

See accompanying CD-Rom

Tectonic and structural.ppt

PHOTO: GERRY LUCAS

Since1996, there is evidence of a new island (Loihi) forming some 30km to the south-east of Hawaii on the Pacific ocean floor, showing the next phase of activity above the hot spot site. All the islands in the Hawaiian chain are large shield volcanoes producing lava lakes and rivers of basalt. They are among the largest mountains on the planet when taken from the floor of the Pacific Ocean to the top of their volcanic cones. Our third example, Yellowstone National Park (figure 1.15), is a huge caldera within which sits the entire national park.

Figure 1.15:
Hot spring activity, Yellowstone

See accompanying CD-Rom

Tectonic and structural.ppt

PHOTO: RG JOHNSSON

Although not producing lava at present, the geysers and mud volcanoes of Yellowstone provide clear evidence of continuing hydrothermal activity. This type of activity, plus that of the minor earthquakes that are often felt in the region, are clear evidence of the presence of hot, subterranean magma here and hence possible eruptive behaviour in the future. Indeed, it is now thought that Yellowstone National Park is the site of a supervolcano. An eruption 600,000 years ago resulted in a layer of ash 12m thick being deposited up to 1,200km downwind of the present national park. A major eruption today, which is a possibility, would generate a significant environmental disaster.

Regional and local structural landscapes

Having considered major landforms linked to plate boundaries, it is important not to lose sight of the importance that smaller-scale tectonic events can have on landform development. A look at a simple, structural map of the British Isles enables straightforward identification of major fault controls on our landscape. Both the Highland Boundary Fault and the Great Glen Fault have been enhanced by glacial erosion to create features such as Loch Ness. Both of these faults have produced major structural landforms at a regional scale, and both are the result of past plate tectonic processes. The folding of the crust that produced the Downs of south-east England is the result of the northward push of the African Plate against the Eurasian Plate, while the Alps are the more obvious, largest-scale result of the same plate movement.

Teaching idea 1.6

Using local maps and their knowledge of their local area, ask your students to build up a physical background for their area. Does it have rolling hills or even mountains? Is there a sudden change from plain to upland or are there any structural elements buried beneath the more recent deposition of glacial, periglacial or river sediments?

The West Pennine Moors

Local to the author is the West Pennine Moors area of Lancashire, bounded by the M65 motorway to the north and the M61 to the west (see figure 1.16 on p24). This area, some 4km to the east of Chorley, includes places like Winter Hill, Anglezarke and Wheelton Moors. It is an area of carboniferous gritstone, sandstone and shales on the western edge of the Rossendale Anticline. The main landforms of this area are controlled by faults. The Brinscall Fault has caused softer and more thinly bedded grits and sandstones of the Haslingden Flags and Rough Rock groups to be downthrown to the west of the coarse gritstones of the Fletcher Bank Grits. The area to the west is also more heavily faulted than the relatively horizontal rocks of Anglezarke and Wheelton Moors. Erosion, especially during the last glacial period, has removed much of the more faulted and finely bedded rocks, leaving the Brinscall Fault as a major escarpment.

Fault control and waterfall, Dean Brook

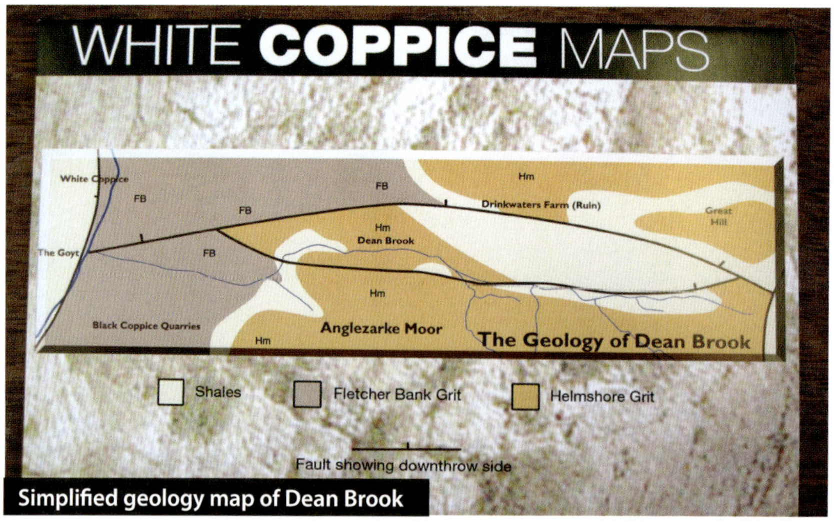

Simplified geology map of Dean Brook

Flood deposit of fragments from jointed and fractured sandstone

Fault controlled stream, Dean Brook

Source: map courtesy of GeoLancashire - Lancashire RIGS Group.

Figure 1.16: Map and images of main fault scarp and fault-controlled drainage at White Coppice in the West Pennine Moors of Lancashire

See accompanying CD-Rom

Tectonic and structural.ppt

As is the case with most fault zones, tension has created a series of minor faults at roughly right angles to the main Brinscall Fault zone. In this area, at White Coppice for example, stream erosion has readily exploited these minor faults to develop the current incised and fault-controlled drainage pattern from the uplands across the main fault zone and out onto the glacial lowlands to the west. This lower land to the west, the downthrow (side of the fault with downward relative movement) from the fault, has therefore been the site of most glacial deposition, producing a drumlin landscape dissected by meltwater channels. The clay-rich deposits of these has produced poor drainage in the area, and led to the siting of a series of water supply reservoirs to the south. The upthrow side of the fault has a thin veneer of glacial and fluvioglacial deposits beneath extensive blanket peat. The fault itself has undergone a degree of periglacial frost shattering, producing scree-covered surfaces, now largely covered and stabilised by vegetation. The landscape is clearly one in which faulting is the main control over subsequent processes. Of note is the resource use that has been made of this area, from the way in which this fault scarp has been exploited by a number of quarries and by historic lead mining along the mineralised fault zones, to the poorly drained lowland adjacent to the faulted uplands being exploited through the construction of a series of water supply reservoirs, using locally quarried stone. This is a good example of geological and geomorphological processes over time providing useful local physical resources [☞].

MAKING THE LINKS

See ch 2, Rivers (p61).

Land and sea-level changes

Land and sea-level changes can be a result of plate tectonic processes at a variety of scales. As we have seen, plate movements, the creation and destruction of ocean crust, and the creation of mountain belts in continent-to-continent collisions, all have an effect on the shape of the ocean basins, and through this on the relationship between the level of sea water and the land. Also, because the continents are in an isostatic equilibrium floating on the mantle, as erosion takes place releasing sediment from the mountains down rivers to the sea, isostatic readjustments of the mountains occur and they rise at the same time as deposition in the sea builds out the continental shelf into the ocean basin. This results in a change in sea level relative to the land in that region. This is known as an isostatic change in sea level.

A second factor that can influence this process of isostatic change is the presence or absence of glacial ice on the surface of the Earth. During a glacial period, much ocean water is locked up on land, or floating in the sea as ice, hence the volume of water in the ocean falls, sea level drops worldwide and, where the oceans retreat across the continental shelves, dry land is formed. At the present day, we are still in a period of rising sea levels, as ice sheets and glaciers worldwide continue to retreat. This global effect is called a eustatic change in sea level.

Along much of the west coast of Britain, as shown, for example, by the coastline of the Isle of Arran or along the southern coast of Dumfries and Galloway, we can see the results of sea-level change in a range of ways. Here many of the coastal features are linked to changes related to sea-level rise since the last glacial period. Examples clearly show the interplay between eustatic factors of melting ice globally, causing sea level to rise relative to the land, and then subsequent isostatic changes of the land locally allowing the land to rise relative to the sea. A series of raised shore platforms, sometimes covered by raised beaches, raised cliff lines and other features can all be seen in these locations (figure 1.17).

Figure 1.17: Evidence of sea-level change from Mallorca (top) and Dumfries and Galloway (bottom)

See accompanying CD-Rom

Tectonic and structural.ppt

As sea level has risen globally, then similar features would be expected elsewhere, for example on the island of Mallorca (see figure 1.17 on p25) in the western part of the Mediterranean. Here we can see raised shoreline features, the result of the interplay between eustatic sea-level rise and the local tectonic regime, Mallorca being sandwiched between the African and Eurasian Plates.

Rock types and materials

This section considers the nature of the materials that make up the Earth, especially those of the Earth's crust that are sculpted by surface wind, water and ice to produce the variety of surface landscapes we see today. The nature of the interior components of the Earth has already been mentioned; the iron/nickel inner core, the iron with 10% oxygen/sulphur outer core, and the peridotite mantle. Only the nature of some of the mantle material, the source of much of the molten material that cools and becomes solid at or near the surface of the lithosphere, concerns us now, as we focus on the main rock types that make up the crust.

There are basically three main groups of rocks: igneous, metamorphic and sedimentary, though there are many individual rock types in each group. Igneous and metamorphic rocks are largely crystalline, being made up of interlocking minerals in the form of individual crystals. Sedimentary rocks are mostly made up of mineral/crystal grains and/or rock fragments, all derived from existing rocks by a range of chemical and mechanical weathering processes. How these groups of rocks are linked together as a continual flow of Earth materials from one physical and chemical state and location to another, by means of the rock cycle, is a fundamental concept in our understanding of how the Earth works. This concept is, in turn, explained by the theory of plate tectonics.

Igneous rocks

This is the name given to any rock formed from molten material which cools and becomes hard in the form of interlocking crystals (see figure 1.18 on p27). Molten rock is termed magma when it is molten and within the lithosphere, but lava when it is erupted and found on the surface of the crust. The temperature of this molten material is typically around 1,000°C or above (magmas can begin to solidify from 1,300°C down to 600°C depending on the chemical composition of the magma). If it cools quickly, as lava usually does when it is erupted into a much cooler environment than that in which it originated, it will harden very rapidly (effectively it freezes) producing very fine crystals. Such rocks are so finely crystalline that their constituent crystals can only be seen under a microscope. Sometimes they cool so rapidly that they produce a volcanic glass. Basalt is an excellent example of a finely crystalline igneous rock, cooling rapidly as lava at the Earth's surface as it contacts air, water and cool surface rocks. If, however, it remains within the lithosphere for a long time, then it cools much more slowly, being insulated within the warmed lithospheric rocks, and so individual crystals have time to grow to a larger size; one that can be seen with the naked eye. A good example of this slower cooling process is gabbro, a coarse-grained igneous rock of the same mineral and hence chemical composition as basalt, but one which has simply cooled much more slowly. Both of these rocks are abundant as

Figure 1.18: Examples of igneous rocks

See accompanying CD-Rom

Igneous rocks.ppt

ocean crust material, and are derived from the partial melting of mantle peridotite (see figure 1.2 on p7) as it heats up in a mantle convection cell. They are, therefore, very common at divergent plate boundaries and as deeper ocean crust material.

When we are dealing with ocean floor material that is subducted, it heats up, and so the minerals that melt at the lowest temperatures again melt first. This is another phase of partial melting and therefore chemical differentiation from the parent material. As with basalt being derived from the partial melting of peridotite, in this instance magma of a slightly different composition to the basaltic ocean floor is produced. The minerals rich in iron and magnesium melt at higher temperatures, and therefore fewer of these melt as the rock heats up, and the magma is enriched in other elements such as calcium, sodium and potassium as well as silica. These are the components of minerals like feldspar that melt at lower temperatures. This magma produces andesite where lava is found at the surface, and diorite from magma cooling slowly at depth. It is worth noting that the term 'andesite' comes from the Andes Mountains where the Nazca Plate is being subducted underneath the South American Plate.

A third set of igneous rocks are those where the material that becomes molten is largely derived from continental crust, and so has even less iron and magnesium. This further set of partial melting produces finely crystalline rhyolite from lavas and coarsely crystalline granite from magmas.

These rock suites are usually termed acid (granite type), intermediate (andesite type) or basic (basalt type) igneous rocks. The mincral crystals formed depend on the original chemistry of the magma, and the temperature at which it is cooling. As we can see, both of these are related to the magma's plate tectonic setting. A recognised sequence of the more common rock-forming minerals crystallisation is known as Bowen's reaction series (see figure 1.19 on p28).

Figure 1.19:
Bowen's reaction series

See accompanying CD-Rom

Igneous rocks.ppt

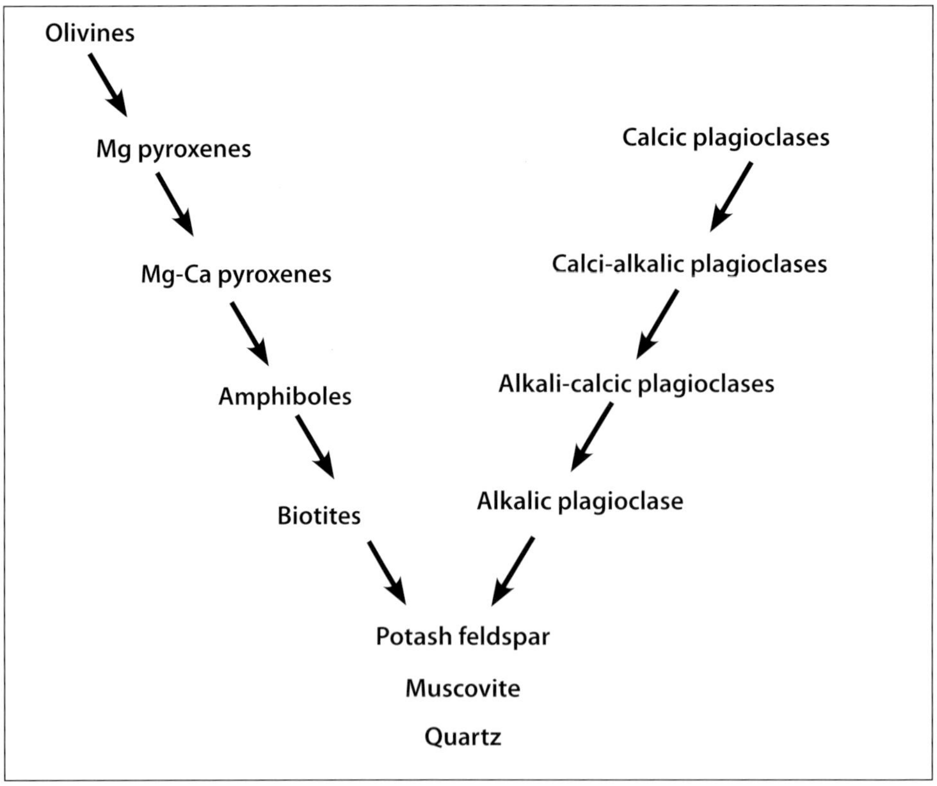

Metamorphic rocks

Metamorphic rocks are also largely made up of crystals, but ones that are often banded or aligned in appearance, gneiss being an excellent example (figure 1.20). This is due to the presence of directed pressure as they are being recrystallised from any type of existing rock. This directed pressure may be due to stresses set up by plate motions, or the weight exerted by hundreds of metres of overlying rock. Metamorphic rocks may also form due to movements of the crust resulting in crushing and increases in temperature due to friction along the faults. This movement can sometimes cause localised melting of rocks. The rocks produced in these settings may be less banded, and have a more fractured and sometimes glassy appearance where local melting and subsequent crystallisation has occurred. A good example is a pseudotachylite. The level of foliation in a metamorphic rock can be used to tell us the number of times it has undergone metamorphism, and so the number of times potential mountain building or other plate tectonic forces have affected the location, even where no other evidence survives. Both the degree of temperature and pressure and the chemical composition of the original rock material play a part in the metamorphic rock produced.

Figure 1.20:
Examples of metamorphic rocks

See accompanying CD-Rom

Metamorphic rocks.ppt

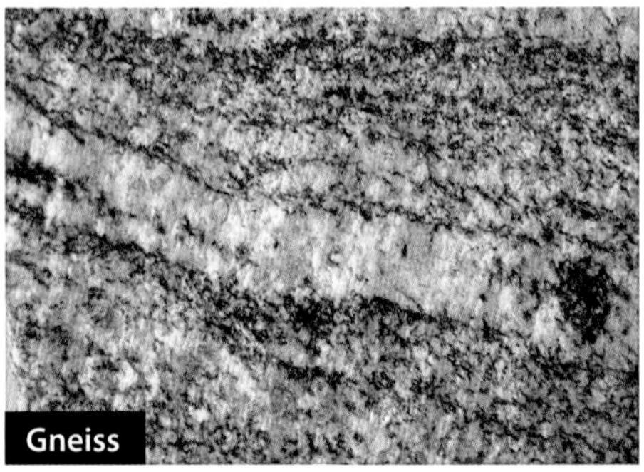

In terms of metamorphic temperatures, those above 600°C are generally regarded as leading to melting, and so the processes of crystallisation of the material produce an igneous rock. At high pressures and temperatures, gneiss can be formed from original layers of muds and sands, and schist from muds and clays, whereas at lower pressures these muds will produce slate.

Sedimentary rocks

The sedimentary group of rocks are probably the ones we are most familiar with in Britain, especially in England, as they are the surface rocks throughout much of the country. They are formed by the physical and/or chemical weathering of *any* rock exposed at the Earth's surface. A summary of these processes is presented in figure 1.21.

Chemical weathering
Removes the more soluble rock/mineral constituents
Bases are the most soluble, *sesquioxides* the least
Physical weathering
Mechanically breaks rock and regolith into smaller fragments
Most important are *freeze–thaw, salt crystal growth weathering* and *thermal cracking due to expansion and contraction*
Biological processes (biochemical and biomechanical)
Most important are *faunal digestion* and *root action* (basically chemical and physical as above)

Figure 1.21: Summary of main weathering processes

See accompanying CD-Rom

Sediments.ppt

The wide range of weathering processes discussed above occurs at the surface for a variety of reasons, related both to the environments in which rocks form, and the nature of the surface environment itself. Environmental conditions such as pressure, temperature regime, moisture conditions, and the presence of organic as well as other acids in solution at the Earth's surface, are different from those where any rock type was formed. All rocks can therefore be regarded as being out of equilibrium with surface physical and chemical conditions. Igneous rocks cool and solidify from higher temperatures and are completely solid while still being several hundreds of degrees in temperature, metamorphic rocks have readjusted to high pressures and/or temperatures. Even sedimentary rocks themselves have usually only become solid after burial by later sediments, in an environment of slightly increased temperature and pressure, often between 100°C and 200°C (at most) and a few kilo bars pressure. The physical and chemical changes of compaction and cementation, along with any further mineral growth that converts loose sediments or fresh precipitates (see p31) into a solid sedimentary rock, are termed diagenesis.

Physical weathering processes, such as freeze-thaw or salt crystal growth due to evaporation, bring about the mechanical break-up of existing rocks by the exploitation of cracks or voids within them to produce broken rock fragments. Thermal expansion and contraction, such as in a hot desert where the night time temperature plummets, can have the same effect. Chemical weathering is brought about by a range of chemical reactions between rocks and chemicals normally dissolved in water in surface environments. A summary of some of the types of chemical weathering reactions that occur can be seen in figure 1.22 on p30.

Figure 1.22: Examples of common chemical weathering reactions

See accompanying CD-Rom

Sediments.ppt

a. Limestone solution

b. Salt pan production

Solution - Dissolution:
Solid mineral + acid or water = ions in solution
Example: $NaCl + H_2O\ Na^+ + Cl^-$ (halite + water ⟶ ions in solution)

Hydration:
Solid mineral + water = new (hydrated) mineral (including chemically bonded water)
Example: $Fe_2O_3 + 3H_2O\ 2Fe(OH)_3$ (hematite + water ⟶ limonite)

The chemicals involved mainly come from dissolved atmospheric gases in rainwater, organic acids in soil moisture, and ground and surface waters acquiring and transporting chemicals from weathering processes elsewhere. These chemical reactions remove bases, silica and sesquioxides (the main chemicals forming rock minerals) in that order. This shows a progressive move to silica-rich sand and silt, residual minerals that are resistant to chemical weathering, and to new minerals such as clays and iron oxides that are the product of weathering changes along with the removal of dissolved material as solutes. Figure 1.23 shows some of the common weathering products.

The outcomes of these processes provide us with two main sets of solid materials to be transported across the Earth's surface to new locations, where materials will accumulate to produce sedimentary rocks. A further component of these sediments can be the remains of organisms, such as bone fragments, shells, leaves, plankton and algae.

Figure 1.23: Common weathering products of main rock-forming minerals

See accompanying CD-Rom

Sediments.ppt

		Weathering products	
Weathering process	**Materials attacked**	**Soluble**	**Insoluble residue**
Physical or mechanical	Rock outcrops	⟶	Rock fragments get smaller
Disintegration		⟶	Undecomposed silicate minerals
Chemical weathering	Silicate minerals		
	Olivines	⟶ Mg^{2+}, SiO_2 ⟶	Fe^{3+} oxides, hydroxides
	Pyroxenes	Mg^{2+}, SiO_2 ⟶	Fe^{3+} oxides, hydroxides
	Amphiboles	⟶ Mg^{2+}, SiO_2, Ca^{2+}, Na^+ ⟶	Fe^{3+} oxides, hydroxides
		⟶	Clay minerals
	Biotite mica	⟶ Mg^{2+}, SiO_2 ⟶	Fe^{3+} oxides, hydroxides
		⟶	Clay minerals
	Muscovite mica	⟶ K^+, SiO_2 ⟶	Clay minerals
	Feldspars	⟶ K^+, SiO_2, Ca^{2+}, Na^+ ⟶	Clay minerals
	Quartz	⟶	Quartz grains
	Calcareous cements and limestones	⟶ Ca^{2+}, HCO_3-	Impurities

The solid fragments of weathering processes are generally gravel, sand, silt and clay-sized materials, and are all particles that are physically transported. They produce clastic sediments that are compacted and cemented together over time, from loose sediment into a solid sedimentary rock. Often the structures produced within such sediments, as they are being deposited or shortly afterwards, give us clues to the nature of the environments they formed in. (Think of the ripples seen on a beach, the footprints left by birds or people, the shrinkage cracks as water evaporates and the sediment dries out). Such clastic sedimentary rocks include conglomerates made up of large rounded fragments bound together by a finer grained matrix of material, sandstones made from sand-sized grains, and shales and mudstones composed of silt and clay-sized fragments, along with fossiliferous limestones made from fossil fragments bound together with a lime mud matrix.

Figure 1.24: A range of sediments and sedimentary rocks

See accompanying CD-Rom

Sediments.ppt

The dissolved materials are carried in solution until the water transporting them finds itself in chemical disequilibrium with the environment it has moved into. Because of this disequilibrium, chemical reactions occur to precipitate out some of the solutes and so restore the chemical equilibrium of the solution. In chemistry this is called Le Châtelier's Principle. It may be that the water moves into a more acidic environment, one with less dissolved oxygen, or is simply evaporated producing precipitation from a saturated solution. The sedimentary rocks produced by these processes are called precipitates and include gypsum, rock salt and some limestones such as tufa (see figure 1.25 on p32).

Figure 1.25: Examples of gypsum and tufa

See accompanying CD-Rom

Sediments.ppt

Rock cycle

The rock cycle concept seeks to illustrate how the major groups of rocks are all related to each other, and how these relationships can be explained by the theory of plate tectonics. A simple diagram of the rock cycle is shown in Figure 1.26.

If we take as our starting point a hot liquid magma, as it cools the chemical compounds within it start to become solid, forming small crystals. Depending on the speed of cooling and the chemical composition of the magma, it can cool rapidly to form a range of coarse-grained igneous rocks, or slowly to produce finer-grained ones.

Figure 1.26: The rock cycle

See accompanying CD-Rom

Rock cycle.ppt

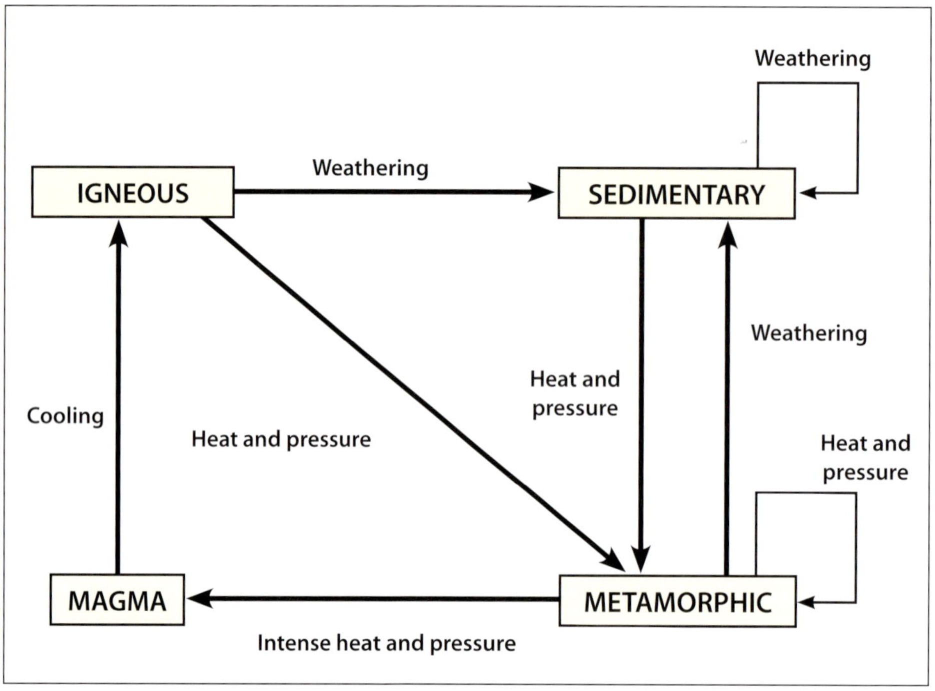

Teaching idea 1.7

Figure 1.27 on p33 shows some mobile phones and provides information about the minerals involved in their production. Ask students to research the production of one of the minerals in the diagram from source to end product.

Acrylonite Butadiene Styrene/Polycarbonate alloy (ABS/PC) – the production of 1kg of ABS – used in the plastic casings, requires 2kg of oil.

Lithium – used as the electrolyte in mobile phone batteries.

Copper – an excellent conductor of electricity. Chile mines more than one-third of the world's supply.

Cobalt – used to create the battery's cathode.

Silica – superheated silica is the most common form of glass, used in the mobile phone camera.

Graphite – used as the anode in most Li-ion batteries. Graphite is the most stable form of carbon.

Aluminium – part of the mobile phone electronics. China produces around one-fifth of the world's supply, followed by Russia, Canada and the USA.

Tin – used as solder holding together the electronic parts of the phone. China and Indonesia are the world's largest producers, although current estimates suggest the world has only 40 years' supply remaining.

Iron – stainless steel is used as a rust-proof metal finish; it is an alloy of iron, carbon and chromium.

Nickel – found in the microphone; 30% of the world's supply comes from the Sudbury region of Canada, an oval basin formed when a meteorite smashed into the Earth1.85 billion years ago.

Silicon – is crucial to the microchip and the liquid crystal display. Silicon dioxide is central to the phone's circuitry.

Figure 1.27: Mobile phones and their mineral components

See accompanying CD-Rom

Mobile phone.doc

The type of rock produced depends not only on the cooling history, but also on the source of the parent magma in the mantle, and the nature of the processes at the type of plate boundary or hot spot the magma finds itself associated with (see *Igneous rocks* on p26). These rocks may be found initially at the Earth's surface as lavas or other volcanic products, or exposed at the surface later from plutonic solidified magmas. Once exposed, they may then be subjected to a range of weathering processes (see *Sedimentary rocks* on p29) and the weathered products may be transported to form clastic sediments or precipitates, which are then further weathered and/or transported to eventually be converted into sedimentary rocks. These sedimentary rocks may themselves undergo subsequent weathering, to produce a further generation of sediments and sedimentary rocks, or they may undergo deep burial and/or increased tectonic pressures to form metamorphic rocks. Similarly, these metamorphic rocks may become exposed and undergo weathering to form a new sediment, or they may be subjected to different temperature and pressure conditions at a later date, and so undergo a second phase of metamorphism. If the environment is such that their temperature is raised to above 600°C, then the rocks will begin to melt and become magma, and so pass back into an igneous rock. Additionally, the original igneous rock may have undergone metamorphism after it became solid, and then melted again and returned to magma without ever becoming sediment.

It is a useful exercise to try to visualise the journey of magma from mantle through the various aspects of the rock cycle back to magma again. Although rock changes continually on its journey through the rock cycle, the chemicals that rocks are made from are not being created or destroyed but simply changing their chemical combinations and crystal form to adapt to the new environments they keep finding themselves in.

Landscape change over time

In this section we are going to consider how our landscapes evolve over time. We shall be thinking about how rapidly changes take place and about what controls these changes. Firstly we must consider the rate of change of the landscape: is it rapid or slow? Does the rate vary? Rapid change may be seen with flooding on a river and what happens in a flood event.

The frequency of occurrence is the key to how rapidly most surface processes operate. Floods recur roughly every 2.5 years somewhere within a particular river system, but perhaps only once in every 50, 100, 500 years or longer at a particular location. Over the rest of the time, lower-key, more typical processes of erosion, transport and deposition are leading to the evolving changes we see in that river system. Here the magnitude of operation of a geomorphic process and the frequency with which that magnitude of process operates are key factors. Low magnitude events are common, while high magnitude events are rare. In this context, landscape change can be seen as a balance between the amounts of change achieved, say, over 500 years by the normal everyday processes, and the sometimes catastrophic, dramatic changes wrought by an extreme, rare event lasting a few hours. In terms of the movement of material along the stream bed, fine material can move at moderate flows within the channel, mainly when the water level is a little higher after a rainfall event, while coarse bedload, especially in an upland stream, usually only moves in flood flows and may well never move throughout an entire lifetime.

Teaching idea 1.8

Ask students to think of a recent river flood and to find out how long the flood lasted, what stretch of the river it affected, how much of the flood plain was covered and how often a flood occurred in that location. The Boscastle flood of 2004 is a suitable event: *http://en.wikipedia.org/wiki/Boscastle_flood_of_2004*

Figure 1.28: Stream bedload

See accompanying CD-Rom

Landscape change over time.ppt

Figure 1.29: Slope failure above a stream

See accompanying CD-Rom

Landscape change over time.ppt

The idea of processes operating at different rates is fundamental to the understanding of landscape change. We need to be able to consider slow evolution, catastrophic change and the balance between the two. One concept linked to this, and especially important when we are thinking about hazards in the environment, is the idea of processes operating completely differently when a certain condition is exceeded. For example, a river may be operating under normal, low-magnitude, high-frequency conditions but eventually just removes enough material on the outside of a meander bend to weaken the support of the valley floor sediments for the valley side slope above. Without this crucial support, gravity acting on the slope material is now able to overcome the resistance to movement of that slope material; the slope fails, a small landslide occurs, which in turn feeds material into the stream channel to be sorted and transported within the channel itself. Material has undergone a sudden move from its place of rest because a condition stopping that movement, the river bank at the bottom of the slope, is no longer effective, so a threshold to the movement of the slope, the forces resisting movement, has been overcome.

Threshold values abound in the operation of surface processes, with entirely different results either side of the threshold. Examples of such thresholds include the velocity of flow needed to start a pebble moving, the temperature that would cause snowfall to melt and run off as liquid water or to collect and be converted to glacier ice, and the velocity of wind needed to strip the leaves off a tree or blow someone off their feet.

Teaching idea 1.9

Ask students to do a library/web search through past news articles for any extreme event that has caused a sudden change to a normal process in your local area or in a chosen study area (a Google search [event/location] should provide a reasonable start for such an activity). Having identified an event, use maps to decide what are the main physical processes operating, and what problems extreme events might lead to – for example, flooding or slope failure. A fairly recent example was the severe flooding in north Cumbria which occurred in 2009 (see the BBC news website: *http://news.bbc.co.uk/local/cumbria/hi/people_and_places/nature/newsid_8366000/8366661.stm*)

The nature of change that takes place is not only a product of magnitude, frequency and threshold values, but also of the materials and landforms on which the processes under that climatic regime are operating. Therefore, we should also consider the materials of the landscape, the geology, soils and covering vegetation, the climate operating at the time, and the nature of the landforms that already exist. Landscapes rarely evolve from a blank canvas, a sudden fault producing a cliff or fresh rock is extremely unusual. Most of the landforms in Britain are currently being modified under our present moist, cool, temperate environment, but are still largely the result of glacial, periglacial or even cold, arid processes and the landforms they produced from the end of the last Ice Age, a mere 16,000 to 18,000 years ago. If you live in Scotland, most of Ireland or Wales, or north of a line roughly from Birmingham to London and the Thames Estuary, your landscape was glacial; to the south of here it was periglacial. This idea of the landscape being in continual change and renewal, of a continuous journey with changes in the rate of landform evolution, with variations in climate throughout this time, gives us our current landscape, a polycyclic landscape.

Teaching idea 1.10

Ask students to look at the area around their home and see if they can pick out elements of past landscapes still present in the modern environment. How are they being modified?

Landscape geodiversity

The geosciences of geology and physical geography provide us with essential tools and information to enable us to study the history and evolution of our planet, and even of life itself. Their study underpins our understanding of the variety of landforms, materials and processes in our natural environment, and provides explanation to many of our iconic landscapes.

If we consider the northern part of the English Lake District for a moment, we see a landscape rich in geological and geomorphological history. If we look from the summit of Skiddaw to the south-east, along its periglacially formed plateau (felsenmeer) we can see the dissection of Roughton Gill and the northern slopes of Saddleback or Blencathra. Moving our view more to the south, we look across Little Man to Walla and Falcon Crags and the summit of Bleaberry Fell. Although this summit plateau feature probably started forming some 10,000 to 11,000 years ago in the Late Glacial, most of the main landform elements owe their form to a succession of glacial advances and retreats separated by periglacial and cool temperate conditions.

Figure 1.30: Landscape elements seen from above St John's in the Vale, Cumbria

See accompanying CD-Rom

Landscape change over time.ppt

Looking south to St John's

Looking north from St John's

Further, the rocks we are standing on, the Skiddaw Slates (see Teaching idea 1.2 on p11) are some 480Ma Lower Ordovician silt and mud deposits that formed from submarine landslips (turbidites) off the then continental shelf into deep ocean water. At this time England and Wales were on the southern edge of a large sea, the Iapetus Ocean, lying some 20°S of the equator on the surface of a planet with no land vegetation, a completely different world from today.

Teaching idea 1.11

Ask students to imagine how different such a landscape without land vegetation might be. What would surface run-off processes and river valleys be like in a world with no vegetation? How different might slope processes be?

Continuing our views of the Lake District, if we move to the south and look back towards the south side of Blencathra, with Skiddaw in the distance to the north-west, we get a different scene. This view takes us across a major east-west glacial trough; we can see the cirques modified by periglacial activity on the south face of Blencathra, and the cnoc and lochan type of hummocky landscape due to glacial scouring in the foreground above St John's in the Vale. In the glacial trough we see Threlkeld village and the surrounding farmland, a landscape whose more obvious surface features have evolved over thousands of years of human activity - from early Neolithic woodland clearances to modern agriculture with the recently restructured A66 major east-west route running across the landscape. This is one small area with some 480Ma of history, from the times of a vegetation-free tropical globe, to an ice and snow-covered landscape, and then to one experiencing continuing modification by people. Landscapes are by their nature dynamic, evolving and changing through time, while keeping a record of some of the changes they have experienced for us to appreciate. Views from Skiddaw summit, from St John's in the Vale, from Threlkeld itself, all will give us something different to enjoy, appreciate and interpret.

The geodiversity of our environment also underpins our economy directly, through the exploitation of natural resources, such as groundwater and aggregates, and indirectly through activities such as education, tourism and recreation [☞]. Blencathra boasts a long-standing outdoor education centre, while Threlkeld has both old quarry workings and mine shafts. Long-distance footpaths, such as the Allerdale Ramble and the Cumbria Way, cross Skiddaw and Blencathra. A coast-to-coast cycle route passes along the dismantled railway tracks and roads through the glacial valley past Threlkeld.

See Volume 1: Human Geography, ch2, Tourism (p50).

Summary

In this chapter we have shown how the plate tectonic paradigm is a unifying theme throughout the geosciences. We have looked at the nature of plate tectonic processes and how they and the rock materials produced by them form the basis upon which our present landscape has developed. We have commented on the importance of tectonic structures and the processes of weathering at the Earth's surface. The concepts of landscape polycyclicity and the balance between magnitude and frequency of operation of geomorphic processes have been introduced. Finally, the concept of geodiversity within the landscape introduced us to consideration of the landscape as a whole entity.

Useful websites

United States Geological Survey: *www.usgs.gov*

British Geological Survey: *www.bgs.ac.uk*

USGS: Earthquake Hazards Programme: *http://earthquake.usgs.gov*

USGS: Volcano Hazards Programme: *http://volcanoes.usgs.gov*

Plate tectonics: *www.platetectonics.com/index.asp*

Palaeomap Project: *www.scotese.com*

International Union of Geological Sciences: *www.iugs.org*

USGS Dynamic Earth website: *http://pubs.usgs.gov/gip/dynamic/dynamic.html*

Plate tectonics and sea floor spreading information: *http://vulcan.wr.usgs.gov/Glossary/PlateTectonics/framework.html*

Heezen and Tharp map of Ocean Floor: *www.earthinstitute.columbia.edu/news/images/TharpMapLarge.jpg*

Further reading

Christopherson, RW (2009) *Geosystems: An Introduction to Physical Geography* (7th Ed). Pearson Prentice Hall, New Jersey.

Holden, J (Ed) (2008) *An Introduction to Physical Geography and the Environment (2nd Ed).* Pearson, Harlow, England.

Skinner, BJ and Porter, SC (2004) *Dynamic Earth – Introduction to Physical Geology* (5th Ed). Wiley.

2

Rivers

Introduction

River processes operate, to a greater or lesser extent, in all continental environments, and are the dominant surface processes throughout much of Britain today. These processes operate within the fluvial environment, that is to say, the river channel itself, and in the wider alluvial environment encompassing the flood plain. Rivers show an amazing variety of forms and patterns, both along a single river system from its source to the sea, and between different river systems. It takes little imagination to contrast a gentle brook flowing through farmland with a rapid flowing mountain stream full of coarse blocky bedload, or to contrast both of these with a river meandering through a wide valley containing a broad floodplain. Rivers are among some of the most dynamic of landscape features. They are indispensable to us for water supply and for transport, and they replenish our flood plains with nutrients for farming, yet at the same time they provide one of the most ubiquitous of natural hazards. For these reasons, they are one of the most managed, or mismanaged, process-landform suites we have.

This chapter will provide a clear introduction to river systems. It will consider the catchment hydrology inputs to the river system, and how these are reflected in both normal and flood flows. We shall view rivers as the main continental transporting agent in most climatic regimes; the means of erosion, transport and deposition of material on its journey from mountain to sea. Variations in river channel form and river channel pattern changes will be covered, and we shall look at the responses of river systems to environmental change along with the main scenarios of river management schemes.

Figure 2.1: Different characteristics of rivers

See accompanying CD-Rom

Rivers introduction.ppt

Teaching idea 2.1

Ask students to consider a range of images of different types of river such as the ones shown in figure 2.1 on p41, and of flood events such as the 2009 floods in Cumbria [☞] or the flash flood in the small Cornish village of Boscastle in 2004 [☞]. What can they identify by way of variations within the river systems and in terms of the processes that are taking place?

See ch1, Restless Earth, Teaching ideas 1.9 (p36) and 1.8 (p35).

Inputs to river systems

The principal inputs to river systems are water and sediment. Each will be discussed in turn after first giving a brief consideration to the catchment hydrological cycle itself. Figure 2.2 shows the basic inputs, throughputs and outputs of water in such a drainage basin system, as well as identifying locations where water may be temporarily stored.

Figure 2.2: Basin hydrological cycle

See accompanying CD-Rom

River inputs.ppt

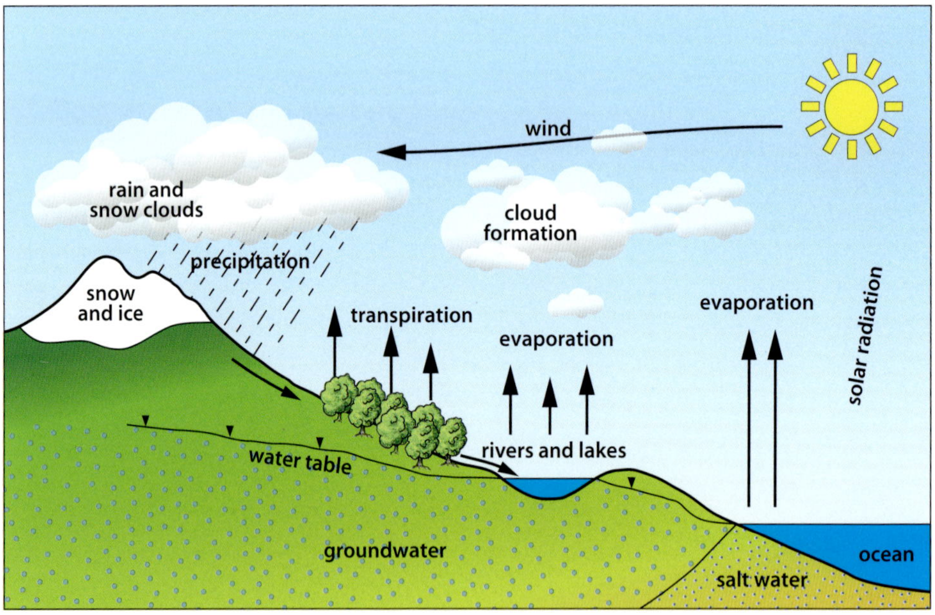

Water inputs

Water run-off to a catchment is controlled both by the nature of precipitation input in the region and the nature of the catchment itself. Water run-off may vary dramatically. Issues under consideration here might include: seasonality of rainfall or snowmelt (seasonal snowmelt in northern Scotland and monsoon rains in India to cite two extremes that have very different impacts); amount of water lost by the nature and seasonality of vegetation (in the case of woodland, for instance, there are significant differences between coniferous and deciduous tree cover in terms of interception of rainfall and use of soil moisture); variations due to farming practice (arable or grazing land, amounts of hedgerow, etc); the steepness of slopes in the catchment (the steeper the slope the more rapid the overland flow or throughflow); the amount of bare rock (a control on infiltration and surface run-off), and the thickness and nature of the soil cover (again a control on throughflow or overland flow characteristics).

Water flowing over the surface, just below the surface and sometimes in soil or peat pipes (eroded subsurface channels), is the first to reach the river channel and is termed 'quickflow'. Another important source of water input to the river channel is groundwater discharge from precipitation that has infiltrated down to the water table (and so varies seasonally and over shorter timescales related to rainfall patterns). This source of water is particularly important in providing the baseflow component to river discharge between rainfall events. The relative amounts of quickflow and baseflow reaching the river channel determine the shape and size of the run-off hydrograph (the graph of discharge against time) and the lag time (time delay) between peak rainfall and peak run-off. Of value in cold environments [☞] is the length of seasonal melting of permafrost or of glacial melt, and in more humid tropical [☞] and subtropical locations, monsoonal rainfall patterns. All of these water inputs vary over both space and time, and so need consideration on a catchment-to-catchment basis. The resulting pattern of water input to the stream is usually described in terms of plotting daily or monthly water discharge against time (figure 2.3 depicts both annual and storm hydrographs). These plots are known as run-off regimes. Five main annual global patterns can be seen in figure 2.4.

See ch 5, Ice (p117).

See ch 6, Geohazards (p141).

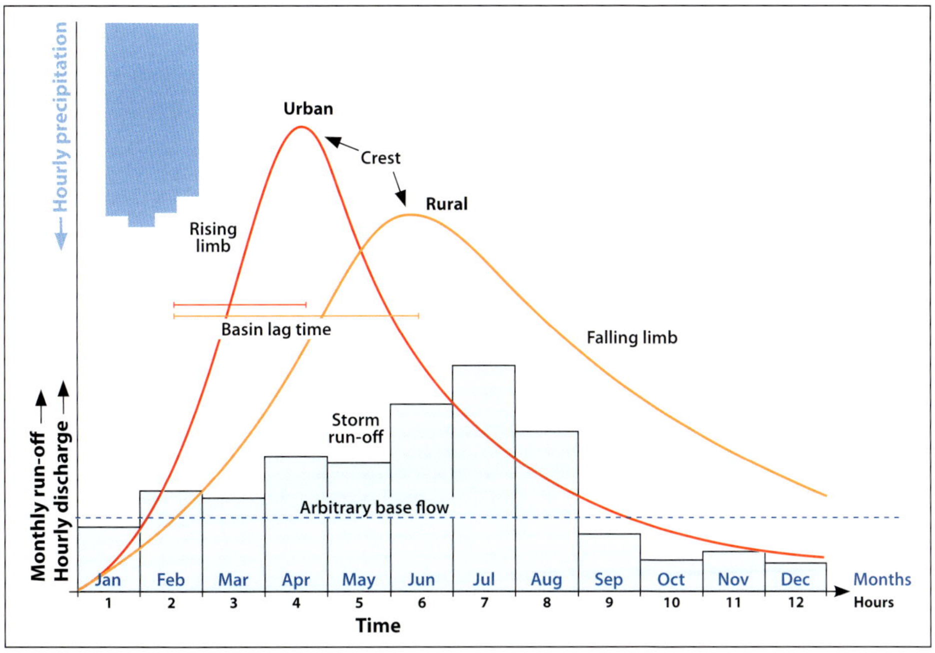

Figure 2.3: Annual and storm hydrographs

See accompanying CD-Rom

River inputs.ppt

Figure 2.4: Global run-off regimes

See accompanying CD-Rom

Global run-off regimes.doc

Equatorial (double maximum)	Heaviest rain in spring and autumn, no dry season
Tropical (single maximum)	Marked seasonal high rainfall (June/July to October/November) and low (December to May)
Temperate – oceanic	Evenly spread rainfall influenced by snowmelt/evapotranspiration in some locations
Snow/ice melt – mountain	Late spring to early summer maximum commonly related to snow/ice melt
Arid	Highly infrequent and short-lived discharges, ephemeral channels

See Volume 3: Environmental Geography, ch 7, Environmental management, figure 7.3.

At the scale of global climate regimes, certain characteristics of river flow can be identified. In temperate maritime locations like the British Isles, precipitation occurs fairly regularly all year with a late autumn to winter peak, but the generally higher evapotranspiration rates during the summer are the main control on the pattern of river flow. It is worth noting that, regionally in England, the very high demand for abstracted water for public supply [☞] exacerbates low summer discharge in many of the south-eastern counties.

See ch 5, Ice (p117).

On the other hand, in regions where stream flow is dominated by seasonal snowmelt or glacial ablation, a marked peak in discharge occurs. This peak is in late spring for snowmelt and mid to late summer for glacier-fed streams where the seasonality of ice ablation is the main control [☞]. Tropical river systems similarly show a marked peak in mid to late summer, coinciding with main rainfall input, evapotranspiration rates being high all the time. River systems in equatorial regions have a more complex double peak: a low one in late spring and a higher one in autumn, following the equinoxes.

See ch 1, Restless Earth (p23) and ch 8, Globalisation (p180).

Superimposed on these global regimes are local factors, which may be of greater importance. For example, in the upland areas of the West Pennine Moors [☞] of Lancashire, steep rocky catchments with high rainfall events produce rapid flood discharges with high peaks, termed a 'flashy' regime. Such a regime contrasts with the more subdued regime of lowland streams on the permeable chalk rocks of the North and South Downs, where high infiltration rates and greater infiltration capacities can lead to greater water storage and so run-off to streams is slower, with flood peaks rising more gently, and generally being lower in magnitude.

Teaching idea 2.2

Local river regime

Ask your students to use the data in figure 2.5, from three Sussex rivers and associated regional rainfall statistics (or by using your own local data). Plot this data of discharge against time as a graph. Calculate the standard deviation and coefficient of variation of the data. In addition, calculate the Spearman rank correlation coefficient for each of these three sets of river discharge against the rainfall data. Comment on the results. Use all this information to comment on the type of river regime shown by these examples. Is there any correlation between each of the three rivers and the rainfall data?

Figure 2.5 : Sussex river data

See accompanying CD-Rom

River inputs.ppt and Sussex rivers.doc

Monthly flow of three rivers in Sussex along with average monthly rainfall statistics (10-year average) for the Sussex Weald

River discharge (m^3 sec)	Jan	Feb	Mar	Apr	May	June	July	Aug	Sept	Oct	Nov	Dec
Ouse	8.81	7.97	5.38	4.10	2.83	2.06	1.09	1.48	2.63	3.75	8.27	7.78
Arun	6.7	5.65	5.03	3.04	3.10	1.52	0.74	0.85	2.38	2.46	5.20	6.16
Rother	3.64	3.28	2.88	1.92	1.66	1.22	0.94	0.87	1.37	1.38	2.56	2.94
Rainfall (mm)	90	64	60	56	64	55	62	78	80	84	104	96

For each river:

- Construct histograms to show the above information
- Calculate the standard deviation
- Calculate the coefficient of variation
- Discuss what these results tell you about the behaviour of each of the three rivers
- Calculate the Spearman rank correlation coefficient for each of these three sets of river discharge against the rainfall data. Comment on the results.

Flood events

As well as consideration of the annual run-off regime and the typical storm hydrograph (see figure 2.3 on p43), we also need to concern ourselves with the nature of flood flows, as these produce periods of major geomorphological change and are responsible for major hazards [☞] in riverine locations. A flood event may be defined as a high discharge that exceeds the capacity of the river channel, and so flows beyond bankfull discharge (where water fills the river channel to the top of the channel banks) onto the adjacent flood plain. Different sizes of floods are defined in terms of discharges above a stated flood level for that river within that location, or in terms of a height above bankfull. Large flood discharges are less frequent than smaller ones, and so floods are described in terms of their magnitude (size) and frequency (how often a flood of a specific size might be expected to occur). The return interval is an estimate of the time between floods of a given size, for example a 20-year flood event would be much smaller than a 100-year event. Expressed as a probability this means a 5% chance of a 20-year flood in any one year, but only a 1% chance of a 100-year event. In semi-arid environments, high-magnitude low-frequency floods can produce more extreme changes than in humid environments, as there is less protective vegetation and probably higher quickflow values. Large differences can be seen in the frequency of flood flows, but above bankfull discharges typically have a return period of one to two years for most alluvial channels.

See ch 6, Geohazards (p141 and p158).

Teaching idea 2.3

Flood characteristics and local flood frequency

Produce a database of information on local or other specific flood events using flood discharge data, historical and press records. Ask students to use discharge data to construct a plot of recurrence interval against discharge and to look at the frequency of specific flow events, including flood discharges. Ask them to comment on this. Comparison with another catchment from a different region or on a different land use type might be interesting here.

A useful starting point might be the Environment Agency website section on flooding, for example the summer 2007 floods at: *http://www.environment-agency.gov.uk/research/library/publications/33903.aspx*

Sediment inputs

Sediment input to a catchment may be within the stream channel itself, as a result of bed and bank erosion, most commonly during higher – especially flood – flows. Sediment may also be delivered to a stream channel externally by a range of slope processes culminating in sediment falling, sliding, slipping or being washed downwards across the surrounding slopes and floodplain. Figure 2.6 on p46 shows examples of these types of sediment input from the River Lostock in Lancashire and the River Derwent in Borrowdale, Cumbria. Such processes may be enhanced by any rill and gully network present. Much of this sediment movement is initiated by rainfall and so sediment supply can also have a staggered delivery, much like a flashy river regime where higher and/or more prolonged rainfall events produce more erosion and sediment loss from the land surface to the river channel.

Figure 2.6: Sediment input from selected rivers

See accompanying CD-Rom

Sediment inputs.ppt

The loss of sediment after weathering and erosion is termed the sediment yield, and catchments with moderately low rainfall, in the order of 250 to 300mm per year, and with sparse amounts of vegetation cover, have the highest natural sediment yields. High rainfall tends to promote more vegetation growth, and so more surface protection, with the lowest sediment yields being in forested catchments receiving 700 to 750mm of precipitation per year. If we combine these considerations with the influences of steep topography, low permeability and a snow or ice melt regime, then it is hardly surprising that rivers like the Kosi in India, which drains much of the Himalayas, has one of the highest sediment yields in the world, some 3,130t km^{-2}yr^{-1} of sediment. This can be contrasted to the British average of somewhere between 30 and 40t km^{-2}yr^{-1}. [1]

As well as the total amount of sediment, it is also very important to take note of the size or calibre of the material, variations of which are shown in figure 2.7 on p47. The calibre of the material has implications for the speed of transport of sediment through the river system, the rate of channel change, and for the uses people are able to make of the river system. In areas like Britain, silts and clays are well represented in the lowlands along with sands, gravels and boulders in the uplands. Tropical environments tend to produce more silts and clays due to the prevalence of intense chemical weathering resulting in these materials. Glacial environments [☞] tend to produce all sizes, due to the range of glacial erosion processes, but with a particularly high silt input in terms of the mechanically ground-up rock flour from subglacial erosion.

MAKING THE LINKS

See ch 5, Ice (p127).

Figure 2.7: Sediment calibre in selected rivers

See accompanying CD-Rom

Sediment inputs.ppt

An interesting and somewhat cautionary note here is to consider how much of the sediment yield in upland Britain is from the erosion of glacial sediments relating back to the recent Glacial Period, rather than from the weathering and erosion of the underlying bedrock.

River system throughputs

In this next section, we are going to consider the movement of water and sediment along a river system. As can be appreciated from the study of any river system, stream channels consist of a drainage network built up over time where, on each occasion new channels join, there is an increase in the dimensions of the stream and in its discharge. Although this is the situation in much of the world, there are anomalies produced in arid and semi-arid environments, where extremely high evaporation rates lead to decreases in discharge, and the presence of ephemeral streams which only flow for part of the year, normally after the infrequent rainfall events. Here we are going to consider channel networks, and subsequent changes in the channel dimensions and planform, as we follow water along river systems in a temperate environment like the British Isles.

Channel network

The channel network that develops is a function of the combined effects of geology, soils, vegetation and topography on catchment hydrology. It has been shown to have an ordered internal composition and so we can use this to describe and compare drainage networks in a numerical manner. The system commonly used today is that of Strahler (1957). Here headwater tributaries are termed 'first-order' streams, where two first-order streams meet a second-order stream is formed, two second-order streams meet to form third-order and so on (figure 2.8). The higher the order, the more complex and well developed the drainage network for water transfer. Other parameters used include the main stream length, the distance along the main channel from its source to its mouth along which the channel long profile is measured, the total stream length of the whole channel network, and the drainage density – that is to say, the drainage area divided by the total stream length. These measures help us to compare and contrast drainage networks, as well as identifying aspects of the hydrology of the drainage basin. For example, the higher the drainage density, the more rapid or flashy the river discharge is.

Figure 2.8: Strahler stream ordering system

See accompanying CD-Rom

Channel parameters.ppt

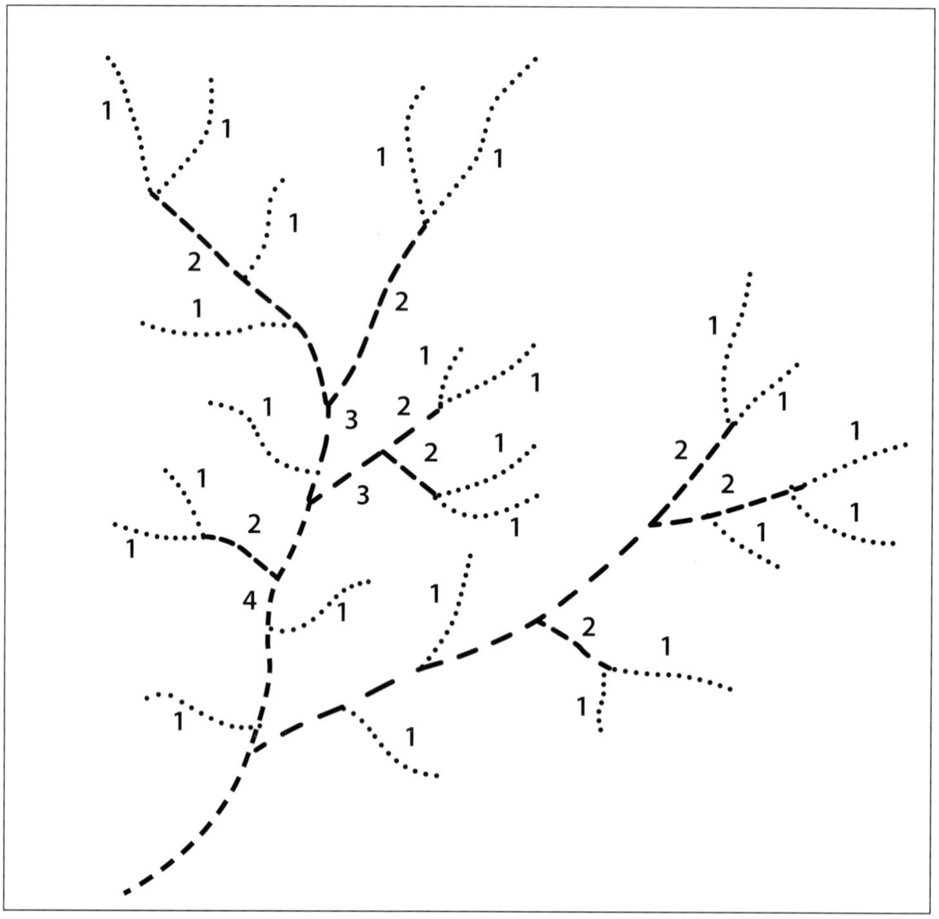

Teaching idea 2.4

Channel networks

Ask your students to plot the drainage system for a local river system from Ordnance Survey 1:50,000 maps and apply Strahler's stream ordering system to it. They can compare this to an upland, lowland, larger or smaller river system from elsewhere in the country. They can look at precipitation records for these locations (records and links can be found on the Meteorological Office website: ***http://metoffice.com/weather/uk***). Get them to identify the main differences between the stream networks; do they think these mirror differences in rainfall between the locations or something else such as geology or land use?

Channel long profiles are plots of the slope of a river between its source and where it enters the sea or a lake at its mouth. They are normally concave in shape with a decreasing gradient downstream. This concave profile can be disrupted by a range of factors such as local changes in geology (resistant rock bands and faults, for example), and also by changes in the nature of the existing landforms, possibly ones inherited from a previous climatic regime. Bed material erosion or deposition due to climate change can cause the profile to become steeper or shallower locally. A change in base level as sea level changes can also affect the long profile as a whole, causing both erosion and river down-cutting or deposition and floodplain aggradation to occur.

Channel dimension changes

The channel dimension is the shape and size of the channel cross-section at a particular location (usually termed a river station) at bankfull discharge, which is when the river channel is full of water to the top of the banks. This is used because at this bankfull stage the friction of the bed and banks in slowing the flow of water is at a minimum with regard to the volume of water passing along the river channel. Water flow here is at its most efficient. The basic morphological measurements of the stream cross-section are shown in figure 2.9: bankfull width **W**, depth **D**, wetted perimeter **P** (bed plus banks cross-section), channel cross-section area **A**. From these we can also calculate the width to depth ratio **W/D** and the hydraulic radius **R** (**A/P**). These are measures of channel efficiency: the more semicircular the channel (**W/D** ratio 1), the smaller the wetted perimeter in relation to the volume of water passing along the channel, and so the more efficient the channel is at transporting water, as a result of the reduced friction levels. Similarly, the higher the hydraulic radius, the lower the friction and the more efficient the river channel becomes.

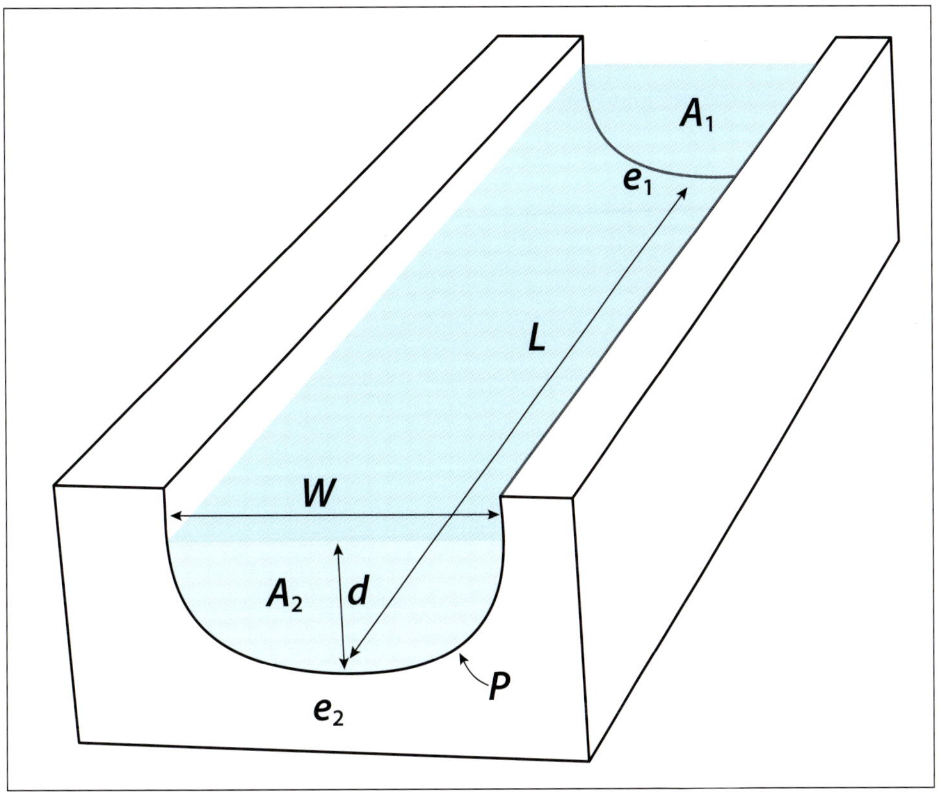

Figure 2.9: Basic stream cross-section morphometry

See accompanying CD-Rom

Channel parameters.ppt

Figure 2.10: Velocity measurements

See accompanying CD-Rom

Channel parameters.ppt

Channel dimension changes are often linked to changes in river discharge. Discharges increase downstream in normal rivers as more tributaries and drainage area contribute water to the main channel. Thus, we can consider changes in hydraulic geometry in a downstream manner at bankfull stage. Alternatively, we may wish to understand the behaviour of a stream as discharge increases at a specific location (termed 'at-a-station' as opposed to 'downstream'). In either case we need some measurement of the velocity of water flow to compute the bankfull or other discharge value. At particular stages of water depth in the channel this may be done by current meter or surface float methods. For bankfull stage or when it is unsafe to enter the channel, estimates of velocity using Manning's equation can be used. These are detailed in figure 2.10.

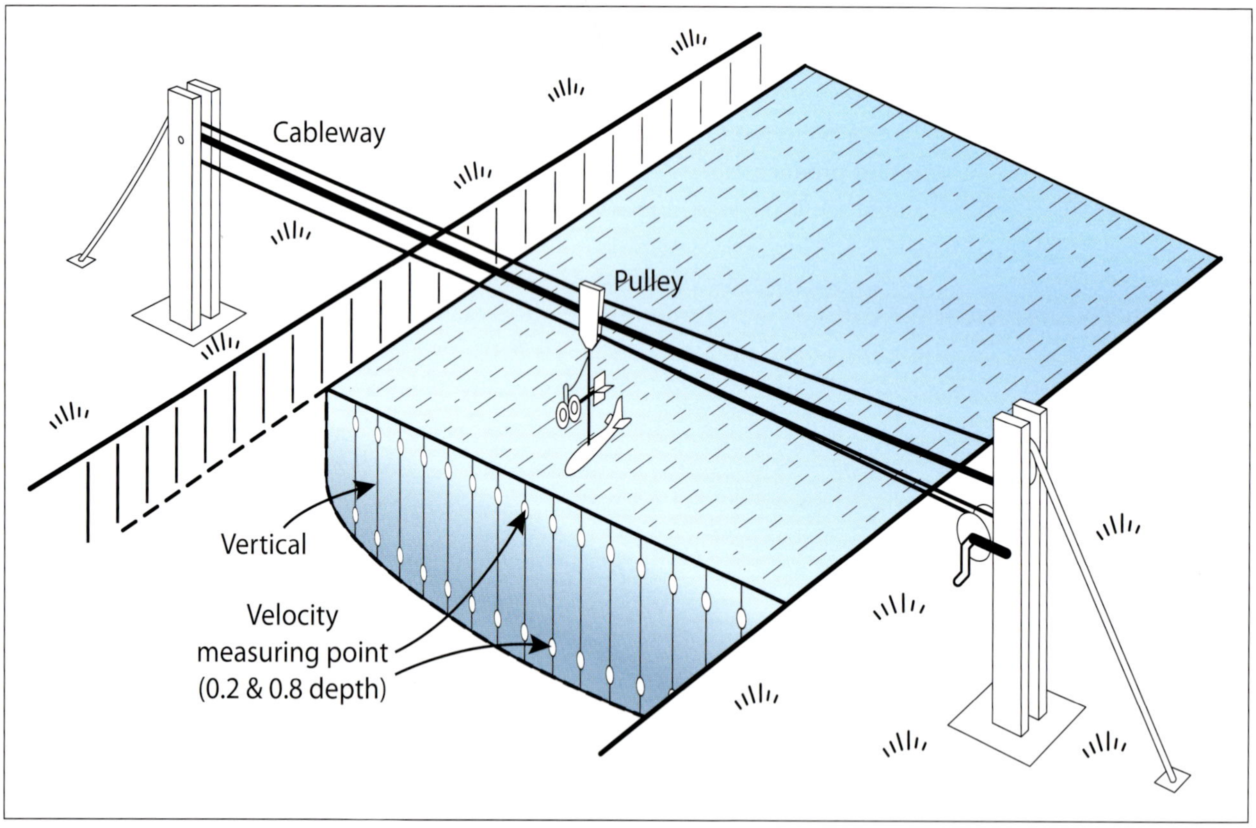

Teaching idea 2.5

Channel cross-section change

Analysis of change may be done in the field, or from data previously collected. Your students could tabulate data on width, depth, wetted perimeter and hydraulic radius for parts of a river system near you and then look at how these change from small tributaries along to the main channel, and then at different stations along the channel (as far as safety permits). Students could see if there is a gradual or more sporadic change in the parameters. Do they all increase or decrease in the same pattern or not? Students could calculate the bankfull discharge at each of the stations if possible and see how this relates to (controls) the other changes.

Generally, channel dimensions increase as we move downstream and, as this leads to increases in hydraulic radius, the channel becomes more efficient, and so there is a relatively greater increase in channel discharge capacity at bankfull stage. Similarly, bed and bank materials tend to reduce in size downstream due to increased weathering and erosion of the material, and so the roughness of the channel boundary decreases, again promoting faster flow. These factors help to offset the reduced channel slope (see *Channel network* on p47), which would tend to lower the flow velocity. Such changes as these are termed 'downstream hydraulic geometry changes'. They show how channel shape changes with the channel becoming broader and deeper with increased friction and reduced hydraulic radius at bankfull and especially below bankfull discharges. Velocity increases more slowly than width or depth here. Gravel and sand bed streams tend to be wider and shallower than silt and clay ones. The higher bed friction mobilises coarse bedload, whereas channels with more efficient flow maximise finer calibre suspension transport. A further aspect that can also affect channel shape and erodability of material is the nature and amount of vegetation. Where vegetation root systems bind sediment together and produce more cohesive and less erodible banks, the channel becomes deeper rather than increasing in width. As we can see from this discussion, changes in channel shape dimensions are the result of the combined effect of discharge and water flow velocity (themselves due to climatic control), along with sediment calibre, transport and vegetation. The interplay of all these aspects needs to be considered in understanding how and why channel dimensions change.

Channel planform changes

There are three basic channel planform styles or patterns: straight, meandering and braided. Channel sinuosity (ratio of river channel length between two points to valley length between the same two points) is the common measurement used to distinguish between these three basic patterns. Straight channels have a sinuosity ratio of less than 1.5 while meandering channels have a ratio above 1.5. Braided or divided channels are multiple channels divided by sand, gravel or vegetated bars or islands at low flows but which can be drowned out during higher discharges. Braided channels thus tend to be wider and shallower than other channels. River planform is largely controlled by channel slope and discharge, with sediment calibre also being important.

Straight channels are not stable in nature due to channelled flow being deflected by centrifugal forces, as a result of the Earth's rotation (termed 'helical flow' as the deflected velocity of flow decreases with depth due to increased friction from the channel perimeter), and so meandering rivers develop as flow velocity erodes alternating banks and produces a more sinuous channel. Any river channel, including a straight reach, tends to develop deeper and shallower areas, termed 'pools' and 'riffles' respectively. These can be readily duplicated in a flume with a constant input of water. The spacing of one pool to the next is generally between five and seven times the channel width. It is at the site of these pools that flow deflection and helical flow patterns seem to become established. Flow through the pools is slower, while it is more rapid over the steeper riffle sections. The sediment eroded from the outside of a developing meander bend is deposited on the inside of the next meander bend downstream creating a point bar. Figure 2.11 on p52 shows examples of these morphological features.

Figure 2.11 (right): Pool and riffle and meander sections

See accompanying CD-Rom

Channel planform.ppt

Figure 2.12 (below): Meander migration

See accompanying CD-Rom

Channel planform.ppt

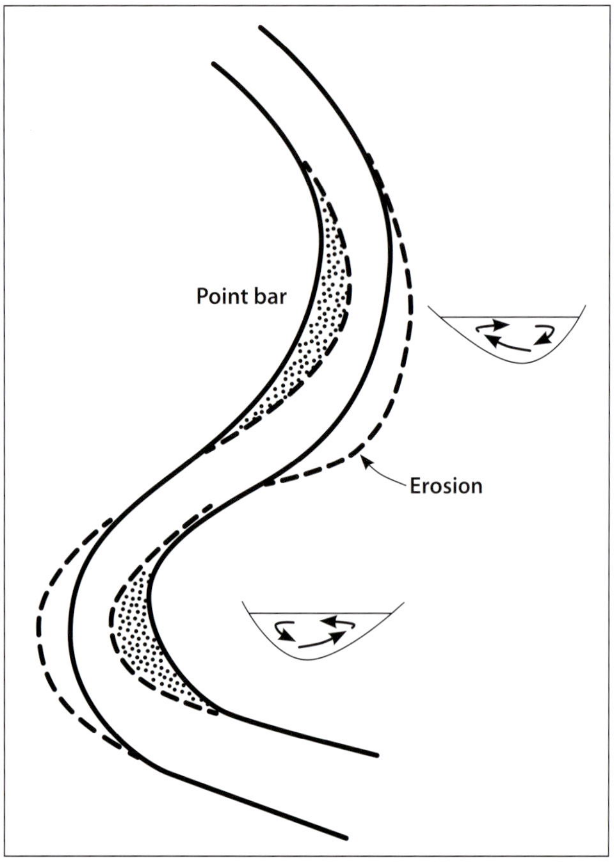

Meandering rivers can be characterised by relatively low channel slopes, cohesive bed and bank deposits, and a relatively high suspension load to bedload transport ratio. The style of meandering channel migration is shown in figure 2.12. The number and size of meanders increases through time, with a corresponding lowering of channel slope as the river takes a longer course. Meanders also increase in amplitude and migrate downstream. Differences in the rate of meander migration, plus high levels of erosion during flood flows, can lead to dramatic meander pattern changes, such as channel avulsion as meander necks are breached, with the subsequent formation of oxbows in abandoned meanders. Similarly, during flood flows natural levées (small build-ups of material on the floodplain adjacent to the channel banks) can be formed because of higher friction and therefore sediment deposition. When floods breach these levées, crevasse splay deposits form as small sediment fans adjacent to the main channel.

Braided channels are characterised by steeper channel slopes with flashy hydrological regimes, showing wide variations in discharge and highly mobile bedload transport. This means that new channels are rapidly cut through existing bars and islands during high discharges, building these up again as sediment is deposited in waning flows. The overall efficiency of the stream is maintained as the flow is dispersed through a number of individual high-efficiency channels (see figure 2.13 on p53, which depicts a number of braided scenarios). These conditions are found commonly in arid and semi-arid environments, especially where streams discharge from heavily dissected uplands onto lowland plains (see *Alluvial fan development* on p53), and in areas of high seasonal discharge such as snow and ice-melt-fed channels and monsoon-affected regions. In such environments, mechanical weathering and erosion is active and the high flow velocities, discharge and steep gradients tend to rapidly sort and remove the finer-calibre sediment in suspension. This leads to channels dominated by sand and gravel bars and islands.

Figure 2.13: Braided stream scenarios

See accompanying CD-Rom

Channel planform.ppt

Variations to the characteristic braided channel occur where there is a series of interconnected stream channels separated by stable, often vegetated alluvial islands, or occasionally by bedrock. These are termed 'anastomosing' channels. Similar to this is the rare occurrence of vegetated and semi-permanent islands cut into relatively cohesive floodplains or built up within channels by sediment accretion on low angle slopes with irregular flow regimes. These multiple channel settings are termed 'anabranching' rivers.

Alluvial fan development

These are localised landforms and deposits that occur when streams with a high sediment yield emerge from topographically constrained uplands onto a major valley or lowland plain. They form cone-shaped landforms spreading out from the confining valley, where widening of channels and lowering of gradients lead to rapid deposition by fluvial and sediment gravity flows (essentially mudflows). These features are most common in semi-arid and glacial-fed regions with high seasonality of discharge, lack of protective vegetation cover and abundant erodible sediment, but they can also be found in many parts of the British Isles.

In the West Pennine Moors and Rossendale Forest, gritstone uplands with thin veneers of glacial sediments have many structurally controlled channels discharging onto glacial depositional lowlands. A series of photographs of the White Coppice area near Chorley in Lancashire demonstrates the nature of one of these channel and alluvial fan scenarios (see figure 2.14 on p54). These generally contain more varied and poorly sorted deposits than either braided or meandering reaches, though they rapidly become finer down the fan. Such fans are also characterised by rapid channel changes, a good example of which can be seen in figure 2.15 on p54, which shows alluvial fans developing in the Langedalen and Krundalen Valleys, Norway, which exhibit glacier and snow-melt hydrological regimes.

Figure 2.14:
Channel and alluvial fan development at White Coppice, Lancashire

See accompanying CD-Rom

Alluvial fans.ppt

Figure 2.15:
Alluvial fan development, Langedalen and Krundalen, Norway

See accompanying CD-Rom

Alluvial fans.ppt

Channel-forming flows

The geomorphological effectiveness of a given discharge event is dependent on the magnitude of that event, and on the frequency with which it occurs. Larger discharges have more competence to erode and more capacity to transport the eroded material. On the other hand, smaller discharges occur more frequently but have less geomorphological impact. It is necessary to consider a long-term view in estimating which of the two is more important, many low flows or a few large flood discharges. Wolman and Miller (1960) considered such situations and concluded that modest flows occurred most of the time, but that small, high-frequency flood events were the most effective at producing geomorphological change. Many within-channel features such as braid bars, point bars and riffles are controlled by 'normal' below bankfull flows, whereas features such as avulsion chutes producing cut-offs and oxbows or levées are clearly the response to flood flows. One could conclude that channel morphology is a response to a range of conditions, a balance between high-frequency, low-magnitude events – the 'norm' – and low-frequency, higher-magnitude events – the flood condition. During a flood the channel attunes to this 'rare' high-magnitude flood flow, afterwards returning to the slower changes of the more 'normal', frequent flows.

River system response to natural environmental change

We have seen how river channels respond to variations in sediment and water input and how these are also aided by rock type and structure, existing landforms, soils and vegetation. We now need to move on to consider changes over longer time periods, especially ones beyond the scope of the current climates. The current climate is the basic controlling variable for contemporary rainfall patterns and hence present river discharge regimes. A simple consideration of most moderate-sized channels in northern Britain and the valleys they flow through will immediately show that many of them could be classified as 'misfit' streams – ones incapable of cutting their existing river valley. The nature of the controls on the existing stream channel is not the same as those on the stream channel that produced the river valley. The processes operating have been affected by changes over time, and so we need to consider the past history of the river channel, and of the drainage basin itself, if we are to fully appreciate the current river and how it is modifying its valley. For example, the floodplain of a river is made up of sediments deposited over time, by former sediment and flow regimes, and by former climate and vegetation influences. The overall river valley is the result of previous phases of erosion and slope development, periods of river aggradation, and of river rejuvenation and incision as base levels change.

A look at the River Lostock in Central Lancashire near to the author's home will illustrate this (see figure 2.16 on p56). The photographs demonstrate how this stream flows through a valley that is much wider and deeper than the current floodplain, channel meander belt and stream channel. Terrace remnants of former flood plain levels can be identified, showing that river incision due to changes in base level has occurred here. Similarly, palaeochannel remnants (traces of old abandoned channels) exist away from the modern channel zone, along with evidence of more recent oxbow formation and floodplain erosion and deposition. When we consider the materials that make up the valley sides and much of the valley floor, we encounter fluvioglacial sands and gravels with occasional patches of glacial till (see chapter 5, Ice), thus suggesting a glacial origin to some of the landscape as well. A view of the local region shows abundant evidence of glacial and fluvioglacial landforms and materials to support this contention. This regional picture shows initial post-glacial drainage patterns flowing to the south and south-east. The current River Lostock flows northwards, the opposite way through the valley (as indeed do several other streams in the region). The present stream is reworking some of these landforms and materials within a rather limited meander belt zone on part of the valley floor. Also of importance here is the nature of the material being eroded. Much of the eroded material in the River Lostock catchment is of glacial origin and already bears the imprint of processes of glacial erosion and deposition, along with some fluvioglacial reworking, and subsequently one or more phases of more recent fluvial modification. This makes interpretation and even description of modern fluvial sediments difficult. In this context, it is essential to consider the polycyclicity of the materials (reoccupance and reworking of materials and landforms over time), as well as the processes operating upon them. Similar examples of river valley polycyclicity and current misfit situations can be found throughout the north-west of England (see figure 2.17 on p56).

Figure 2.16: River Lostock and its valley

See accompanying CD-Rom

Channel change.ppt

Figure 2.17: Polycyclic and misfit valleys in north-west England

See accompanying CD-Rom

Channel change.ppt

PHOTO: CHARLES RAWDING

Changes such as those discussed above are termed 'allogenic' changes, and are adjustments of the river system and drainage basin as it responds over time to external factors that produce changes in the catchment water and sediment budgets. In essence, as water input patterns change, so the river's discharge hydrograph changes. This changed catchment flow regime operates on the channel bed and bank materials, on the adjacent slopes, soils and vegetation (which themselves may have adjusted to the new conditions) to produce changes in catchment run-off, in channel cross-section, planform and gradient. There are differences in the response times of various elements within a catchment to external changes. Run-off responds rapidly in cooler, wetter climates, whereas vegetation may have a response time of tens or even a hundred years. Different parts of the river system have different sensitivity to change, often depending on how close to a change threshold the system already is. A meandering stream carrying a high bedload may change to a braided channel after an increase in rainfall leads to increased discharge and hence stream power. A stream carrying little bedload, and so little material for braid bar formation, is unlikely to undergo such a response.

Teaching idea 2.6

Identification of polycyclicity in river catchments

Using local or regional Ordnance Survey maps, ask students to investigate drainage networks in your region by mapping river valleys and producing cross-valley profiles at various points along the main channel. Compare and contrast these cross profiles. For example, can you identify any past flood plains by river terrace remnants still preserved? Can you identify any palaeochannel remnants from this information? Look at the landforms and materials outside this zone and suggest what is currently happening and what has happened in the past to produce the rest of the valley.

Autogenic changes occur where thresholds affecting how internal processes operate within a catchment are crossed. These can lead to notable channel planform changes, for example channel avulsion events and the formation of cut-offs or the dissection and erosion of braid bars and river banks. A good example of this is shown by the River Till in Northumberland, where a major flood event caused increased surface erosion, extensive floodplain inundation and local extensive bank erosion. Figure 2.18 demonstrates these effects. Over timescales of hundreds or thousands of years we see river floodplains being built up by the sporadic deposition of recurring flood events, but it only takes one major flood, the 500-year event perhaps, to produce catastrophic erosion and dramatically alter the floodplain, stripping much of the sediment away. This is called a 'pulsed disturbance', where a short-lived, episodic, high-magnitude event leads to run-off and erosion thresholds being crossed with dramatic results. This is then followed by a return to the original, normal conditions. Again, this illustrates the need to understand the balance between magnitude and frequency in fluvial processes.

Figure 2.18: Flooding and erosion of the River Till in Northumberland

See accompanying CD-Rom

Channel change.ppt

Teaching idea 2.7

Historical channel pattern change

Collect past editions of Ordnance Survey maps and choose sections of river channel to provide the basis of a channel-mapping exercise. Ask students to trace the plan of the same section of the river channel from each edition of the map. Get them to superimpose or compare side by side to identify changes through time. On the basis of these, try to predict where future changes might next occur. This could be extended by trying to find old photographs, historical documents, survey plans and so forth. Look through old records and press comments on flood events to try to identify the scale of change from these specific high-magnitude events. Do you think they cause greater changes than lower-magnitude but more common conditions? (Historical map data is available from the Ordnance Survey: *www.ordnancesurvey.co.uk/oswebsite/products/historicalmapdata* and some from local authorities, for example in Lancashire try *www.lancashire.gov.uk/environment/oldmap*).

River response to anthropogenic influences

Human activity over several thousands of years has modified general drainage basin and river channel processes. These process changes include aspects of overland flow and throughflow, infiltration rate and channel form, and pattern behaviour. One of

See Volume 3: Environmental Geography, ch 1, Ecosystems (p22) and ch7, Environmental management (p166).

the earliest examples of such human interference in fluvial systems dates back some 6,000 years in Britain, to forest clearances and agricultural development and expansion. Deforestation [☞] removes a lot of the ability of the vegetation to intercept rainfall and to bind the soil together. This leads to the removal of exposed soils producing higher sediment input to the river channel. Also, the reduction in soil cover produces reduced infiltration capacity within the remaining soil and so increased quickflow, especially enhancing storm run-off and flood peaks. Phases of increased flood plain build-up are seen, along with increased sediment load, producing shallower, more braided channel reaches. Particularly notable changes can be identified that relate to the extensive increase in agriculture (anthropogenic influence), coupled with the colder temperatures, increased snowfall and hence higher seasonal flood peaks of the Little Ice Age (a natural cold period during the 17th and 18th centuries in Europe).

Increasing levels of urbanisation, and the change to more intensive agricultural practices over the past 150 to 200 years, have resulted in growth in both run-off and sediment yield. During urban construction, the removal of vegetation and disruption of surface materials leads to increased run-off and sediment yields locally. After construction there is usually only a partial return to previous conditions, the flow regime has been permanently altered. Buildings, paved areas, car parks and roads feeding into gutters, drains and sewers produce rapid quickflow into rivers, greatly enhancing discharge values. This has a particularly noticeable effect on the lower-frequency flood incidence and peaks, where generally a tenfold increase in the one to two-year event has been identified. Urbanisation has much less impact on the higher-magnitude events where infiltration rate rapidly becomes exceeded and quickflow established.

Intensive farming often includes the provision of field drains to remove excess water, thus increasing run-off as well. Increased cropping and ploughing also enhances soil erosion and thereby increases sediment input via the 'improved' drainage system, which also allows for more rapid removal of applied fertilisers, so bringing about a reduction in water quality.

Teaching idea 2.8

Recent changes in channel discharge

By using local discharge records, ask your students to compare drainage basins with different flow regimes. Acquire monthly discharge figures to plot and compare both between catchments and within the same catchment over time. Local records or newspaper articles can be used to supplement such studies. Alternatively, use records and articles from different parts of the country to bring out regional differences, for example, lowland arable farmland catchment against upland managed forest catchment. A further suggestion would be to consider catchments affected by mining or quarrying and suggest what impacts these practices might have on increased discharge, poorer water quality and increased sediment yield, and therefore on the possibility of river channel change. A good source of river discharge data in the UK is *www.nwl.ac.uk/ih/nrfa/river_flow_data/river_flow_data_download.htm*. Annual tables of daily flow data for around 200 gauging stations throughout the UK are available for downloading. *www.sage.wisc.edu/riverdata/* contains a compilation of monthly mean river discharge data for more than 3,500 sites worldwide.

Alongside the catchment changes discussed above, humans have also directly affected river channels by trying to control flooding [☞] and erosion. Most attempts to control flooding in the past have involved civil engineering works, either to straighten the channel and so transmit water more rapidly through the flood-susceptible reach, or to increase its discharge capacity by the use of artificial levées to enlarge the channel cross-section area, or to regulate water transmission by means of a series of dams [☞] with associated flood or multipurpose (river regulation, water supply, hydroelectric power generation) reservoirs. Similarly, engineering works aimed at bank protection, for example gabions (wire baskets filled with rocks) attached together and lining the affected banks, or large quarried blocks, have also been employed. Almost exclusively, such engineering schemes have at best a limited effectiveness, and are sometimes marked failures. They are static elements in a dynamic system and the river channel will respond to re-establish its previous conditions. For example, rivers will erode around bank protection works as channel migration of meanders continues. Artificial levées allow the channel bed to aggrade because they increase the channel's capacity to carry water and so allow more bedload deposition to occur within the channel rather than on the adjacent floodplain. Over time this leads to the channel becoming shallower and so results in an increased likelihood of flooding. The response has often been to increase the height of the artificial levées, and over time this has led to the base of the channel being above the surface of the floodplain. The result is that a high magnitude flood event which overtops the system will be more destructive than any previous event. This has been demonstrated on the Mississippi at New Orleans and along the Rhine in Europe. In this latter case, artificial levées are being removed to allow more flooding, but in controlled locations, returning the river to a more natural hydrological regime. Similarly, river regulation reservoirs are sediment traps with a limited life expectancy (until the river fills them in), and are likely to trigger increased erosion downstream of the artificial knickpoint (break in slope of a river long profile) that has been created. Figure 2.19 shows a selection of engineering works to control channel flow and protect from bank erosion.

See ch 6, Geohazards (p161).

See Volume 3: Environmental Geography, ch 4, Energy (p95).

PHOTOS: CHARLES RAWDING

Figure 2.19: Engineering works to control channel flow

See accompanying CD-Rom

Channel controls.ppt

River channel management

Humans have always used river valleys for transport, food supply, water supply, waste disposal and power supplies, while low-lying fertile floodplains have been developed for agriculture and for settlement. As our demands on these river channels, floodplains and valleys have increased, so we have turned to traditional civil engineering works to solve our problems. Floodplains are so named for a reason: they are built up by repeated flood flows, and so, as we increasingly encroach upon these floodplains, the flood hazard increases. It was noted above how anthropogenic influences such as deforestation and land drainage have exacerbated flood flows. As a result, engineers have turned to flood control structures to lessen flood impacts. Artificial levées, channel straightening and vegetation removal all have long traditions. Cross-section enlargement to produce multistage channels, flood diversion channels, flood storage reservoirs and flood meadows are more recent, more environmentally sensitive techniques.

River channelisation for navigation purposes includes engineering works, re-sectioning of channel cross profiles and dredging aimed at keeping a minimum depth of water for navigation along the required section of a river channel.

The latter part of the 20th century has seen a marked change in methods of river management. Traditionally, river management has tried to meet its demands largely through civil engineering solutions with little regard for natural systems. As our understanding of river catchment processes and of channel behaviour and change has increased, so has our appreciation of the importance of environmental constraints in river channel management. River management is now regarded as a multidisciplinary affair, needing inputs from experts in such fields as geomorphology, ecology, civil engineering, economics and sociology.

Increased urban and industrial demands for water supply have led to increased use of groundwater, river water abstraction and reservoir construction. All of these have direct impacts on the hydrological cycle [☞] and ensuing river discharges. Integration of these sources and inter-regional transfers are becoming more commonplace.

See Volume 3: Environmental Geography, ch 2, Climate and weather (p44).

Greater environmental awareness, together with our improved understanding of catchment and channel processes and a concern for the decline in fluvial ecosystems have resulted in the development of much more environmentally sensitive approaches to river management. A key part of this modern approach is to view the catchment holistically rather than only considering the impacts on a particular section of channel, no matter what the scale of project being considered. Management strategies need to cope with conflicting demands: for water supply by agriculture, residential and industrial users, for flood alleviation and channel stability, for navigation, for recreation and to meet ecological requirements. Besides coping with this demand problem, management strategies also need to work with the existing river and catchment conditions themselves. Few rivers today are in natural or even near-natural conditions. Most rivers have been affected indirectly by changes in land use within the catchment, if not directly by some form of channel protection or channelisation. For instance, human-induced alterations in sediment budgets, flow regimes and water quality occur in most of our streams in Britain.

One of the first priorities in catchment and channel management is to identify any remaining natural channel reaches and maintain them. A second priority is to restore channel reaches to a more natural state where possible, while a third priority is to try to improve severely degraded reaches when resources permit. Baseline assessments need to be carried out involving catchment and stream reconnaissance surveys to establish the valley and channel characteristics, and to identify the particular needs of channel reaches in terms of restoration and management. To successfully understand the nature and functions of such specific channel reaches we need to link them to the drainage basin and its overall history. Only by using such integrated approaches can the dual functions of channel restoration and successful drainage basin management be achieved. One consequence of such approaches has been the replacement of single-purpose dams by multipurpose dams. An interesting example of this approach can be seen in the recent dual purpose Styggevatn reservoir and dam scheme in south central Norway, aimed at flood alleviation and hydroelectric power generation. Figure 2.20 shows the location and nature of this dam and reservoir. The rock metalling of the dam face blends sympathetically with the bare rock and scree slopes of the surrounding valley. The rocks used here were acquired from the tunnels driven through the hillside to transport the water from the dam to the hydroelectric turbines, which in turn have been buried in the hillside. The water used here is then transported further down valley to exit into Sognfjord at Gaupne, meeting the dual objectives of flood alleviation for the Jostedal Valley and helping to keep this part of Sognfjord more ice free during the winter by increasing the water discharge into it.

Figure 2.20: Styggevatn dam and reservoir and view of Sprongdalen stream control

See accompanying CD-Rom

Channel controls.ppt

Summary

In this chapter, we have covered the basic elements of the catchment hydrological cycle and the fluvial system it feeds. The complexity of the linkages within the whole drainage basin system has been demonstrated, and the system has been shown to be in a state of continual flux between rapid response to infrequent high-magnitude flood discharges and slower, long-term response to the frequent within-channel discharges. The final sections of the chapter showed how the fluvial system both affects, and is affected by people. It is a system strongly intertwined with human society.

Endnote

1. t $km^{-2}yr^{-1}$ = tonnes per square kilometre per year.

Useful websites

Environment Agency: *www.environment-agency.gov.uk/default.aspx*

Meteorological Office: *http://metoffice.com/weather/uk*

Centre for Ecology and Hydrology: *www.ceh.ac.uk/data/nrfa/river_flow_data.html*
An excellent site for data sponsored by the Natural Environment Research Council.

A good source of river discharge data in the UK: *www.nwl.ac.uk/ih/nrfa/river_flow_data/river_flow_data_download.htm* Annual tables of daily flow data for around 200 gauging stations throughout the UK are available for downloading.

This site contains a compilation of monthly mean river discharge data for over 3,500 sites worldwide: *www.sage.wisc.edu/riverdata*

Google Earth can be used for examining river planform: *http://earth.google.com*

Further reading

Charlton, R (2008) *Fundamentals of Fluvial Geomorphology*. Routledge, Oxford, England.

Holden, J (Ed) (2008) *An Introduction to Physical Geography and the Environment* (2nd Ed). Pearson, Essex, England.

Smithson, P, Addison, K and Atkinson, K (2008) *Fundamentals of the Physical Environment* (4th Ed). Routledge, Oxford, England.

Coasts

3

Introduction

The coastal zone is probably the most intensively used area by humans. More of the world's largest cities are sited on coasts than inland, and it has been estimated that roughly 50% of the world's population live within 60km of a coast. The coastal zone is an extremely dynamic environment. This dynamism can be seen by the clear evidence [☞], throughout the British Isles, for higher and lower sea levels than those currently present. Contemporary concerns relate to trends in sea-level rise. Sea levels are currently rising by roughly 3mm yr^{1}, with a predicted rise by the end of the century of between 18 and 59cm (Intergovernmental Panel on Climate Change – IPCC). In terms of coastal processes and landforms, erosion along current coastlines and a landward shift in the location of these coastal processes and landforms (a marine transgression) will follow. In terms of coastal zone management, and how severely coastal communities are affected, of greatest significance are the rate of sea-level rise and the length of time that this rise continues.

MAKING THE LINKS
See ch1, Restless Earth (p25).

This chapter will firstly consider what constitutes the coastal zone, and how this links into sea-level change scenarios, including the nature of our current sea-level rise, before considering the general nature of coastal systems, and especially the energy and materials driving these systems: waves, currents and tides. The chapter will then investigate the main elements of clastic (mud, sand and gravel) soft sediment systems and rocky hard coastlines, before turning finally to consider examples of the increasing problems faced in coastal zone management.

The coastal zone and sea-level change

The coast or coastline means different things to different people. To holidaymakers and for recreation purposes, it may be the beach for sunbathing and the shallow water zone of breaking waves for surfers and bodyboarders. This area is termed the 'shoreface'. For other users, the coast may also include the deeper water zone for sailing and fishing. Coastal managers consider the zone in terms of the ways in which different areas are used (figure 3.1).

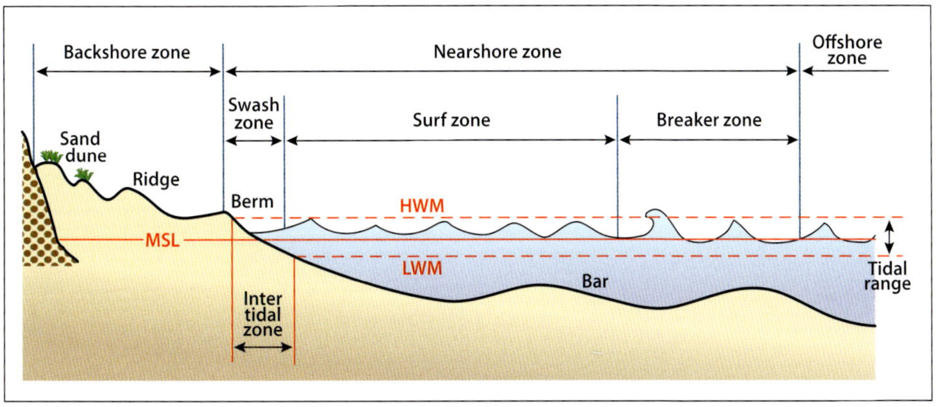

Figure 3.1: Definition of coastal zones

See accompanying CD-Rom

Coasts intro.ppt

For coastal geomorphologists to understand the development of coastal landform features, it is essential to view the historical context of the development of coastal landforms and materials, along with the changes in sea level that have occurred over the last 2.4 million years of glacial expansion and contraction. These changes have caused sea levels to fluctuate over 100 metres in vertical extent. The recent glacial fluctuations have caused coastal processes and landforms to migrate landward from their present location during high sea levels (warm interglacial times) and seaward towards the edge of the continental shelf during low sea levels (cold glacial periods).

Global sea level is rising at an accelerating rate, from around 1mm yr^{-1} in 1850 to 3.1mm yr^{-1} today (IPCC, 2007, observed data to 2003). The IPCC's *Fourth Assessment Report (AR4)* identifies four main contributing factors: thermal expansion of seawater due to increased temperature, melting of Antarctic ice, melting of Greenland ice and melting of ice elsewhere around the globe. These estimates account for all but 0.3mm yr^{-1}, though there is a considerable degree of uncertainty about the contributions of the Antarctic and Greenland ice sheets, and how these may alter in the future.

Teaching idea 3.1

Sea-level change

Provide students with maps showing sea-floor and land topography and contours around the British Isles, or of your local or chosen coastal area. Ask your students to plot sea-level change scenarios. Get them to draw the configuration of these islands, or the chosen coastline area at 5, 10 or 50m below present, at 1, 5 or 10m above present. How might these changes affect people today? How do they think a rise from 5m below present to present sea level affected our ancestor hunter-gatherers some 6,000 years ago? What impact might their possible migration have had on the landscape elsewhere? A useful website is: ***http://coastobs.pol.ac.uk***

Coastal systems

As implied in the introduction, when we consider the landforms and processes operating within coastal systems, we need to be aware of both spatial and temporal elements, that is to say, the spatial context of where the processes have been operating, and the historical context in which they were taking place. Figure 3.2 on p65 shows contrasting examples of these elements from the island of Mallorca in the western Mediterranean, which are the results of global eustatic sea-level changes and a local tectonic component, and from western Scotland, where local glacial isostatic and global eustatic changes have occurred. Eustatic changes are due to changes in the volume of water in the oceans and are global in nature; isostatic changes are those brought about by the natural buoyancy of the Earth's crust. For example, if the weight of an ice sheet melting were to be removed, then the crust would slowly rise to gain its new buoyant equilibrium (Archimedes' principle in physics). The returning meltwater in this case would cause a eustatic sea-level rise. Further, the stresses initially set up in the crust, because of the disequilibrium of the ice melting, might well then cause local tectonic movements, until the isostatic recovery had been completed. Both raised shorelines due to sea-level fall (regression) and flooded river valleys or rias due to sea-level rise (transgression) can be seen. In coastal zones there is a strong link between process, materials and form producing a linked morphodynamic system.

Figure 3.2: Examples of features related to sea-level change from Mallorca and western Scotland

See accompanying CD-Rom

Coasts intro.ppt

The coastal morphodynamic system

In order to understand the coastal system, it is essential to include all the processes involved in sediment production, movement and deposition, as these are what produce the evolving landforms we see. Weathering contributes material directly, or via the weakening of materials, thereby allowing erosion by other processes. Wave action and coastal currents are important in redistributing these materials, while tidal action governs where these operate within the coastal zone. Wind processes can be equally important in aiding weathering, by distributing salt spray and by transporting dry materials at low water. In some coastal locations, biological aspects are the leading process, as in salt marshes, mangrove environments and coral reefs [☞]. Where forces of gravity, water and wind are able to overcome particle inertia, then transport of material will result. If more sediment comes into a region than is transported out of it, depositional processes are dominant; on the other hand, if more leaves than enters, then erosional processes are dominant, with the coastline becoming prograding (depositional) or retrograding (erosional) respectively. This idea is termed 'the sediment budget' for the region in question. Examples of prograding and retrograding sections of coastline are shown in figure 3.3.

See Volume 3: Environmental Geography, ch 7, Environmental management (p169).

Figure 3.3: Prograding and retrograding elements of the Sefton Coast in Lancashire

See accompanying CD-Rom

Coasts intro.ppt

Source: (top left) Sefton Metropolitan Borough Council Coastal Defence Team; (top right, bottom far left) Steve Suggitt; (bottom centre and right) Vanessa Holden.

The final element of this morphodynamic system is the landform suite that is produced by the processes, materials and historical development of the particular region under study. Features such as dune complexes, beaches and barrier islands, salt marshes, deltas and estuaries can be seen in prograding or depositional situations; cliffs, stacks, arches and shore platforms on retrograding or erosional coastlines.

In addition to studying the environmental controls of materials (geology), and the external forcing agencies that modify and redistribute these materials (wind, waves and tide), it is also necessary to consider how sea-level change has affected where these driving forces operate, and the varying influences of these forces on the coastal system. Having said this, within any modern coastal system we also have to take account of anthropogenic influences. Such influences might incorporate aspects such as coastal protection works, land reclamation and beach nourishment schemes. Figure 3.4 demonstrates some of the differences between a natural coast and one heavily influenced by humans. Although, at the same time, it should be pointed out that elements such as anthropogenic influences on climate change [☞], with its knock-on effect on sea-level rise, also modifies the external forcing agencies themselves.

MAKING THE LINKS
See Volume 3: Environmental Geography, ch 3, Climate change.

Figure 3.4: Natural and anthropogenically controlled elements of the Lancashire coastline

See accompanying CD-Rom
Coasts intro.ppt

Source: Sefton Metropolitan Borough Council Coastal Defence Team.

A strong link between morphology and process is provided by the movement of materials, and this can be seen to exhibit both negative and positive feedbacks, which may either prevent landform change or enhance it. For instance, during storm conditions, down-combing of the beach, as material is removed seawards, may result in the formation of an offshore bar or island. This bar will then reduce the incidence and strength of wave action on the beach, thereby reducing further erosion and possibly even leading to deposition, as shown behind the barrier island on Benbecula in the Western Isles (see figure 3.5a on p67), an example of negative feedback. This development can be contrasted with the situation at Mangersta beach on the Isle of Harris, just to the north of Benbecula in the Western Isles, where storm activity has produced a coarse storm beach protecting the inner part of the bay from further erosion (figure 3.5b). This depositional event has led to further deposition in the form of increased sand dune and sand sheet development behind the storm beach. Stability (almost a steady state) is now developing here, as vegetation is establishing itself with minimal movement and entrapment of windblown sand now taking place.

a. Benbecula

b. Mangersta

Figure 3.5: Barrier and storm beaches in Scotland

See accompanying CD-Rom

Coasts intro.ppt

Coastal classification

All early coastal classification systems were based around the idea of sea-level change being the main control (producing emergent or submerged coasts), or of distinguishing between primary coasts (non-marine processes being the dominant control) and secondary coasts (dominated by marine processes including marine organisms). The problem with such classifications is that although they may be a useful concept for rocky coastlines, especially ones of erosion, they take little account of river, wave or tidal factors, which are the main controls behind clastic coastlines. A more process-based coastal classification balancing these three factors is therefore desirable and will be discussed below.

Waves, currents and tides

Waves

Waves are the dominant agent of erosion and transport within the nearshore coastal environment in most settings. Wave motions are generated by the friction between wind movements and surface water; the stronger the wind, the greater the disturbance of the water surface, and the higher the resulting wave motion. Such waves tend to have a regular motion but, as wind speed and direction varies, so does the wave height and direction. At a coastline, waves from different sources, as well as variations from the original source, may come together, producing a more random or irregular pattern as wave crests and troughs interfere or reinforce each other. Because of this, although regular waves can be described in terms of height, wavelength and period to gain insight into their character (see figure 3.6 on p68), they are not usually what is experienced at the coast, and so for practical purposes it is much better to consider the significant wave height (H_s), the average of the highest one-third of the wave heights recorded at the coast. This indicates the energy the waves have for erosion and transport of material.

The motion of water particles, as waves move across the water surface, can be determined according to linear wave theory. Figure 3.7 on page 69 shows how this translates in practical terms. As waves move onshore, friction at the wave base (the maximum depth of wave motion) increases. This slows down water movement, and leads to the circular orbital wave motion becoming more elliptical, eventually producing a horizontal motion as waves become more peaked and break at the edge of the surf zone. This increase in wave height, due to interaction with the seabed, is called 'wave shoaling' and leads to waves losing their sinusoidal shape. The waves become more

Figure 3.6: Morphological parameters of waves

See accompanying CD-Rom

Waves.ppt

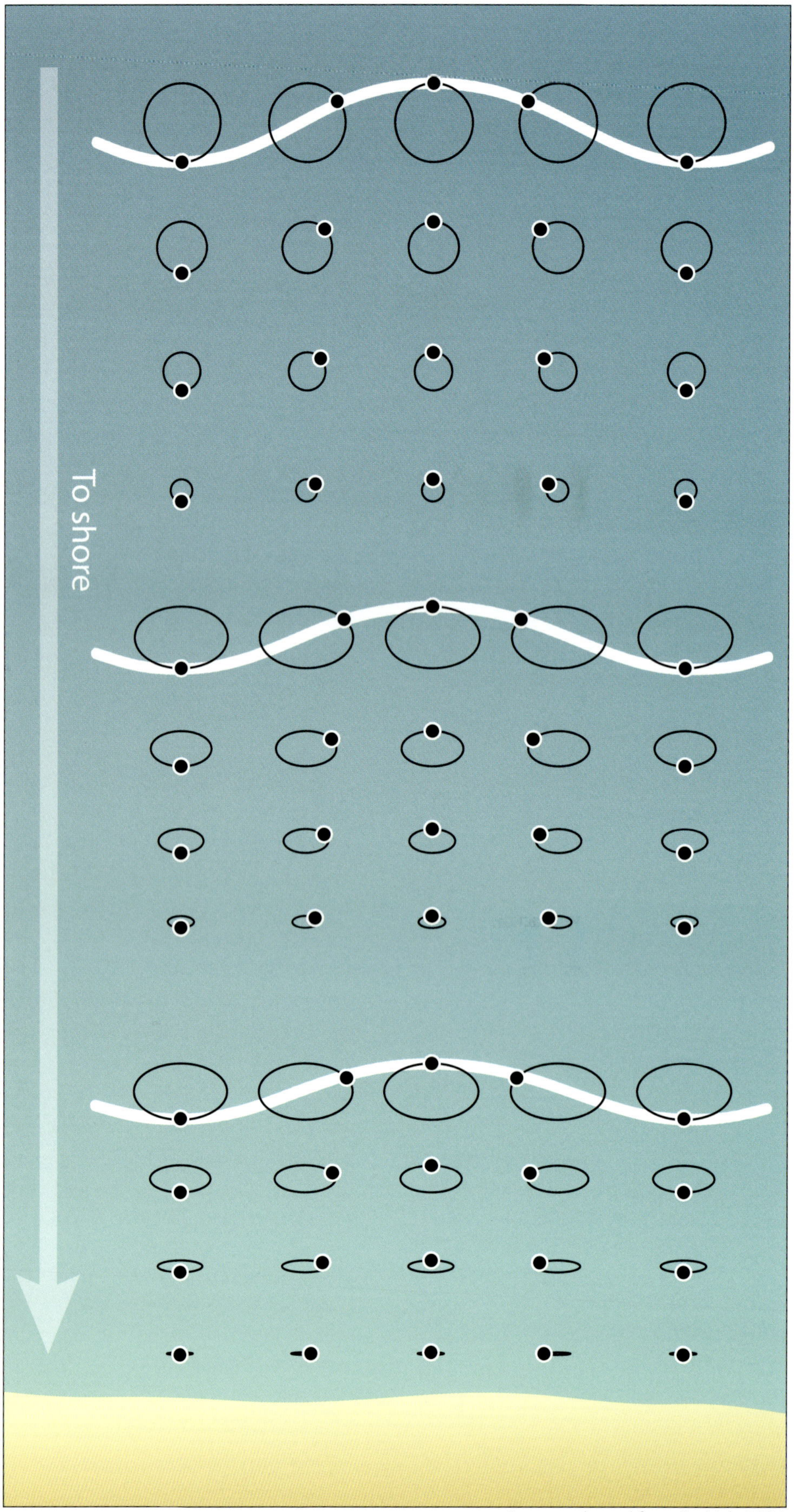

Source: adapted from Pethick, 1984.

Figure 3.7: Changes in wave morphology as the shoreline is approached

See accompanying CD-Rom

Waves.ppt

asymmetrical with flatter troughs and peaked crests. The symmetrical flow velocities also alter with the onshore direction of movement being shorter but faster than the offshore movements. Faster onshore velocities produce sediment movement in an onshore direction; without this change in wave symmetry, sand and gravel beaches would not exist, as there would be no net shoreward sediment movement.

Where the seabed topography is uniform, then waves will proceed onshore in their direction of movement. However, any variations in seabed topography will vary the efficiency of wave shoaling. Waves will slow more rapidly in shallower water than deeper water. This will result in waves being pulled in towards shallower areas (wave convergence), but spreading out over deeper water (wave divergence, figure 3.8). These are examples of wave refraction.

Figure 3.8: Example of wave divergence

See accompanying CD-Rom

Waves.ppt

As waves break they flow up the shoreline as swash. The wave reduces in velocity and moves to higher elevations than those where the still tidal water level would be. This is the wave set-up and is usually about 20% of the significant wave height. At the top of this turbulent swash zone, water has slowed, some has infiltrated into the beach, and water now drains down the beach with increasing velocity as backwash. This onshore asymmetry of swash and backwash maintains the beach gradient until wave energy conditions alter. If waves break against a steep beach, or particularly a cliff or seawall, then they are partly reflected, giving rise to a criss-cross wave pattern.

Breaking waves occur when the horizontal component of the wave motion exceeds the wave velocity and the wave collapses into a mass of aerated bubbly foam. Although breaking waves produce a continuum of shapes, three basic ones can be commonly identified. These are shown in figure 3.9, where we can identify spilling, plunging and surging breakers. Spilling breakers occur where there is a slow peaking of the wave and a slow spilling forward of the crest, usually on gently sloping beaches under steep wave conditions. Plunging breakers occur on steeper beach gradients with less steep wave conditions. Here the waves become more vertical, with the tops often curling over to plunge forward and downward (the ideal wave for surfing!). Steep beach gradients with the shallowest waves produce surging breakers. The crest and face of the wave stay reasonably smooth, though still frothy, as the wave appears to gently slide up the beach. This breaking of the wave motion releases the wave energy for sediment transport, as shown above, and for the generation of nearshore currents.

Figure 3.9: Types of breaking waves

See accompanying CD-Rom

Waves.ppt

Currents

Nearshore currents are generated by the energy from breaking waves. More wave energy produces stronger currents and so the strongest currents are during storm events. Three types of nearshore currents are responsible for the main patterns of movement of water in the coastal zone: the bed return current along the seabed, the longshore current and the rip current as shown in figure 3.10 on p71.

The bed return current is the offshore water flow near the seabed below the surface onshore movement of the breaking waves. These currents are strongest when wave approach is near 90° to the shoreface. When waves break at an angle to the shoreface, longshore currents roughly parallel to the shoreline are produced. These can be enhanced by strong alongshore winds blowing in a similar direction. Strong narrow currents fed by opposing longshore movements and flowing seaward along topographic lows are termed rip currents. The combination of longshore feeder current, offshore rip current and the onshore flow produces a nearshore cell circulation system. One question that

Figure 3.10: Currents

See accompanying CD-Rom

Currents.ppt

remains to be satisfactorily answered is that of which element is in control. Is it the circulation cell that produces the topographic bar and hollow system, with strong rip currents producing net offshore movement of sediment and similar onshore flows with waves breaking depositing sediment to produce the bars, or, alternatively, do variations in the existing bed topography which may have been initially produced by wave refraction cause the pattern of the circulation cell to be set up, which then propagates the landform?

Tides

Ocean tides are the result of the driving forces of gravitational attraction by the Earth-Moon system (dominant partner) and the Earth-Sun system (c. 50% of the strength of the former) on water on the surface of a rotating Earth. These forces of gravity and rotation produce water bulges at either side of the Earth, the size of which depends on the proximity and alignment of the gravitational forces. High spring tides occur when the Sun and Moon are aligned; low neap tides when they are at right angles to each other and their gravitational forces are competing. The Moon rotates around the Earth every 28 days and so a neap-to-neap or spring-to-spring cycle takes 14 days to complete. As the Earth rotates underneath these water bulges, sea level will rise twice a day, roughly 12.5 hours apart. This simple picture is disrupted by the location and configuration of the continents and coastlines producing a large number of individual tidal systems (termed 'amphidromes') around the centres of which the rise in sea level – the tide – produces a rotating standing tidal wave. This tidal wave circulates anticlockwise in the northern hemisphere and clockwise in the southern hemisphere due to the deflection produced by the Coriolis force [☞] as the Earth rotates.

See Volume 3: Environmental Geography, ch2, Climate and weather (p38).

Tidal ranges are categorised in three ways: below 2m is known as micro tidal; between 2 and 4m, meso tidal; and above 4m, macro tidal. The tidal range increases away from the centre of each amphidrome but can also be highly modified by local topographic conditions. The North Sea has three main amphidromes that affect the tides on the British coastline, while more enclosed topographic areas, such as Morecambe Bay, off the Lancashire and Cumbrian coasts, have a particularly great topographic effect, producing a high tidal range in excess of 6m. As these tides rise and fall, water moves to areas of high tide, and so tidal currents are produced: flood currents on the rising tide, ebb currents on the falling tide. As the length of time required for a flood tide is often different from an ebb tide, and because of differences in tidal range and timing of high tides between amphidromes, residual tidal currents are set up. These tidal currents are a dominant factor in sediment movement patterns on a regional scale around the British Isles – for example, Morecambe Bay and the Northern Irish Sea Basin is an area of net sediment gain as a result of these processes.

Storm surge

During severe storm weather conditions, the normal tidal range, wave height and energy can be greatly exceeded leading to high-magnitude, though low-frequency, energy conditions within the coastal zone. Where processes operate at a significantly higher level than normal, landform changes can be dramatic. Figure 3.11 shows the results of a modest storm surge in the vicinity of Formby Point on the Sefton Coast in Lancashire. Three main elements control the height of a storm surge level. As storms are always characterised by low pressure systems [☞], the first element is the low atmospheric pressure with roughly a 1cm rise in water level for every 1 millibar fall in atmospheric pressure. Secondly, wind speed and direction are important determinants, especially where strong onshore winds occur. The final group of elements relate to the

See Volume 3: Environmental Geography, ch2, Climate and weather (p41).

Teaching idea 3.2

Local storm surge effects

Provide the students with local or other 1:50,000 Ordnance Survey maps of an embayed or estuary coastline. Ask students to identify coastal topography contours and the mean high watermark, along with residential and industrial centres and transport routes. Then ask them to plot the high watermark again, with a 5m storm surge superimposed on it. What impacts would such a surge have? Develop the scenario further by asking them to consider a 75 and then a 120km/h onshore wind producing wave heights of up to another 5m on top of the elevated tide level. Where water is travelling up an increasingly narrow estuary or bay, add an additional 5m to the water height. These figures might be slightly high but the scenario is still a valid one, especially with the potential for increasingly stormy conditions that are associated with climate change.

Figure 3.11: Minor storm surge effects at Formby Point

See accompanying CD-Rom

Storm surge.ppt

Line of dune front erosion at Formby Point after minor storm surge, 2008

Detail of dune front erosion at Formby Point after minor storm surge, 2008

location and timing of the event. Enclosed bays and funnel-shaped coastlines such as river estuaries or the southern part of the North Sea, for example, have topographic constraints that increase water levels as incoming tides are fitted into a narrower and narrower area, with a corresponding increase in water depth. As well as the potential constraints of coastal topography, we also have to consider the state of the tidal cycle, low water at neap tide or high water at spring tide.

Tsunami

These are often misnamed 'tidal waves', but are produced by the displacement of a large mass of water in three specific ways. Firstly, a seabed disruption caused by a submarine earthquake; secondly, a large landslide into a water body; and finally, and more rarely, a shockwave generated by a large impact with the water body (perhaps a meteorite). In open water bodies, a tsunami will typically have a wavelength in the range of 200 to 300m with heights below 1m. Once these waves enter continental shelf areas they will shoal quickly, wavelengths will shorten and the heights of the waves can increase to tens of metres in scale. Their impacts on coastal landforms and the whole coastal system can be catastrophic.

Clastic coastlines

Wave-dominated coasts

Wave-dominated coasts contain three main elements with which we are familiar in the British Isles: barriers, beaches and dunes, all of which are shown in figure 3.12. We have already commented on a barrier island system on the island of Benbecula (see figure 3.5 on p67). Here we have the island or major bar (or several of these) separated by tidal inlets from the mainland (and/or each other) and fronting wide, shallow lagoons backed by a coastal plain, or estuaries or beaches. Most barrier systems

Figure 3.12: Example of barrier, beach and dune

See accompanying CD-Rom

Clastic coastlines.ppt

are sandy, but gravel barriers are found in some locations, mainly at high latitudes where flooded glacial deposits have provided the necessary parent material. Spits are good examples of drift-aligned barriers. Beaches are accumulations of sand or gravel deposited along shorelines. They represent the upper part of the shoreface and have generally concave, upwards profiles. Beaches often have smaller, superimposed forms such as berms (accumulation of sediment at the landward edge of swash processes) and cusps (rhythmic features caused by deposition of sand or gravel) with divergence of wave action. Coastal dune systems are common in wave-dominated environments with abundant sand supply. Such systems are common in the Irish Sea Basin and along the coasts of western Scotland, with the Sefton Coast in Lancashire and the Machair of the Western Isles being notable examples (figure 3.13). For such dune complexes to develop there is a need for dominant onshore winds and the stabilisation of the developing dunes by vegetation.

Teaching idea 3.3

Sand dune comparisons

Comparisons of sand dune complexes can be undertaken with various themes in mind. You could ask your students to compare coastal dunes in terms of their morphology across a linear dune belt such as that shown by the Sefton Coast in Lancashire, or in terms of the organisation of dune forms in a foreland dune system such as that at Sandscale Haws north-east of Barrow-in-Furness in Cumbria. Comparisons could be undertaken between the two styles. A good starting point could be Google Earth images followed by Ordnance Survey maps. Vegetation colonisation differences could be included if the images are detailed enough. It might be interesting to compare the differences in scale and form of coastal dune complexes with those of a hot arid desert environment [☞]. Again Google Earth images could be an effective resource in this context.

MAKING THE LINKS
See ch 4, Deserts (p100-105, esp figures 4.19 and 4.20).

Figure 3.13: Dune systems along the Sefton Coast and examples of the Machair dunes in the Western Isles

See accompanying CD-Rom

Clastic coastlines.ppt

Source: (top left) Sefton Metropolitan Borough Council; (top right, bottom) Steve Suggitt.

Tide-dominated coasts

Estuaries form one of the main sites where tidal processes can be seen to be dominant, but they may also be represented by some settings where wave action is a competing activity, producing a bar or barrier at the estuary mouth. Any estuary represents zones of river- and marine-dominated processes interacting in the central reaches of the river. All modern estuaries can be regarded as eustatically flooded coastal river valleys produced at the end of the last Ice Age, especially following the relative stabilisation of global sea level some 6,000 years ago. Since the end of the Ice Age, estuaries have been the site of balances between sediment inputs from marine and terrestrial sources. Where these sources roughly match, we often get estuary meander belts being produced. Salt marshes, sand and mud flats are common elements in estuary developments, and estuaries may be regarded as the lower reaches of drowned river valleys slowly being filled with sediment and returning to their previous fluvial form. Examples of some of the features of estuaries are shown in figure 3.14, where we can see salt marshes, mud and sand flats and tidal creek development.

Figure 3.14: Estuary features

See accompanying CD-Rom

Clastic coastlines.ppt

River-dominated coasts

The classic river-dominated coastal form is the delta, which occurs where the amount of sediment being produced by the fluvial system is in excess of what can be dispersed by tidal and wave activity. Today, British rivers are carrying relatively small sediment loads and drain areas of moderate relief in a cool temperate climate, and the sediment reaching the sea is easily dispersed by coastal processes. As a result, there is little in the way of marine delta development. As river water mixes with sea water and spreads out, velocity is checked and so the coarser-calibre sediment is deposited, the fresh river water interacts with the saline seawater and clays may flocculate and some ions come out of solution. The differences in water chemistry mean that the less dense river water flows over the denser saline water and so the bedload sediment is concentrated nearer to the coast with the finer suspended sediment being carried further seaward. All deltas are composed of three main components: the delta plain, delta front and prodelta. The delta plain is the relatively flat delta top dominated by fluvial, meandering floodplain deposits. As the main distributary channels discharge into the sea at the delta front, bars may build up. Beyond here suspended sediment slowly settles forming the subaqueous prodelta slope (figure 3.15).

Figure 3.15: A typical river delta, the Mississippi, USA

See accompanying CD-Rom

Clastic coastlines.ppt

Source: image courtesy of NASA.

Hard rock coastlines

Rocky coastlines are generally sites of wave attack and marine erosion. They account for some 75% of the world's coastlines and are characterised by a range of erosional processes and features. As rocky coastlines are erosional features, it is very difficult to deduce their evolutionary history, because stages in this are not preserved, and they have a very slow rate of morphological change. Some examples of the iconic landform features of a hard rock coastline, such as the stacks, stumps and arches that are produced, can be seen in figure 3.16.

Figure 3.16: Features of hard rock coastlines – Mangersta, Isle of Harris and Bedruthan Steps, Cornwall

See accompanying CD-Rom

Rocky coasts.ppt

Mangersta – stacks, vertical cliffs and rocky bay

Bedruthan – view southwards depicting stack, stumps and vertical cliffs at mid tide

Mangersta – stack, stumps, vertical cliff line along eroded fault

Bedruthan – view northwards showing stacks and stumps at low water

Mangersta – rockfall debris at foot of vertical cliff

Bedruthan – view of arch forming at mid tide

The main processes operating on a rocky coastline are mechanical and biological weathering, mass movements and wave action removal of debris. Coastal cliff morphology is a balance between downslope transport of material and cliff base removal. Rock lithology, structure and sea-level history are equally influential. The nature of the cliff form produced is often due to lithological control (see figure 3.17 on p77). If material accumulates quicker than wave action can remove it, screes and fans develop. If removal is fast enough, bare rock cliffs are produced. Shore platforms develop in front of these cliffs, where erosion and removal by waves and currents operate on a soft enough rock to leave a flat, gently sloping erosion surface in the intertidal zone.

Figure 3.17: Lithological control of cliffs in Cornwall

See accompanying CD-Rom

Rocky coasts.ppt

Figure 3.18 : Bio-erosion activity at the coast, Cornwall

See accompanying CD-Rom

Rocky coasts.ppt

Physical weathering processes attack pore spaces, cracks and fractures in the rock, aiding chemical weathering, especially salt crystallisation. Bio-erosion by organisms aids mechanical rock weathering and removal, producing local micro features on rock surfaces (see figure 3.18 on p77). Mechanical hydraulic wave action and abrasion by suspended and bedload debris are major agents of erosion.

Teaching idea 3.4

Providing the physical baseline for coastal management

The idea here is to ask students to investigate a section of coastline to determine the main landform elements present and to look at the nature of human occupancy nearby. This can be done using a combination of maps and Google Earth images. If the area is accessible then information on the materials present could be acquired through fieldwork. Students could write a summary report for a coastal management planning committee outlining the main features and what would be the likely impacts under sea-level rise scenarios. Coastal management reports are usually available as pdf files from local authorities. Also the Environment Agency website (*www.environment-agency.gov.uk/*) provides a range of information on coastal flooding and management.

The management of coastal environments

Coastal zones are one of the most dynamic locations on the Earth. The natural processes operating here form the interface between ocean and terrestrial systems. The coast has always been a focus for people, their settlements and livelihood and, increasingly, their recreation. The coastal zone has traditionally provided relatively easy access, food and other natural resources. There is increasing pressure on coastal zones as populations grow around the world, and natural coastal change becomes enhanced by changing sea levels and potential climate fluctuations. Coastal zones are highly dynamic and this means that a good appreciation of coastal landforms, materials and processes is necessary if we are to provide effective management of these locations.

The European Union has a coastline of 68,000km, over three times longer than that of the US and almost twice that of Russia. Maritime regions within Europe, widely used by holidaymakers, account for 40% of Europe's gross domestic product, but cost significant amounts of money to protect. In 2001, it was estimated that more than 70 million people lived in coastal municipalities within Europe, while assets located within 500 metres of the coastline were valued at between €500bn and €1,000bn (Eurosion, 2004a). Public expenditure within Europe to protect against coastal flooding and erosion will average €5.4bn a year for the period 1990 to 2020. Within the United Kingdom, as an island nation, a much greater proportion of our wealth is generated within the coastal zone and a much higher proportion of our population live within a short distance of the coast.

Erosion of the coastline is a serious issue in Europe, with about 20,000km (20% of the coastline) affected by coastal erosion. About 75% of this area has actively retreated, while the remainder is artificially stabilised. This retreat equates to an estimated loss of 15km^2 per year, resulting in serious impacts on coastal communities and coastal habitats (Eurosion, 2004a). Within the UK, the total length of the coast is 17,381km, of which 4,705km is impacted by erosion (Eurosion, 2004b).

Figure 3.19: Guiding principles for coastal management

See accompanying CD-Rom

Guiding principles.doc

Guiding principles for coastal management

- **take a long-term view**
- **consider the bigger picture**
- **ensure we are able to change our approach as our understanding improves**
- **work with nature**
- **get the right organisations to work together**
- **use an appropriate mix of tools**
- **wide involvement of people**
- **reflect local character and need**

In practice, the implementation of these principles for integrated coastal zone management means:

- **take a long-term view**

Management must think further ahead. A long-term perspective is needed, because of the long-term evolution of coastal processes, the natural variability of habitats and species, and the need to take account of the needs of future generations. Strategies for tackling long-term issues may be different to those designed for solving current problems. Forward-looking management approaches are, however, more likely to be cost effective and sustainable in the long-term.

- **consider the bigger picture**

Successful coastal planning and management must look at the big picture, and view coastal problems in the widest context. This means that integrated coastal zone management (ICZM) strategies should take into account the relationship between cultural, economic, social and environmental factors as well as temporal and spatial characteristics. This may mean approaches and policies cut across conventional boundaries and challenge traditional sectoral approaches.

- **ensure we are able to change our approach as our understanding improves**

Uncertainty surrounding future coastal conditions and future demands on the coast make it essential for ICZM approaches and policies to be both flexible and adaptive. Management decisions must be supported by suitable information and be evidence-based, wherever possible. However, since we can never know everything, management has to get on with things and 'learn by doing', while fully applying the precautionary principle. Research, data, information and monitoring (and thus feedback) are prerequisites, enabling adjustments to management with enhanced understanding.

- **work with nature**

Modern coastal management should work with nature rather than battle against it, recognising that the natural dynamics of coastal systems result in a continually changing and evolving coastline. This principle implies that coastal management should take account of the natural limits or carrying capacity of coastal systems, ensuring the maintenance of ecosystem functioning and integrity.

- **get the right organisations to work together**

All relevant bodies (at national, regional and local levels) must be fully involved in the development of any ICZM strategy to ensure that relevant policies and related legal instruments are well coordinated, mutually compatible and coherent.

- **use an appropriate mix of tools**

Successful ICZM requires the combined use of a range of 'instruments', including laws, policies, voluntary agreements, research, education and information provision. Given the need for a coordinated and integrated approach to management, coherence and consistency between these instruments is vital.

- **wide involvement of people**

In addition to government and agency involvement, local ICZM programmes require the participation of non-government organisations and others, particularly local businesses and local people. The full participation of all stakeholders from the outset, and through all stages of the ICZM process, is essential. Stakeholder involvement aids the identification of real issues, harnesses local knowledge and builds and strengthens commitment and shared responsibility.

The objective of UK national government, with respect to flood and erosion risk management, is to reduce risks to people and the developed and natural environment from flooding and coastal erosion, by encouraging the provision of technically, environmentally and economically sound and sustainable defence measures. This risk is made up of probabilities and consequences. Soft and hard engineering options can reduce the probability of damage, but forward spatial planning based on sound knowledge is required to reduce the consequences. A number of guiding principles for good coastal management have been developed to improve approaches to the management of these complex environments (see figure 3.19 on p79). These principles are often referred to as the principles for integrated coastal zone management or ICZM.

Teaching idea 3.5

Ask students to look at a local coastal management plan for their area of study. To what extent does the plan reflect the eight principles listed in figure 3.19? Can they identify any areas of the plan that need strengthening to reflect more effectively the principles listed?

Shoreline management plans

In order to achieve the priorities discussed above, the government has required shoreline management plans (SMPs) to be developed by the appropriate local authorities. It is these that set policy for coastal risk management, and so define the nature of future flood and erosion risk management. The second generation of these (SMP2s), are being developed at present.

Generally speaking, there are four policy options contained within SMPs. Firstly, no active intervention; secondly, managed realignment; thirdly, hold the line; and finally, advance the line. These plans provide a large-scale assessment of the risks associated with coastal processes and a policy framework to reduce these risks to people and the developed, historic and natural environment in a sustainable manner.

SMPs set out the approach to the long-term sustainability of flood and coastal defences for a specific stretch of coastline. Their aim is to provide the basis for sustainable shoreline management policies over the next 100 years within a natural process unit (sediment cell or sub-cell – see figure 3.22 on p84). They will also set the framework for the future management of risks along the coast, ie provide the direction of travel for those responsible for the management of the coast, including maritime councils.

In simple terms, SMPs suggest how the coastline should be managed in the future and form an important element of the high-level strategy for flood and coastal erosion risk management. An SMP may, for example, include a number of communities and a series of sea defences. The plans look at how the maritime local authorities can work with communities to reduce the risks to people, property and land from sea flooding and coastal erosion. SMPs are the coastal equivalent of catchment flood management plans (CFMPs) for rivers. It is essential that such plans are integrated where estuarine, fluvial processes converge with maritime, coastal processes.

The main purpose of SMPs is to identify policies to reduce risk. This is achieved through an assessment of the risks, opportunities, constraints and uncertainties along a given shoreline, using the latest data on the coastal processes, and environmental and human needs and issues involved. Strategy priorities are identified and developed in SMPs. The strategy plan delivers the preferred approach to reducing the identified risk and identifies how best to reduce it while taking full account of both environmental and economic issues. It may be that no method of defence can be justified for technical, economical or environmental reasons. That is to say, coastal defence cannot be shown to be sustainable. In such cases there may be a need to adapt to coastal change rather than attempting to resist it.

The objectives of a shoreline management plan are as follows:

- to define, in general terms, the risks to people and the developed, historic and natural environment within the SMP area
- to identify the preferred policies for managing these risks over the next 100 years
- to identify the consequences of implementing the preferred policies
- to ensure that future land use and the development of the shoreline take due account of the risks and the preferred SMP policies
- to comply with international and national conservation, legislation and biodiversity obligations.

The most appropriate future shoreline position is identified for each policy unit according to the policy options, as set out below:

- **Hold the existing line of defence** – maintain or change the standard of protection. Used to cover situations where works or operations are undertaken to improve or maintain the standard of protection provided by the existing defence line.
- **Advance the existing line of defence** – construct new defences seaward of the original defences. Limited to those frontages where significant land reclamation is under consideration.
- **Managed realignment** – identify a new line for coastal defence and, where appropriate, construct new defences landward of the original defences.
- **No active intervention** – where there is to be no investment in coastal defence assets or operations.

The SMP approach to coastal management is seen as the way forward to deliver sustainable coastal management that involves spatial planning and temporal re-evaluation. It is seen as objective focused and aims to reduce uncertainty through time, as continuing coastal research improves understanding, enabling more effective planning for change.

Teaching idea 3.6

The first generation of SMPs were developed in the 1990s and the second generation (SMP2s) are being developed at present. For a chosen coastal study area, ask students to review the SMP. What is it aiming to achieve and to what extent has it been successful? What do they think ought to be the priorities for the second generation plan? See the Environment Agency website for details of SMPs: *www.environment-agency.gov.uk/research/planning/104939.aspx*

See Volume 3: Environmental Geography, ch 3, Climate change.

An example that illustrates the need to take a long-term view is the need to adapt to climate change [] and to coastal change in general. Attention at a global scale on climate change has mainly been focused on mitigation of climate change instead of adaptation (Safecoast, 2007). Mitigation relates to targeted reductions in the sources or enhancements of the sinks of greenhouse gases (Nicholls and Lowe, 2004) and, in response to climate change, it primarily represents activities to protect nature from society. On the other hand, adaptation constitutes ways of protecting society from nature (Stehr and Storch, 2005).

Defra (2006) highlighted the importance of communicating adaptation to climate change and has developed some key communication messages that environmental managers should be aware of when adapting to climate change:

- climate change is happening and will accelerate despite current mitigation efforts
- we need to revise our approaches to reflect and respond to dynamic systems
- adapt now to minimise impacts
- continue to improve evidence base to be more effective
- due to developing understanding we need to be able to take stock and review and amend approaches
- learn to cope with an uncertain future and act in foresight and unison.

Point for consideration

To what extent should teachers modify their approach to coastal management where students are directly involved at a personal level as a result of their own residential location?

Defra, as the responsible department for adaptation to coastal change (including the effects of climate change), is seeking to develop policy in this area and to learn lessons from the approaches being adopted at various locations around the English coast.

Teaching idea 3.7

Ask students to consider the problems related to adapting to coastal change. This might take the form of a role-play incorporating coastal planners, local residents, local businesses and conservationists. Ask students to consider the role economics plays in such decision making and how economic costs can be equated with environmental value and the personal distress of people losing their homes.

Probably the most important aspect of management at the moment is the problem of coastal stability, especially coastal erosion. Good appreciations of sediment dynamics on the coast, and of the historical changes that have happened, are necessary requirements for successful prediction of change, and to inform future planning. Coastlines are constantly in a state of flux as ice sheets advance and retreat leading to decreases and increases in the amount of water in the oceans, and hence eustatic fluctuations in sea level. Locally, these ice advances may also have an isostatic component due to the weight of ice. At the same time, many places around the world are tectonically active, which also feeds into the local sea-level change [] equation. Nevertheless, coastal managers and decision makers are required to plan and manage the current situation, rather than considering longer-term variability.

See ch7, Globalisation (p187).

For example, the Lancashire coast at Formby has been eroding since 1900 due to increased storminess. Changes in bathymetry due to estuarine dredging on the Mersey and Ribble Rivers are key factors helping to cause current erosion. Future sea-level rise and a predicted increase in storminess are set to further erode the coast at Formby Point (figure 3.20), engulfing tourist car parks and threatening coastal caravan sites. One of the main problems is that, although people demand protection for their local coastline, it is of little use protecting a few key or particularly sensitive sites. What is required is the management of the entire coastline, considering both areas of accretion as well as those of erosion. Solid sea defences have their place, but they do tend to pass the problem further along the coast through their effects on longshore drift and sediment supply.

Figure 3.20: Erosion of the coastline in the Formby Point area of Lancashire

See accompanying CD-Rom

Coasts management.ppt

Coastal management aimed at increasing coastal protection falls into two main types. The first is the use of hard engineering works, such as sea wall defences, aimed at replacing natural materials with protection from more solid structures capable of withstanding the higher-magnitude, less frequent storm events, as well as controlling coastal erosion under normal high-frequency conditions. Alternatively, a second approach is to use soft engineering, where natural materials and landforms such as beaches, bars and dunes are encouraged, as these will absorb the energy of storms and have a built-in natural recovery capacity.

Management case study: the Sefton Coast[1]

The English coastline is divided up into 11 discrete cells (see figure 3.22 on p84) in terms of the nature of the environment and the processes operating therein. Each cell has a set of generic and unique attributes which are subdivided into segments for detailed planning and management purposes. In this section, we shall consider the Sefton Coast as an example of coastal management. An aerial view of the Sefton Coast is seen in figure 3.21 on p84. The Sefton Coast is part of cell 11, and for planning purposes covers parts of cells 11a and 11b (see figures 3.23 and 3.22 on p84).

Figure 3.21: Aerial view of Sefton Coast

See accompanying CD-Rom

Coasts management.ppt

Figure 3.22 (left): Coastal management cells

See accompanying CD-Rom

Coasts management.ppt

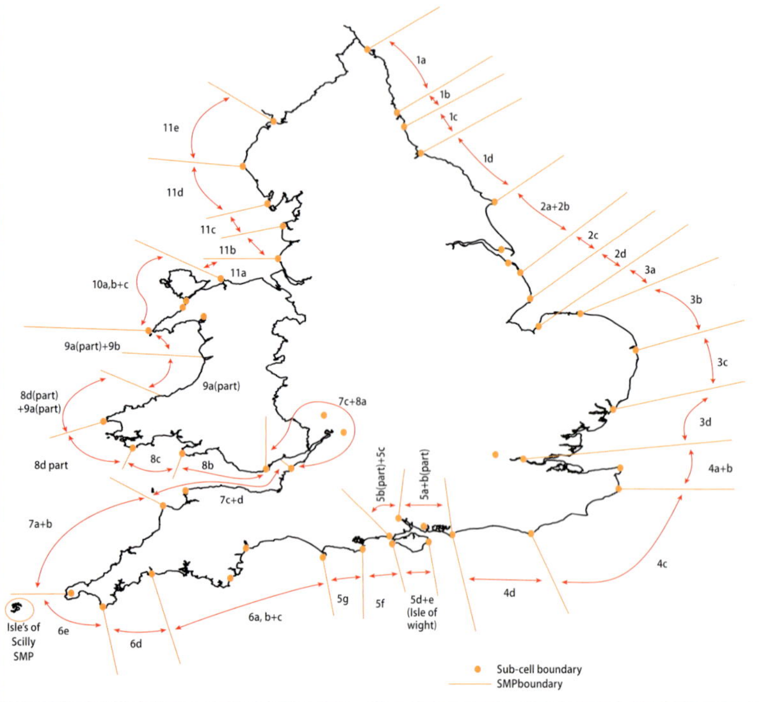

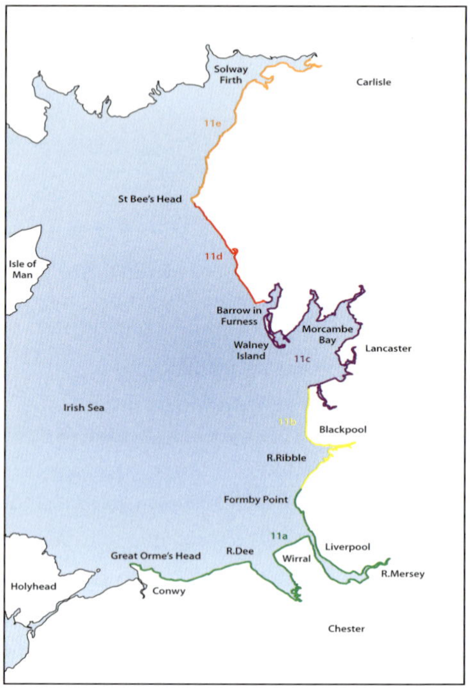

Figure 3.23 (right, inset): Management cell 11

See accompanying CD-Rom

Coasts management.ppt

Along the Sefton Coast, the problem of coastal erosion is such that it is predicted that by 2050 the coastline will be approximately 585m from the urban area at Victoria Road, Formby (see figure 3.24 on p85). The position of the dune toe in 2050 has been calculated using the long-term trend of measurements, combined with the high emissions climate change scenario developed by UKCIP (UK Climate Impacts Programme). Measurements taken at Victoria Road in the past have shown 235m accretion (1845 to 1906), 190m loss to 1945, 310m further loss to 2005 with 315m predicted to be lost between 2005 and 2050. As with all such predictions, this scenario doesn't include all of the potential impacts of climate change. The most notable missing impact is the increased frequency of storms, which could significantly alter the prediction. Other impacts relating to changes in precipitation and wind could be influential in the evolution of the dune system. The prediction will need to be monitored and revised over time.

The management possibilities for this part of the coast include both hard and soft engineering options. A replacement sea wall was completed in 2002. The main impact of this sea wall is to fix the position of the coastline, preventing the natural processes of realignment and vegetation succession that would normally take place. The implication of sea-level rise and increased storminess could see a reduction in the standard of service provided by the sea wall, with increasing risk and frequency of overtopping during extreme conditions. Under current conditions at Southport, serious overtopping might be expected two or three times in a 50-year period. However, it is expected that this frequency will increase. By 2080, it is possible that overtopping might occur once every two years or even annually (figure 3.25). In such a context, it seems unlikely that hard engineering structures are the answer, given that they are costly to build and maintain, and have a limited life expectancy. The way forward would appear to be in terms of a soft engineering option focus, with a management package aimed at greater education and stakeholder engagement being undertaken. Sefton Council is intending to improve understanding of coastal processes and change, and to communicate both with those affected by change, and those who can effect change. At the same time, it aims to systematically review the impacts in order to decide on future responses.

Figure 3.24 (left): 50-year sea-level prediction

See accompanying CD-Rom

Coasts management.ppt

Figure 3.25 (right): Sea-level rise and storminess

See accompanying CD-Rom

Coasts management.ppt

As a society, we have always responded to coastal change, whether to exploit it or adjust to it. Future changes will be more extreme than have been experienced in recent history. As time goes on, coastal communities have developed more fixed infrastructure, and therefore have less scope to adapt. The key to successful management is seen as adaptation. In such situations, the impacts of climate change are assessed (particularly warmer temperatures and increased rainfall/storminess) and suitable anticipatory action is taken to adapt to them. Such measures would include emergency planning, the relocation of threatened assets, sea defences, changes in building design, sustainable urban drainage systems and so forth. This adaptation is seen as an adjustment in natural and human systems in response to actual or expected climatic stimuli or their effects. As such, these responses will moderate the harmful impacts, and allow for the exploitation of beneficial opportunities. In the case of Southport, such strategies may well focus around tourism.

See Volume 3: Environmental Geography, ch7, Environmental management, figure 7.7.

An appreciation of the nature of the coastal processes and changes along the Sefton Coast has led to a combined approach of sustainable management [ ] with no further major hard engineering options being used. This approach is objective-led and addresses a number of timescales in varying degrees of detail, but is founded upon an understanding of the local coastal processes, and the need to involve local stakeholders to as great a degree as possible.

The key to sustainable coastal management is seen as appropriate SMP development. To this end, Sefton has used an understanding of coastal and shoreline processes, along with that of the features and uses of the coastal zone. This has led to the formulation of a series of issues and objectives, along with an identification of how these objectives might be achieved. Policies are initially set, and their implications are reviewed, through studying how the shoreline responds.

One of the key elements in the Sefton approach is that of stakeholder involvement (people with an interest and likely to be affected by the management options) throughout the process, from inputting their initial thoughts, to involving them in improving understanding of the dynamic nature of coastal environments, processes and change. Stakeholders are involved and so feel more ownership of a positive plan with clearly defined objectives. Such a plan needs to be available at a variety of technical levels for use by different groups. As a result of such planning, a clearer understanding of the human-coast relationship is achieved. The issues of future erosion leading to hard defences being breached and left as headlands, loss of beaches, and increased flood frequency and levels need to be understood by all, along with an appreciation of the need for a sustainable management approach. The coast is highly dynamic and so responses to these changes also need to be dynamic. The benefits of such a sustainable approach include a clear representation of future flood and erosion risks, and the recognition of the need to change approaches as climate and environmental changes occur.

Summary

In this chapter we have explored the main processes and landforms of coastal zones such as those around the British Isles. This is an area subject to almost constant geomorphological change, both from everyday processes due to the tidal cycle of the oceans and to the higher-magnitude, less frequent events. We have put a particular emphasis on elements of the coastline related to sea-level change and the need to manage this area effectively due to the amenity and resource use made of it. The coastal zone and its hinterland are often highly populated and so many people with different backgrounds and experiences are interested in its future, a particular problem for coastal managers.

Endnote

1. Many of the images and information are provided by courtesy of Sefton Council to whom grateful thanks are given. For the Sefton shoreline management plan see: *www.sefton.gov.uk/default.aspx?page=4602*

Useful websites

Environment Agency for SMPs: *www.environment-agency.gov.uk/research/planning/104939.aspx*

For coastal images use Google Earth: *http://earth.google.com*

For other data and information, the Proudman Oceanographic Laboratory is a useful hub: *http://coastobs.pol.ac.uk/*

For the Sefton Coast: *www.sefton.gov.uk/default.aspx?page=4730*

A useful educational web portal: *www.physicalgeography.net/*

Further reading

European Environment Agency (2006) *The Changing faces of Europe's coastal areas*. EEA Report No 6. Copenhagen, Denmark: *www.eea.europa.eu/publications/eea_report_2006_6*

Eurosion (2004a) *Living with coastal erosion in Europe: Sediment and Space for Sustainability PART I – Major findings and Policy Recommendations of the EUROSION project: www.eurosion.org/reports-online/part1.pdf*

Eurosion (2004b) *Living with coastal erosion in Europe: Sediment and Space for Sustainability PART II – Maps and statistics: www.eurosion.org/reports-online/part2.pdf*

Holden, J (Ed) (2008) *An Introduction to Physical Geography and the Environment (2nd Ed)*. Pearson, Essex, England.

Safecoast (2007) *Quick scan climate change adaptation with a focus on coastal defence policies in five North Sea countries: www.safecoast.org.uk*

Smithson, P, Addison, K and Atkinson, K (2008) *Fundamentals of the Physical Environment* (4th Ed). Routledge. Oxford, England.

4

Deserts

Introduction

Although our general idea of a desert would be easily recognised from space, deserts are not that easy to define. There are many different types of desert around the globe: in continental interiors, along coasts, at high and low altitude and in high and low latitudes. Deserts cover some 50 million square kilometres, roughly one-third of the terrestrial surface of the Earth, and are presently increasing in size every year. The key feature of any desert is aridity; they all have in common a lack of water, not a total absence, a regular lack. Their average annual precipitation is very low, generally being accepted as below 50mm of rainfall per year. Sometimes precipitation is absent for long periods of time, though all drylands are subject to large variations in precipitation on an almost annual basis. This arid environment results in the processes, materials and landforms that make a dryland largely a balance between the severity of aridity and the frequency and magnitude of precipitation. When we look at deserts, and especially desert materials and landforms, it becomes clear that, somewhat surprisingly, water can be just as important as wind in most cases. Over longer timescales, deserts can be seen as quite dynamic environments, increasing and decreasing in extent and intensity in response to climate changes, but also with margins that can sometimes suffer from desertification induced by anthropogenic influences.

In this chapter, we will be looking at the types of desert and how they form, before concentrating on hot dry desert environments. Here we will consider the surface materials produced by weathering processes in these hot dry lands. We will focus on the interactions between geomorphological processes and these weathered materials, concentrating on the roles of wind and water, and the landforms produced. Though the environment may be hot during the day, night can see temperatures below freezing, and where these high temperature variations occur, they play an important role in dryland geomorphological processes. These regions are some of the most inhospitable in the world, suffering intense erosion by wind and water, and often with a saline or nonexistent water supply. The chapter will conclude by looking at the nature of climate and environmental change and the problem of desertification [☞].

See Volume 3: Environmental Geography, ch 7, Environmental management (p164).

What makes a desert?

Aridity is the main key to understanding what deserts are and why they exist. They are areas that have a net negative water balance for most of the time. Here potential evapotranspiration exceeds precipitation for most of the time, the precipitation (P) to potential evapotranspiration (PET) ratio sometimes being below 0.5(P/PET). This lack of available moisture, with precipitation being highly uneven throughout the year, major dry seasons, and occasional cloudbursts and flash floods, provides for an extremely flashy hydrological regime [☞].

See ch 2, Rivers (p43-44).

In hydrological terms, these drylands include regions where P/PET<0.05. These hyper-arid areas may go for more than 12 months without rainfall and include places such as the central Sahara, parts of Arabia, the Touran, western parts of the Gobi, and the Namib, Karroo and Atacama deserts. At a less severe level, we have arid areas such as central Australia, north and south Sahara, parts of Arabia such as the Sinai, eastern parts of the Gobi, the Kalahari, Patagonia and parts of the south-western United States. Here P/PET is between 0.05 and 0.2. Because of their large precipitation variability on a year-by-year basis, we should also consider the semi-arid areas of the world, such as parts of the Mediterranean, the north and south of Australia, and much of the less arid south-western United States, along with parts of Antarctica where P/PET is between 0.2 and 0.5. Some 4% of the Earth's land surface is hyper-arid, 15% arid and 14.5% semi-arid. In total, almost 50 million square kilometres of the Earth's 135 million square kilometres of land surface – some 34 to 35% – can be classed as drylands of varying degrees of severity. Figure 4.1 shows the disposition of the world's drylands.

Figure 4.1: The world's drylands

See accompanying CD-Rom

Deserts introduction.ppt

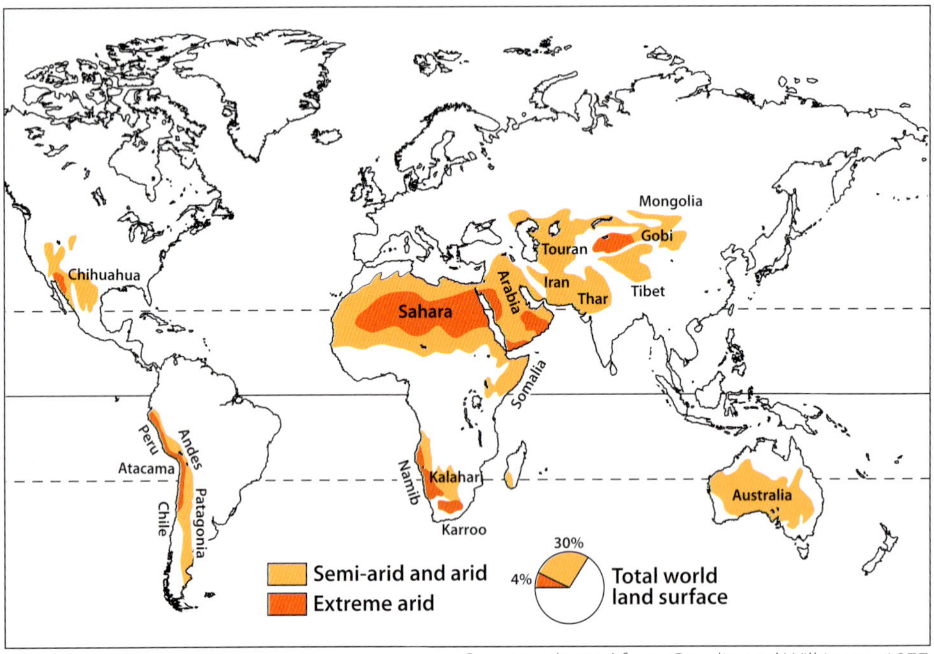

Source: adapted from Goudie and Wilkinson, 1977.

Why this aridity?

See Volume 3: Environmental Geography, ch 2, Climate and weather (p44).

See ch 1, Restless Earth (p8 and p18).

To appreciate how deserts form, and to understand their distribution, we need to consider what brings precipitation [☞] to places on the Earth's land surface. This is where atmospheric circulation patterns come into play, so it is important to consider these briefly before moving on to see how they, and the large-scale geomorphological features of the Earth's surface caused by plate tectonic processes [☞], affect desert formation. As the Earth is a sphere orbiting the sun, incoming solar radiation is spread out over a much greater area in the polar regions than in equatorial ones, resulting in the poles being colder than the equator. This differential heating sets up convections of warmed air between the equator and the poles but, because the Earth rotates, these air mass movements are deflected to the right in the northern hemisphere and to the left in the southern hemisphere. This is known as the Coriolis effect. This breaks up the simple northward and southward circulation from the equator into three major atmospheric cells in each hemisphere. The Hadley cells are made up of warmed air rising over the equator, cooling as it rises and depositing its precipitation over the equatorial rain forests, before moving both north and south to sink between 20° and 30° of latitude, and then returning as trade winds to the equator. In mid latitudes, the Ferrel cells flow towards the poles across the surface (known as the westerlies) to rise and return at high altitude towards the equator. Over the poles we have polar cells with air rising at the Ferrel-polar front and descending over the poles. These basic circulation patterns are shown in figure 4.2.

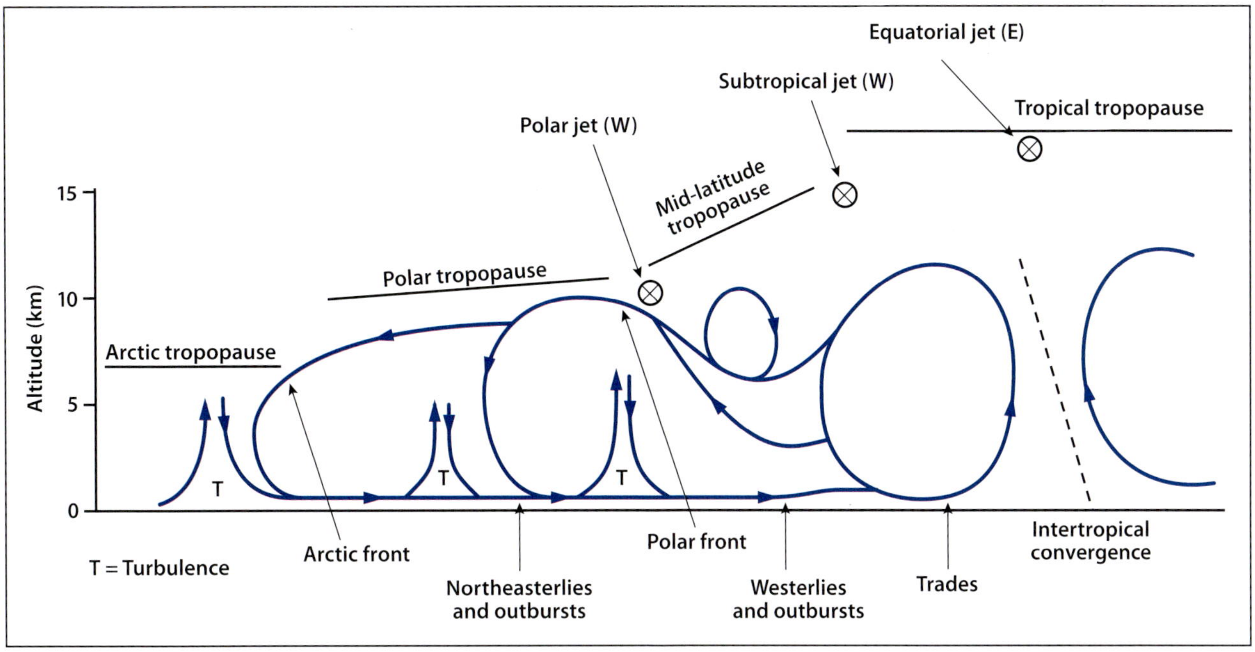

Figure 4.2: Basic atmospheric circulation patterns affecting location of arid areas

See accompanying CD-Rom

Deserts introduction.ppt

As a result of the combination of this global atmospheric circulation pattern and the major geomorphological features of the Earth's surface, it is possible to identify five desert situations. The types of desert associated most strongly with atmospheric circulation are subtropical and polar deserts, both of which are situated where dry, cool air sinks from the Hadley cells at 20° to 30° latitude and from the polar cells over the poles. These promote stable regions of high pressure dominated by dry air. This dry air in turn produces arid subtropical deserts, such as the Kalahari and much of the Sahara, and polar ones, such as much of Antarctica.

Where moist, warm air is moving onshore and encountering mountain ranges, such as the Andes in South America or southern Deccan in India, the air masses cool, condense and deposit precipitation on the windward side leaving the dry air on the leeward side. If the effect is severe enough, rain shadow deserts, such as Patagonia or the Thar in India, form. The Mojave in the USA is a similar rain shadow desert, but with elements of a continental interior. Examples of the landscapes and vegetation of the Mojave Desert are shown in figure 4.3 on p92. Continental deserts occur where the rain shadow process is repeated by a series of mountain belts or high plateaux. By the time air masses reach the continental interiors, such as the Gobi or central Australia, most of their moisture has gone.

PHOTOS: CHARLES RAWDING

Figure 4.3: Examples of the landscapes and vegetation of the Mojave Desert

See accompanying CD-Rom

Deserts introduction.ppt

Coastal deserts form along the west coasts of continents, where air masses have passed over cold ocean currents. These currents have cooled the air mass sufficiently to reduce its capacity to carry moisture. The cold California Current has this effect over much of Baja California in Mexico, while the Benguela Current has the same effect in South Africa. Coastal fogs often form over the oceans from the moisture left behind, as is the case off the Pacific coast of the Atacama and the Atlantic coast of the Namib deserts.

Precipitation in deserts is not only generally lacking, but is also extremely variable in character, both in terms of frequency of rainfall and also in terms of its location. Statistics from average rainfall distributions can easily be acquired from the World Meteorological Organisation website (*www.worldweather.org/index.htm*) for many places around the world. If we compare an area like Khartoum in the Sudan (figure 4.4), towards the margins of the Sahara, with Ghat in the Libyan Arab Jamahiriya (see figure 4.5 on p93), we can contrast the short, sharp rainy season of the former with the almost total absence of rain in the latter. We shall be investigating the effects of intense rainfall over a short period of time, as well as lack of rainfall on geomorphological processes in deserts later (see *Water activity* on p98).

Figure 4.4: Mean total rainfall and mean number of rain days, Khartoum, Sudan

See accompanying CD-Rom

Deserts introduction.ppt

Month	Mean total precipitation (mm)	Mean number of precipitation days
January	0.0	0.0
February	0.0	0.0
March	0.0	0.1
April	0.4	0.1
May	4.0	0.9
June	5.4	1.2
July	46.3	4.8
August	75.2	4.8
September	25.4	3.2
October	4.8	1.2
November	0.7	0.0
December	0.0	0.0

Source: *www.worldweather.org/index.htm*

Month	Mean total precipitation (mm)	Mean number of precipitation days
January	1.1	0.3
February	0.3	0.2
March	0.9	0.3
April	0.5	0.2
May	0.5	0.5
June	1.1	0.4
July	0.0	0.0
August	0.1	0.1
September	0.6	0.4
October	0.2	0.2
November	0.4	0.1
December	0.7	0.3

Source: *www.worldweather.org/index.htm*

Figure 4.5: Mean total rainfall and mean number of rain days, Ghat, Libyan Arab Jamahiriya

See accompanying CD-Rom

Deserts introduction.ppt

Temperature input

When analysing hot arid deserts, it is essential to consider the role of temperature in these locations in enhancing the aridity of the environment. Deserts in subtropical and tropical locations are characterised by extremely high temperatures. Such deserts can be subdivided into coastal and interior locations, with coastal locations having relatively low diurnal and seasonal temperature ranges, and interiors having large ones along with extreme daily maxima. Figure 4.6 on p94 shows mean daily maximum and minimum temperatures for Khartoum, Sudan and Ghat, Libyan Arab Jamahiriya in the Sahara region. These temperatures are well above the 37°C comfort maximum for most animals and humans during the main summer months and, because of the clear skies, diurnal ranges of 18° to 22°C are common. A temperature of 41°C was recorded in Death Valley, California in 1891, when the monthly mean diurnal range was 35°C. These temperature range extremes and surface maxima have important consequences for mechanical weathering (see p95). Coastal deserts are characterised by low daily temperature ranges, generally 10° to 11°C, monthly annual ranges of 5° to 6°C, and mean annual temperatures considerably lower than their interior counterparts. In the Atacama Desert annual temperatures are around 19°C while the Namib Desert is slightly cooler at 17°C.

Teaching idea 4.1

Climate in deserts

Using data from the World Meteorological Organisation website (like that shown in figures 4.4 to 4.6) (*www.worldweather.org/index.htm*) and an atlas, choose a study area in a hot, arid to semi-arid location and compare it to a maritime desert location or to data from Great Britain. What are the main similarities in temperature and rainfall between the two? What effect do you think this will have on the way of life of people living in the contrasting areas?

Figure 4.6: Examples mean daily maximum and minimum temperatures for Khartoum, Sudan and Ghat, Libyan Arab Jamahiriya

See accompanying CD-Rom

Deserts introduction.ppt

Ghat, Libyan Arab Jamahiriya

Month	Mean daily minimum (degrees C)	Mean daily maximum (degrees C)
January	3.5	19.5
February	6.4	23.5
March	10.9	27.7
April	17.2	34.2
May	22.4	38.2
June	24.7	40.5
July	24.6	39.7
August	24.6	39.3
September	22.4	37.1
October	17.6	32.7
November	11.4	26.9
December	5.2	21.0

Khartoum, Sudan

Month	Mean daily minimum (degrees C)	Mean daily maximum (degrees C)
January	15.6	30.8
February	17.0	33.0
March	20.5	36.8
April	23.6	40.1
May	27.1	41.9
June	27.3	41.3
July	25.9	38.4
August	25.3	37.3
September	26.0	39.1
October	25.5	39.3
November	21.0	35.2
December	17.1	31.8

Source: *www.worldweather.org/index.htm*

Effects of past climate change

See ch 1, Restless Earth, figure 1.6.

See ch 5, Ice (p113).

As with all other geomorphic settings, the environments that prevailed in the recent geological past need to be considered. Very few, if any, desert locations escaped the cooling climate of the late Tertiary [☞] (Neogene) over the past 5 to 6 million years, which culminated in the Pleistocene ice advances and retreats. The effects of these global climatic events are well known in the high to mid latitudes [☞]. In the mid to lower latitudes, these fluctuations manifested themselves in pluvial periods of increased rainfall, often leading to the presence of large continental interior lakes, such as Lake Bonneville in the south-western USA. These pluvial periods were separated by inter-pluvial phases, which may have seen even greater aridity than the present day, just as some past interglacials have seen warmer climates than we experience in Britain at the present time.

Pluvial phases are shown by a range of relict materials and landforms. These landforms include deep chemical weathering products known as duricrusts (a hardened and often crystalline surface formed from the precipitation of minerals as groundwater evaporates at the surface), Mediterranean type soils such as terra fusca (brown earth soils forming under tree cover), terra rossa (reddened iron-rich soils formed by the build-up of insoluble residues of limestone weathering), and calcareous tufa deposits formed as a consequence of higher water tables and spring activity. Raised shorelines may also be identified, showing high lake levels and palaeochannels that are now partly buried by dune fields. Lake Chad shows lake levels from 55,000 years BP at 380 to 400m above current sea level, compared to the present 280m. Lake Bonneville now has an area fluctuating between 2,500 and 6,500km^2 whereas in the late Pleistocene, shoreline evidence suggests this to have been in the order of 50,000km^2. Evidence of greater aridity is more difficult to see, but dune fields now covered in natural woodland, or showing deep weathering profiles, can be found around the Sahara.

As these cooler and wetter, and warmer and drier phases interdigitated, so sea level and ocean circulation patterns changed, with many coastal areas becoming further inland and continental interiors becoming even more continental in climate during the cooler phases. The reverse occurred during warmer climate phases.

Teaching idea 4.2

Climate change in deserts

Ask students to use an atlas to choose a study area in a hot, arid to semi-arid location, such as the Namib or Sahara deserts, and then consider two scenarios: firstly, one where sea levels fall at the coast (by 10m) at the same time as precipitation increases (by 100mm per year) and temperatures fall (by 10°C); secondly, where exactly the opposite occurs. What are the likely environmental outcomes for their chosen area under these two contrasting scenarios?

Weathering processes and the materials produced

Weathering processes in hot desert environments produce a range of different products depending on the parent material, location, range of processes and degree of weathering that has occurred. As we have seen above, the landforms and materials these processes are acting on are products of changes between past arid and moist conditions. As a result, many of them may represent polycyclic features and materials affected by multiple environmental settings. Additionally, current processes have been slowly evolving since the last main glacial pulse some 18,000 to 20,000 years ago and, as shown above, present desert environments show great fluctuations in temperature and moisture regimes. In many cases, it is very difficult to separate the polycyclic element of the weathering from the first generation weathering of exposed surfaces.

The major factors that control dryland rock weathering are related to the exposure of the rock surfaces to high diurnal temperature maxima and ranges, along with the rock type and structure. Rock and mineral colours will react differently to incoming insolation. Dark rocks and minerals expand more than light coloured ones, and so adjacent rock types and minerals heat, expand and cool at different rates, leading to varying degrees of thermal weathering. The cracks and fractures produced help to break up the rocks mechanically into angular fragments from mineral grain to block sizes. Intersections with natural bedding and jointing patterns also affect this process. Exfoliation is one variation on this process and produces more rounded surfaces as edges and corners become preferentially weathered. This process is slow, and is undoubtedly enhanced in many cases by the chemical weathering effects of condensing moisture and occasional precipitation in the fractures produced mechanically. This leads to the onion skin development in some rock types, especially igneous rocks. Figure 4.7 shows examples of these weathering phenomena.

Figure 4.7: Examples of weathering phenomena in deserts

See accompanying CD-Rom

Weathering.ppt

In desert regions, salts are often present in soil, in groundwater and in mists and fogs condensing on rock surfaces. Here the moisture in which the salt is in solution will evaporate as temperature rises and the salt crystallises out. Where this occurs within pore spaces and fractures in rocks, the salt crystals produced exert high pressures on the materials adjacent to the spaces they are growing in. This process opens fractures in the rock or causes mechanical granular disintegration of the rock surfaces. If the salts involved become hydrated due to temperature or humidity changes, then the increase in size, as a result of water take-up, further increases the pressure on spaces within the rock.

It should be noted that deserts are never completely dry environments; water is sometimes present because of precipitation or condensation from humid air, and so further mechanical weathering can take place due to wetting and drying of surface rocks and sediments. This process can be particularly effective in fissile rocks such as shales. This presence of moisture, albeit rare, also allows a range of chemical weathering processes to operate. These processes are often enhanced due to the high temperatures warming up solutions and thereby increasing their reactivity. On the opposite side of the temperature spectrum, temperatures can be below freezing at night in some locations, and so frost action may occur during cooler winter periods.

One process that occurs today, and is often related to past wetter conditions, is the formation of duricrusts where specific salts in the rock or sediment are translocated (see *Effects of past climate change* on p94). Laterites, silcretes and calcretes involve the movement of iron, silica and calcium carbonate (lime), respectively, to form hard indurated layers at the surface as water evaporates. Gypcretes forming from calcium sulphate (gypsum) can form in the same way, but can also be produced by deposition of windblown crystals of gypsum derived from the aeolian erosion of dry playa lake deposits. A combination of downward leaching and upward capillary action act to concentrate these deposits as crusts. Such action translocates iron producing rubification (sometimes called rubifaction), which is the concentration of iron compounds as weathering products to give a red coating to the materials. These red sediments and soils can be seen today in many arid and semi-arid areas. Examples of calcrete surfaces and rubification of soils are shown in figure 4.8. However, to add a note of caution, it is probable that many of these weathering features are relict elements from past pluvial phases, or are polycyclic in nature, and so result from a series of different phases of activity.

Figure 4.8: Calcrete surface and rubification of soil formed under semi-arid conditions in Mallorca

See accompanying CD-Rom

Weathering.ppt

Wind activity

The action of the wind is often regarded as the main characteristic of hot dry desert environments, with the sand dune being the main product. This, however, is far from the truth, as many other elements have important roles to play, not least of which is water. Wind, though, does have a great impact on what happens in these environments. The desiccation of surface materials is due to hot dry winds moving moist air away and allowing further evaporation to take place. Wind movement is responsible for the transport of fine sediment, generally silt and sand-sized particles, and also for where they are blown and deposited.

Windblown sediment removal (deflation) is one of the agents in the production of some of the morphological environments discussed below, such as stone pavements and the minor bare rock forms of yardangs and zeugens, which are etched by the windblown sand (see figure 4.9 on p98). Deflation is the process which redistributes sand and silts to produce desert dune systems, examples of which are shown in figure 4.10 on p98. Wind direction is the main control on the form and migration of these systems. Deflation is also responsible for the removal of erodible dry soils, which are often relics from past pluvial environments. In combination with salt weathering, which loosens grains, wind can remove discrete granular material to produce features such as tafoni (see figure 4.11 on p98).

Figure 4.9: Bare rock desert landforms

See accompanying CD-Rom

Wind activity.ppt

Figure 4.10: Desert dune features

See accompanying CD-Rom

Wind activity.ppt

Figure 4.11: Tafoni, Mallorca

See accompanying CD-Rom

Wind activity.ppt

Water activity

The role of water in the development of hot dry desert landscapes is still generally underestimated. Water can be extremely effective as an agent of change in drylands because rainfall events, though infrequent, are often extremely intensive when they do occur. The lack of vegetation cover, allied with desiccated surfaces, aids high run-off values, though notable rates of infiltration can occur in some sandy environments, such as the interior of Australia. In these circumstances, groundwater flow is dominant and, when the water table is high enough, playa lake formation, or at least surface evaporation and crust formation, may occur. Overland flow is dominant over throughflow elsewhere in these high run-off, quickflow environments [☞], especially in areas of bare rock, and where crustings are present, or where the intensity of the rainfall causes compacting of the surface. Although high evaporation rates can occur, flashy, high run-off, ephemeral stream regimes tend to produce gulley, wadi and badland topography (see figure 4.12 on p99). Flash floods are common in these environments though wadis may be completely dry for 10 years or more. Evaporation and infiltration usually mean that streams

MAKING THE LINKS

See ch 2, Rivers (figure 2.4 and p45).

eventually dry up, depositing sediment on the surface, infiltrating the fines into the surface, and precipitating solutes on the surfaces of sediment grains. This is notable as the origin of the red iron staining of desert sands as iron oxides (haematite) precipitate out, as shown in figure 4.13, on the grain surfaces to produce a stable coating.

PHOTOS: GERRY LUCAS

PHOTOS: STEVE SUGGITT

Figure 4.12:
(top) Piping in soft sediment, Sorbas Basin, Spain
(bottom) Examples of badland topography, South Dakota, USA

See accompanying CD-Rom

Water activity.ppt

Figure 4.13:
Examples of desert gravel and sand grains

See accompanying CD-Rom

Water activity.ppt

Channel flows are usually irregular, and of short duration, because of the localised nature of rainfall events and infiltration rates. Due to the high run-off amounts when it rains, but the short duration and infrequency of such rainfall, sediment movement along desert river systems is usually highly limited. It is this limited water availability that is the deciding factor, not the production of material by weathering processes and its initial transport down slopes by mass movement phenomena. River systems tend to be endoreic (flowing to a central position), not producing estuaries at coastlines, but evaporating or soaking into the ground en route, or terminating in playas or sabkhas to produce evaporites and salt crusts. Another factor worth a passing mention is that not all river systems in deserts originate there. Rivers like the Nile, the Indus and the Colorado, for example, have their headwaters and main source areas outside of the desert environment in more humid mountainous areas. Views of the Colorado River flowing through an arid environment can be seen in figure 4.14 on p100. As such, these rivers can be regarded as superimposing an alien hydrological regime, leading to alien geomorphological processes within the desert environment.

Figure 4.14: Colorado River

See accompanying CD-Rom

Water activity.ppt

PHOTOS: SYLVIA WOODHEAD

Morphological environments of hot dry deserts

The seven main morphological environments identified within deserts are areas of bare rock outcrop, arid alluvial fans, stone pavements, aeolian sand dunes, playa lakes, sabkhas and depressions (see figure 4.16 on p101). Although most people tend to think of deserts as sand-dominated environments, only about 25% of the world's deserts are covered by aeolian sand; indeed, deserts in the USA only contain about 1% aeolian sand. It is important to appreciate the wide range of geomorphological settings present to gain a better grasp of the characteristics of hot desert environments.

Bare rock outcrops are generally characterised by rough, shattered rock surfaces, more rounded, exfoliated forms, and gully and wadi features. Scree development occurs towards the bottom, leading down into alluvial fans, or ending abruptly as a sharp boundary where they pass into stone pavements or sand dunes, as shown in figure 4.15a. Gully development is especially enhanced in a softer, more erodible sedimentary bedrock situation, with a badland landscape developing as seen in South Dakota, USA (figure 4.15b). Aeolian processes can sandblast bare rock outcrops, producing a range of minor landforms, such as the classic yardangs and zeugens, from resistant bare rock outcrops (see figure 4.9 on p98), though exfoliation, salt weathering and the variable lithology of the rock itself may all play a part in the development of such forms. The Algerian Ahaggar massif, a high granite plateau topped in parts by thick basalt and occasionally phonolite lavas, and dissected by wadis, is a major area of bare rock in the northern Sahara. Here, intense weathering by wind and water through Quaternary climatic cycles has produced a landscape of fluted peaks and deep canyons, with scree slopes and occasional water pools in the valley bottoms, resulting from the sporadic short rainfall events.

Figure 4.15: Examples of bare rock outcrop

See accompanying CD-Rom

Environments.ppt

Figure 4.16: Morphological environments of deserts

See accompanying CD-Rom

Environments.ppt

PHOTOS: A: ANDREW GRANT; B-E & G: GERRY LUCAS; F: NASA.

a. Bare rock outcrop
Rough shattered rock surfaces, scree, wadi, wind-etched rocks

b. Arid alluvial fan
Pyramid-shaped fan, apex to mountains, coarse sediment, ephemeral streams

c. Stone pavement
Armoured surfaces of rock fragments set in a sand or mud matrix

d. Aeolian sand dune
Sand and coarse silt in dune form, various shapes controlled by wind direction

e. Playa lake
Inland drainage basins where ephemeral stream flow evaporates to leave salts

f. Sabkha
Similar to playas but found at coasts and periodically inundated by sea

g. Depression
Deep topographic hollow, formed by wind deflation, fault movement, subsidence. Desiccated, occasionally flooded floors

Arid alluvial fans are found as cone-shaped deposits whose apex leads into a gulley, and whose base often spreads onto a stone pavement. These fans are composed of sieve deposits of coarse, often angular rock fragments, sometimes infilled by fines and with ephemeral channel developments across their surfaces. Where they attain regular development below upstanding bare rock outcrops, they may begin to coalesce forming a bajada (figure 4.17).

Figure 4.17: Alluvial fans forming a bajada, Sinai Desert

See accompanying CD-Rom

Environments.ppt

PHOTO: ANDREW GRANT

Stone pavements are often the most common feature in hot dry desert regions, and are an excellent example of the principle of equifinality, where similar landform types may result from a wide variety of processes and settings. Stone pavements are armoured surfaces, composed entirely of rock fragments, either set in or with matrices of sand or mud. The northern half of the Namib Desert from the Kuiseb River along the Skeleton Coast (a name coined by a journalist in 1933) is one of the largest single examples of such a land surface. Here, sporadic sand dunes cover this vast expanse of pavement. Sea-level change has eroded part of it into offshore reefs. It is the combination of these reefs and the fogs commonly associated with this desert (see *Why this aridity?* on p90) that have caused many shipwrecks throughout history, with the desert environment then proving fatal to most survivors. Traditionally, these pavements are identified as forming from wind deflation of fines leaving the coarser grade as a lag deposit. However, other processes may produce the same types of result. Occasional flushes of water flowing across the surface can remove fines, leaving similar lag deposits, and the rare occurrence of freeze-thaw processes, or the movement of salts and clays by alternating hydration and dehydration, can produce partial stone pavements with a patterned ground style. Often such developments are incomplete, and we see occasional lag or heaved clasts littering a hardened mud or sand surface, as shown in figure 4.18 on p103.

PHOTO: GERRY LUCAS

Figure 4.18: Stony desert, Death Valley, USA

See accompanying CD-Rom

Environments.ppt

Aeolian sand dunes epitomise what most people consider to be a desert environment, despite their presence in only 25% of hot dry deserts. The variety of sand dune types is great, much greater than the generally considered longitudinal, seif and crescentric barchan varieties. Figure 4.19 shows images of desert dunes. Differences in local wind patterns, and in the supply of sand-sized material, produce these different types of dune system. Sand and coarse silt grains move by saltation and rolling, and when they encounter an obstacle such as a pebble, twig, plant or even a patch of moist sand, their trajectory can diverge, causing eddies which allow sand to be deposited. This may result in the formation of an embryo dune. The increased size of these features causes greater flow divergence and dunes grow, sand being moved up the windward side and cascading down the lee. As a result, the dune moves in the general direction of the dominant wind movement. Most dunes are the result of either a dominant (eg barchans) or a set of conflicting (eg star dunes or rhourds) wind directions, or are related to topographical interference (eg climbing and echo dunes).

Figure 4.19: Desert dunes

See accompanying CD-Rom

Environments.ppt

PHOTO: JITZE COUPERUS

Sinusoidal dune

PHOTO: GERRY LUCAS

Complex dune

As noted in the introduction, deserts cover one-third of the Earth's land surface, and so it is no surprise that some of the largest single landforms and specific landscape areas can be found in these sand dune areas. The largest single dune field or sand sea on our planet is the Rub'al-Khali, or Empty Quarter, on the Arabian Peninsula: some 560,000km^2 in extent, the dune field is slightly larger than France. The most common dune types, linear seif dunes, can attain lengths up to 300km as parallel ridges in the Simpson Desert of South Australia. Some of the highest dunes in the world are found in the Sossusvlei Sea in the Namib Desert, where they attain some 300m in height and migrate downwind between 10 and 20m per year, with a maximum rate of 50m per year being recorded. At a high speed of transport, a sand storm can rapidly change the dune disposition in a desert area. In the Sahara, such storms have been recorded as extending up into the atmosphere for as much as 1km. Where dunes become cemented by percolating groundwater, or the precipitation of salts by evaporation, we can see their internal cross-bedded structure, as shown in figure 4.20. The study of such features can be particularly useful in determining palaeowind directions, and so help toward palaeoclimatic reconstructions.

Figure 4.20: Internal cross-bedding structure of aeolian dune, Mallorca

See accompanying CD-Rom

Environments.ppt

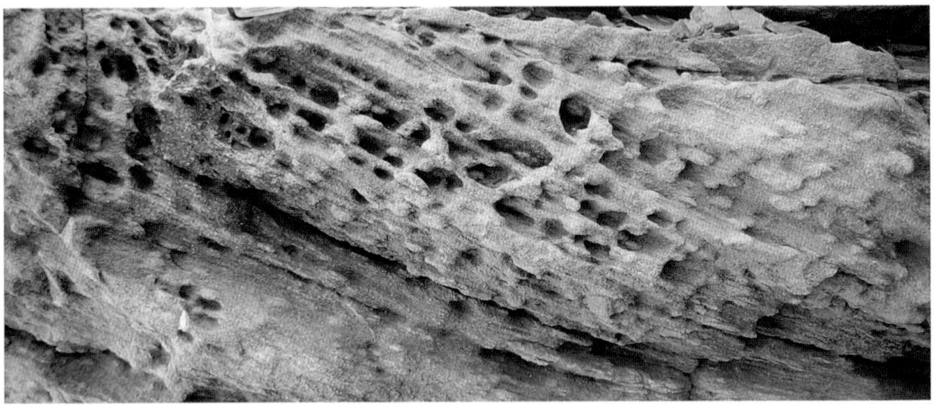

Playa lakes and salt crust developments occur when ephemeral stream flow ends in an inland basin, or where the water table rises to the surface after rainfall input and subsurface groundwater flow. These shallow, temporary lakes suffer evaporation leading to increases in the salinity of the water and hence the precipitation of weathered solutes at the lake margins. These solutes eventually cover the whole basin as the water completely evaporates (see figure 4.21 on p105). These salt crusts may desiccate into polygonal crusts, but these crusts may also become disrupted if capillary action leads to the evaporation of subsurface groundwater brines. Here precipitation may take place at the edges of the polygons, adding salt crystals, and so enlarging the features until they thrust over each other producing spaces, thereby allowing further activity to produce small salt pillars at these junctions.

Sabkhas are in some ways similar to playa lake situations, but as they occur at the coasts they are periodically covered by the sea during high tides, as well as by surface run-off or groundwater elevation. They are characteristically between 0.5 and 3.0m above mean tide levels, and so their frequent flooding and proximity to the water table (often only between 20 and 100cm in such coastal settings) provides a regular input for the high temperatures and evaporation rates to concentrate large spreads

PHOTOS: GERRY LUCAS

Playa basin, Uyuni, Bolivia

Evaporite salt flat, Laguna Colorada, Bolivia

Figure 4.21: Playa basin and evaporite deposits

See accompanying CD-Rom

Environments.ppt

of evaporates such as gypsum (calcium sulphate) and halite (sodium chloride). This chemical precipitation is joined by the presence of microbial biological activity, producing calcium carbonate precipitates. Onshore winds may carry some of these salt crystals inland, and so add them to the chemistry of inland desert materials, thus enhancing salt weathering processes in inland areas.

The final morphological form to be considered is the depression. The depression is a classic example of equifinality as these topographic lows can have many origins, both modern and historic. Some may be initially fault-controlled, or the result of solution processes and subsequent collapse of rocks such as limestone or gypsum, while others may have formed in erodible rocks by wind deflation. Pleistocene pluvial lakes that have subsequently dried up are another cause, as are old river systems that have been blocked by more recent dunes. Whatever their initial origin, these depressions tend to have fine mud, silt or evaporite surfaces, which are often desiccated and occasionally flooded.

Desertification and environmental change

We have already discussed some of the impacts of past Pleistocene climate changes on the production of modern desert landscapes, but we will now consider the effects of these changes, and more recent climate fluctuations, on the increase in desert conditions. Climate fluctuations involving increases in temperature and reductions in precipitation are often the trigger that moves an area over the desert threshold. Natural climate changes, with durations that last for hundreds or thousands of years, dramatically change the global distribution of the main climate zones that control the location and timing of desert conditions. The Medieval Warm Period, when Britain enjoyed a warmer, more Mediterranean climate, was mirrored by an increase in desert conditions in northern Africa. The margins of all deserts expand outwards and contract inwards in parallel with such global and regional precipitation and temperature changes.

MAKING THE LINKS

See Volume 3: Environmental Geography, ch 7, Environmental management (p164).

Shorter-term fluctuations, such as the extremely low rainfall in the Sahel [☞] region of northern Africa between 1968 and the late 1980s, can initiate drought conditions, leading to vegetation reduction and increased erosion of bare land. In this instance, the southward

See Volume 3: Environmental Geography, ch 2, Climate and weather (p38).

movement of the Westerlies [☞] stopped the northward movement of warm, moist air from the West African coastline, resulting in rainfall in the Sahel being below the annual average every year between 1969 and 1990. The annual rainfall here is between 100mm and 200mm. This rainfall is seasonal, with most falling between June and September. The shortfall in the rains, coupled with high temperatures and evaporation rates, resulted in a major drought and an increase in the spread of desert conditions.

Desertification, the long-term problem of soil degradation, is usually initiated by the reduction and then complete absence of natural vegetation. This change in surface conditions reduces the input of organic material into soils, bringing about a reduction in soil moisture-holding capacity, and so a degradation of the soil structure. Poorer soil structure leads to further reduction in vegetation amounts. This process produces bare, erodible soil surfaces, ripe for wind and water erosion. The result is large areas of bare, badly eroded and infertile soils. Although these soils form as a result of natural climate changes, any climate changes exacerbated by humans will inevitably lead to a greater incidence of such conditions. Further, human impacts in these marginal lands from overgrazing, poor crop cultivation practices and deforestation of desert margins will all increase the problem of desertification.

Humans and desert environments

Undoubtedly, water is the single most important resource in desert environments. Human settlement in these marginal lands can be related to several factors. Socio-economic and political needs, such as the development of Nellis Air Force Base in the United States for nuclear testing, or the presence of mineral resources such as oil, nitrates and phosphates, may cause people to move into desert locations. Coastal deserts are often juxtaposed to fishing grounds, such as the Namibian and Peruvian coastlines, where upwelling cold waters bring up nutrients leading to increased phytoplankton growth, enhancing the start of the marine food chain. Tourism [☞] and the promotion of health resorts are modern stimuli to desert occupancy. In such cases, the economic and political factors become the most important and so water is piped in, brought by tanker or desalinated in situ, although in many cases environmental costs may accrue as a result of these location decisions.

See Volume 1: Human Geography, ch 4, Urban (p90).

In most desert areas, people earn their livelihood from traditional cultivation [☞] and livestock farming. In such cases, the quantity and quality of water are of overriding importance for their existence. In deserts, water supply is from groundwater or rivers, the most populated areas being along river systems which have their sources in non-arid areas beyond the desert margins. These rivers may eventually flow into the sea, like the Nile, or end up in an inland lake, as with the drainage into Lake Eyre in Australia. This means that most river basins have a set of distinctive geological and geographical factors, which in turn leads people to specific solutions to issues such as flood control, drainage, water sharing, desalination and so forth.

See Volume 3, Environmental Geography, ch 7, Environmental management (p161).

Teaching idea 4.3

Ask your students to use Google Earth (or possibly NASA) images to gain a background view of river water in typical desert areas. What do they think would be the main water supply problems in the chosen areas based upon this evidence?

A further notable source of water in desert regions is that of groundwater, though in most cases this is in the form of fossil water from past pluvial periods, rather than water being recharged by current rainfall events. Most of the sites where groundwater is exploited are artesian springs where surface depressions have led to oases tapping water-bearing formations, such as the Nubian sandstones in western Egypt. Here the confined aquifers have groundwater sources that are often between 25,000 and 50,000 years old. Mining of such groundwater is limited because of the low recharge potential, and is in no sense a solution to water supply problems in desert areas in the long term.

A further problem for the provision of water in coastal desert settings is that of saline intrusion. Due to the higher density of saltwater than freshwater, saltwater can support a column of freshwater some 2.5% higher than itself, a ratio of 40:41. Freshwater thus forms a lens with a thickness some 41 times the height of the water table (piezometric surface) above sea level on top of the saline groundwater level. If the hydrostatic pressure produced by the freshwater drops, for example due to over-extraction from wells during extremely dry weather, then for every 1m drop in the water table around the well head, the saline groundwater will rise 40m at the well base.

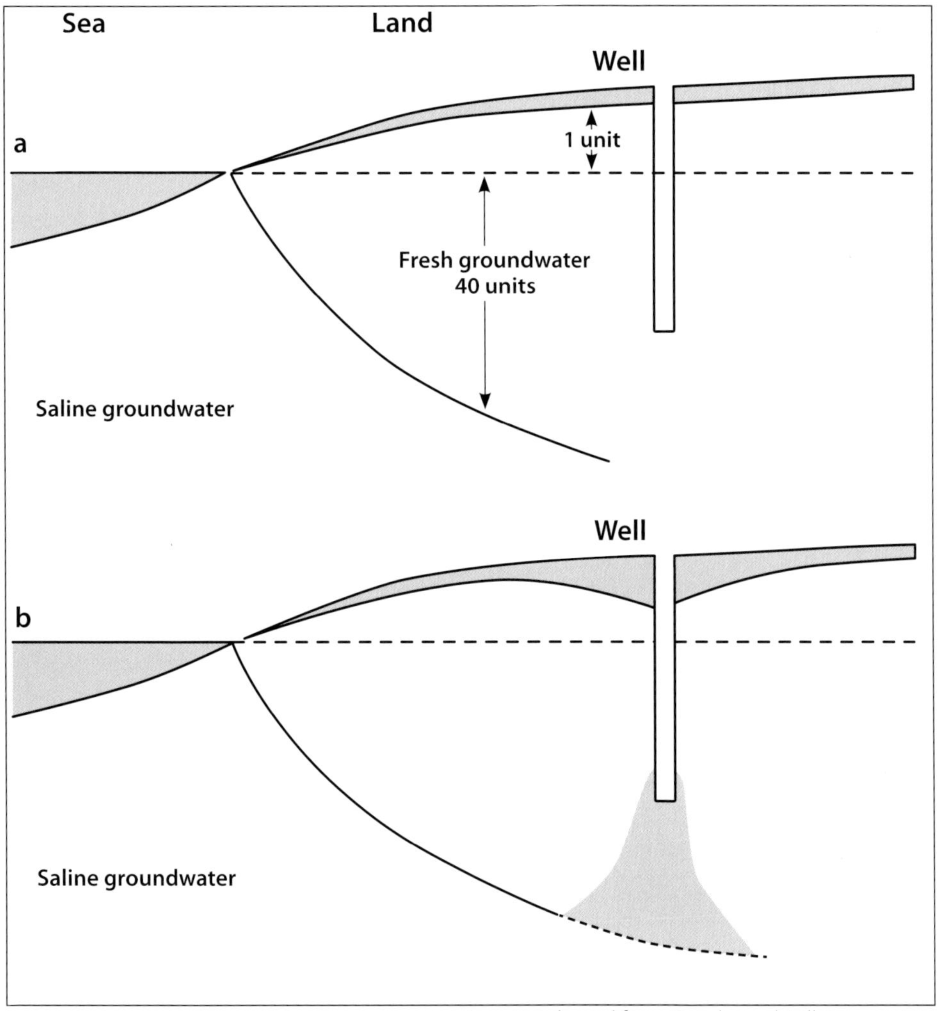

Source: adapted from Goudie and Wilkinson, 1977.

Figure 4.22: Saline groundwater incursion

See accompanying CD-Rom

Human interactions.ppt

This problem of water quality manifests itself in other ways in desert environments. As we have seen, few desert areas are totally without access to water, and so it is often the quality of the resource that is the limiting factor to the use of these locations by people. Salinity is the major factor that limits human use of these areas. Evaporation and concentration of salts in the upper parts of the soil profile, the presence of endoreic drainage systems (see *Water activity* on p98), the lack of removal of salts to the sea, and the input of salts carried by the hot dry winds, all add to the salinity problem. This produces the build-up of evaporite deposits, which themselves can be internally recycled in desert areas.

Salinity can be measured in total dissolved solids (TDS) in ppm (parts per million) or in electrical conductivity (EC) in milli-mhos (10^{-3}) or micro-mhos (10^{-6}) (mho is the reciprocal of the ohm measure of resistance). Unlike the camel, humans are not adapted to life in desert environments. Humans need to drink at frequent intervals, and require some 50% more water per year than camels. We can tolerate up to 3,000ppm TDS for a short period, but this is well above the 500 to 750ppm recommended by the World Health Organization for potable water. Natural vegetation can tolerate drought (xerophytes) and salinity (halophytes), but cultivated plants require both higher quality and quantities of water. As a result, the possibilities for agriculture in deserts are limited. Livestock herding is more of a possibility, as all domesticated desert animals drink relatively small quantities of water and can cope with higher levels of salinity.

Dust storms, produced by the transport of silt grade material in suspension in drylands, is a particular problem for road and air transport in terms of visibility, blocking roads, clogging engines and other mechanical parts, and being a human health hazard. This is particularly important in areas where the dust is contaminated by fertiliser and other residues. This has developed into a major problem in the Aral Sea region in Central Asia, with the sediments now exposed due to the shrinking of the Aral Sea as a result of the dramatic reduction of its inflows. Water was diverted for irrigation purposes leading to environmental disaster.

On the other hand, dust has recently been seen to have a beneficial role. Dust generated by strong winds acting on the dry and erodible lake bed of the Bodele Depression within the Lake Chad Depression contributes significantly to the 66% of global dust generated by the Sahara. Total Ozone Mapping Spectrometer (TOMS) satellite data shows persistent movement of this dust across the Atlantic Ocean to produce plankton blooms in the ocean or to be deposited on the Amazon Basin. Estimated at some 40 million tonnes per year, this deposition affords a critical source of fresh nutrients to the Amazon rainforests (see figure 4.23 on p109).

Flash floods in deserts are major problems to communication and transport networks. It is not only the total water inundation, flooding wadis and filling playa lakes whose surfaces act as transport routes for most of the time, but also the speed of the quickflow into the channels, and the erosive capacity of these floods, that produce the problems. In many instances, there is very limited forewarning of the event. The redistribution of sediment by these events is both a problem and a benefit. Traditionally Egypt's main agricultural areas have survived due to the seasonal flooding of the Nile along its desert margins bringing in fresh nutrients.

Figure 4.23: Windblow from Angola

See accompanying CD-Rom

Human interactions.ppt

Source: image courtesy of NASA. *http://veimages.gsfc.nasa.gov/747/S2000158101720.png*

Summary

Far from the dry, windswept sandy wastes that it is all too easy to imagine dryland and desert environments as being, they are much more complex places, affected by a wide range of natural processes and an increasingly diverse set of human interferences. This chapter has investigated the nature and range of the major causes of aridity, and their links with atmospheric and hydrological processes, as well as mentioning the impacts this has on soils and vegetation. Dryland environments are subject to high rates of weathering and transport of weathered and erodible material by wind and water. Both of these transport processes are important in the formation and modification of landforms, and the continual redistribution of sediments. Characteristic rock and dune forms can be seen. Climate fluctuations within the Quaternary, more recent Holocene variations, and anthropogenic influences, have all contributed to an ever changing balance between arid phases and pluvial periods in the history of desert environments.

Useful websites

The NASA Visible Earth site contains some desert images: *http://visibleearth.nasa.gov*

Australian-based physical geography website Earth Science Australia: *http://earthsci.org/index.html*

Intute: *www.intute.ac.uk* Excellent search engine site, the geography and environment specific part being at *www.intute.ac.uk/geography*

Further reading

Holden, J (Ed) (2008) *An Introduction to Physical Geography and the Environment (2nd Ed).* Pearson, England.

Smithson, P, Addison, K and Atkinson, K (2008) *Fundamentals of the Physical Environment* (4th Ed). Routledge, Oxford, England.

Ice

5

Introduction

Our present glacier ice environments are the current stage in some 2.4 million years of expansion and contraction of glaciers and ice sheets. Today, glaciers cover some 10% of the Earth's land surface. At the peak of the last glaciation, between 18,000 and 20,000 years ago, this figure was closer to 32%. However, the impact of glaciers and glacial processes was much greater globally than this figure suggests. For example, if all today's glacial ice melted, it is estimated that global sea level could rise by up to 75m. Glacier-fed meltwater streams provide valuable water supply, transport and hydroelectric power resources in many parts of the world. Glaciers are charismatic tourist and recreation honeypots. Their former presence provides valuable aggregate resources, and has helped sculpt the landscape of much of the mid latitudes. In fact, there is none of the British Isles that has escaped the impact of glacial or associated periglacial processes in the recent past – our entire current land surface has both material and geomorphological heritage from these cold environments.

Glaciers and climate are inexorably linked. Climate controls glaciation and glaciation in turn affects climate. In this chapter we are going to be looking at this interlinking of glaciers and climate, at how and why glaciers form, at glacier types and movement, the glaciohydrological system, and at the main ways in which glaciers produce, transport and deposit materials leading to the development of glacier landscapes. In considering these latter elements, we shall concentrate for a while on the close linkage between glacial and non-glacial processes, and show how these operate in time and space. Finally, we shall consider the glacial heritage of our landscape, and consider some of the resource and hazard implications of past and present glaciations.

Glaciers and glacier dynamics

Glacier ice formation

Glaciers occur wherever the climate is cold enough to produce snowfall that does not melt in the summer. Both snowfall and temperatures low enough to maintain this snow are needed. Cold is not enough on its own, it will simply produce cold, arid permafrost deserts. Once this build-up of snow has occurred, it can be converted into glacier ice by straightforward weight compaction as the snow pack becomes deeper. This process may be aided by either surface or pressure melting of snowflakes, and the refreezing of the meltwater produced as it infiltrates down into the cold snowpack. Wet compacted snow that has survived more than a year is called firn, and slowly this firn becomes denser as more compaction and refreezing of meltwater takes over the air spaces. When most of these air spaces and interconnecting pathways have gone, the ice mass will have started to deform under its own weight. The result is glacier ice.

Fresh snow has a density[1] of around 50 to 70kg m^{-3}, with settled or drifted snow reaching the 300kg m^{-3} mark. The density of firn ranges from 400 to 800kg m^{-3} and glacier ice from 830 to 910kg m^{-3}. Glacier ice still contains some air bubbles and is less dense than fresh water (1,000kg m^{-3}), therefore it floats, on both fresh and saline water. As we can see in figure 5.1, most glaciers consist of a zone where ice is continually being produced, as snowfall lasts all year; this is known as the accumulation zone. The glacier also has an area where snow melts in the summer (the ablation zone), but where the glacier is still being nourished by movement of ice out from the accumulation zone. The junction of these two zones is the equilibrium line (ELA). If climate gets cooler, the ELA moves downhill to a lower altitude, the accumulation zone increases and so more ice is formed each year and glaciers advance. If climate ameliorates, then less snow survives throughout the year, the ELA moves higher, the ablation zone reduces in size, ice production is similarly reduced and so glaciers retreat.

Figure 5.1: Glacier accumulation and ablation zones

See accompanying CD-Rom

Glacier dynamics.ppt

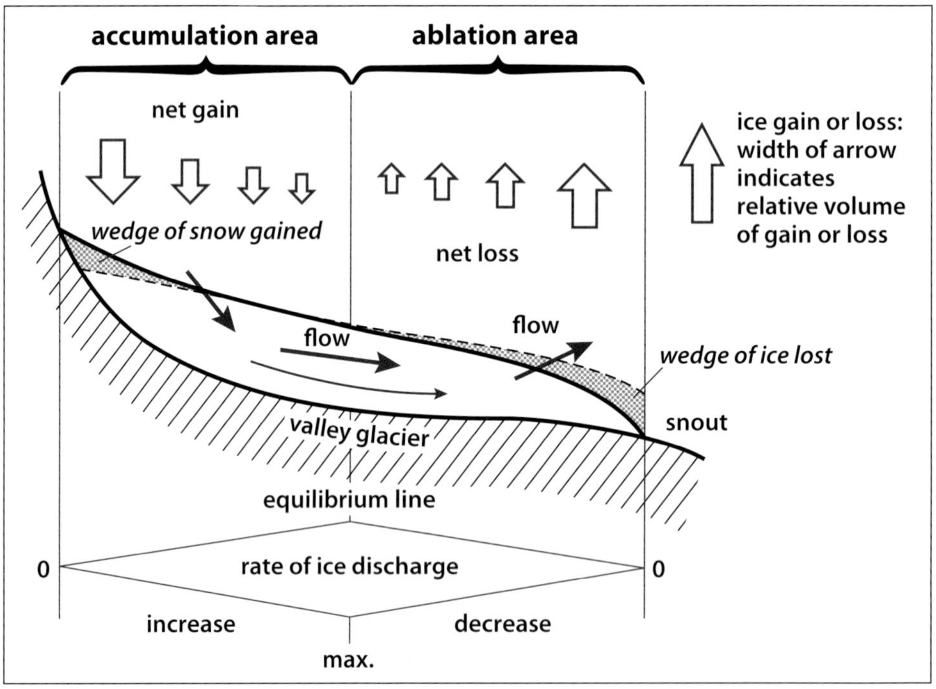

Source: based on King, 1984.

It is possible to distinguish three main types of glacier mass. Ice sheets contain the greatest volumes of ice – for example, Antarctica contains 11.97 x $10^6 m^{-3}$ glacier ice[2], while Greenland contains 1.74 x $10^6 m^{-3}$. These ice sheets can be either terrestrial or marine based, and usually contain both forms. They generally deform and flow very slowly because of their very low temperatures, but they do contain some faster flowing ice streams, which mostly feed ice shelves that break apart around the margins and so calve into the oceans. Ice caps are much smaller but still cover sizeable areas – for instance, Vatnajokull in south-east Iceland covers 8,100m^2. Valley glaciers occur as outlets from larger ice masses, or may build up in glaciated mountain ranges as isolated or later connected glacier systems in their own right. Flow rates and glacier regimes depend on the type and location of the ice mass. The smaller and more maritime the glacier is, the more responsive to climate it will be. Glaciers on steeper gradients are similarly more responsive to climatic fluctuations, with small steep maritime glaciers being the most responsive.

Glacier fluctuations

These fluctuations in glacier length are termed the 'advance' or 'retreat trend' of the glacier, and can be considered in terms of glacier mass balance. This is where we look at the amount of mass (in terms of water equivalent to allow for variable amounts of air or sediment in the snow/ice) either gained or lost per balance year (minimum mass one year to minimum mass the following year). For a typical alpine style valley glacier, this is a function of winter temperature and precipitation against summer temperature and incoming solar radiation. Many methods have been applied to estimating mass balance, including changes in the extent and depth of snow and ice by mapping from aerial photographs and, more recently, satellite images and meltwater discharge measurement, as this is the main ablation product. The simplest and most widely used method is the measurement of the terminus or snout position of the glacier on an annual basis. This is the basis of the type of data seen in figure 5.2, which shows some typical glacial terminus fluctuations from a range of Norwegian glaciers.

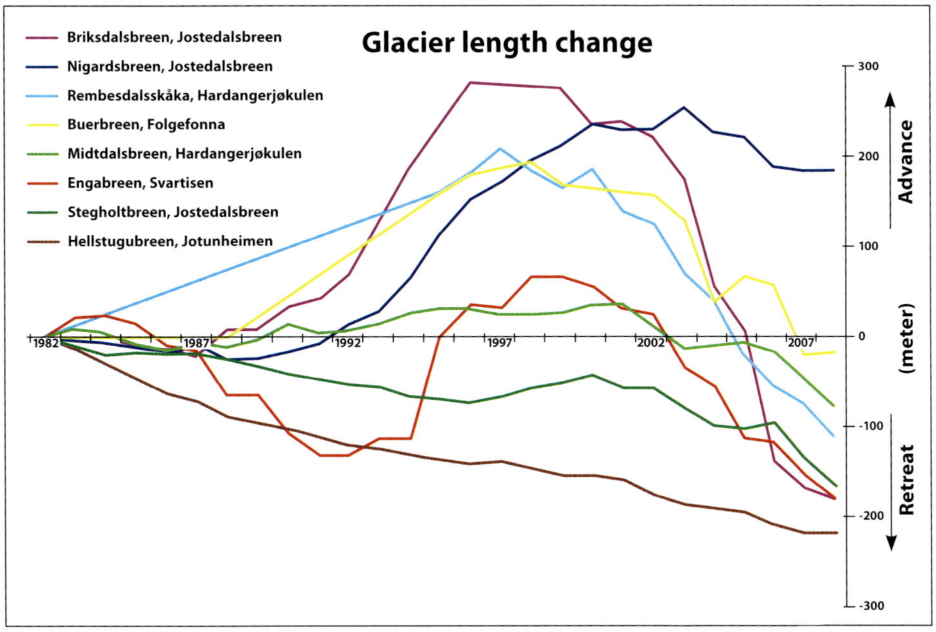

Source: adapted from *www.energimerking.org/FileArchive/79/Glacier%20length%20change%20 1982-08_int.pdf*

Figure 5.2
Examples of typical glacier fluctuations from selected Norwegian glaciers

See accompanying CD-Rom

Glacier fluctuations.ppt

If we look at the data for these Norwegian glaciers (figure 5.2), it can be clearly seen that the behaviour of glaciers differs in that the more maritime glaciers respond to small fluctuations in climate much more than continental ones. The Jostedalsbreen outlet glaciers responded to increased snowfall and cooler, wetter summers in the late 1980s and early 1990s by advancing, while those in the Jotunheimen, further inland to the east in a more continental setting, maintained a steady retreat as climate continued to follow a slight but steady warming trend. Since this late 20th century advance, the Jostedalsbreen glaciers have generally suffered a marked retreat, due to less winter snowfall and warmer summers. Figure 5.3 on p114 shows how the smaller glaciers with steeper gradients, such as the Bergsetbreen glacier, have retreated dramatically, while those larger glaciers with lower gradients, such as the Nigardsbreen glacier, show a much slower and less pronounced response.

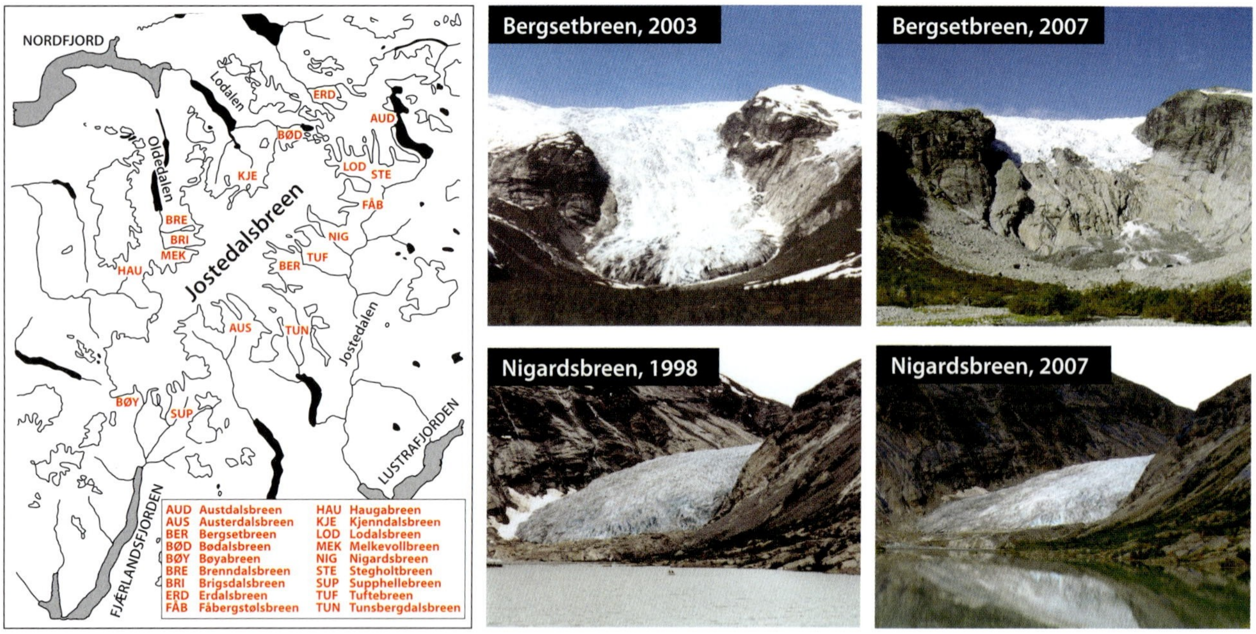

Figure 5.3: Comparison of the recent retreat behaviour of selected Norwegian glaciers

See accompanying CD-Rom

Glacier fluctuations.ppt

Teaching idea 5.1

Glacier mass balance – a climatic response: Ask students to acquire data for glacier mass balance for a variety of glaciers, either in one country or in different parts of the world, and compare their behaviour over different time periods. The pattern identified should then be related to the location of the glaciers. Data is readily available from the World Glacier Monitoring Service at *www.geo.unizh.ch/wgms*

When we consider modern glacier response rates to small climatic fluctuations, it becomes possible to build up a picture of a very climate-sensitive system, where rather than a steady, inexorable build-up of ice followed by an equally steady retreat, in reality we have a much more dynamic system showing many fluctuations. Some of these fluctuations are at a global scale, some regional and some local; all occur over both long and short timescales. This means that areas like Antarctica and the Greenland Interior, at the centre of large ice sheets, have been ice-covered for hundreds of thousands, even millions of years. The margins and outlet glaciers from these regions, however, will show a much more dynamic behaviour related to smaller-scale climate fluctuations. These fluctuations are shown by the glacial to interglacial period variations, as with the interglacial period we are living in today. Such periods occur within any major glacial phase. A table of these major phases for the Holocene is shown in figure 5.4 on p115. Within each of these glacial and interglacial periods, we also have even smaller-scale, though still significant, warming and cooling trends. Small ice caps such as Vatnajokull in Iceland, and valley glacier systems like the outlet glaciers from the Jostedalsbreen ice cap in Norway, show these more dynamic trends, producing regions where glaciers may disappear completely at times, and show marked advances at others. The Jostedal region was ice-free some 7,000 to 8,000 years ago, the modern ice cap and outlet glaciers such as Nigardsbreen and Briksdalsbreen have appeared since this time. Their maximum advance was during the Little Ice Age which peaked in Norway between1745 and 1750. Figure 5.5 on p115 shows the status of the Austerdalsbreen glacier in 1748 and its retreat between then and 2000. Other moraine remnants can be seen along the valley floor.

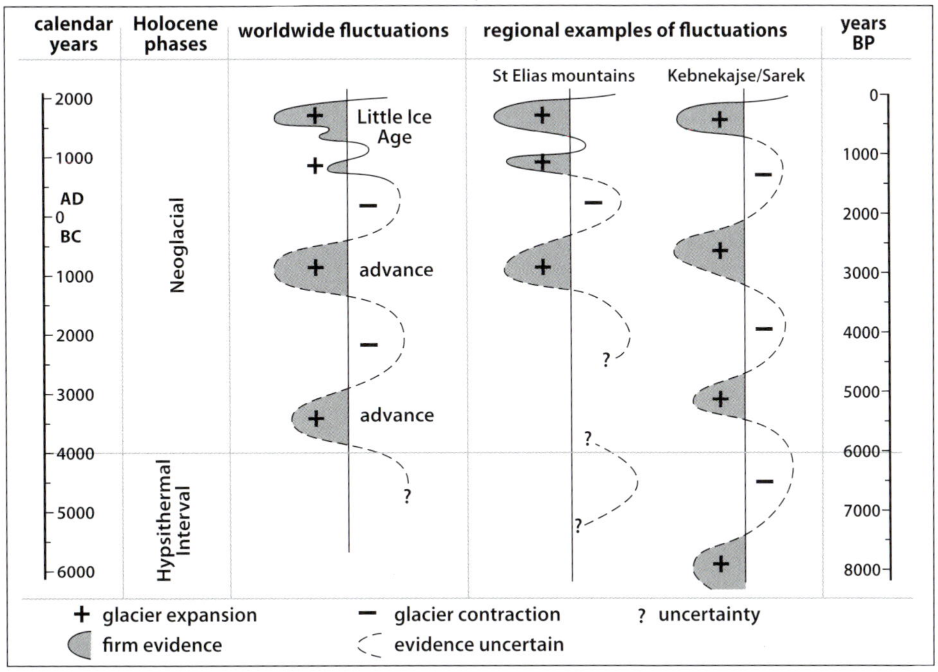

Source: adapted from Sugden and John, 1976.

Figure 5.4: Examples of worldwide Holocene glacial fluctuations

See accompanying CD-Rom

Glacier fluctuations.ppt

Figure 5.5: Little Ice Age glacial limit of Austerdalsbreen, Norway, compared to 2000 position

See accompanying CD-Rom

Glacier fluctuations.ppt

Teaching idea 5.2

Comparison of Little Ice Age glacial limits: Using a combination of Google Earth images and topographic base maps (atlas or route planner maps could also be used), try to identify the distance of moraines in front of the glaciers chosen. Valley glaciers give the best differences. Compare these for glaciers with different aspects in the same region. Suggest how the landforms outside and inside these limits might vary. What effect might this have had for farmers in these valleys?

Glacier ice character and flow dynamics

Having discussed aspects of glacier mass balance and fluctuations that involve ice being moved from one place to another, we now need to consider how glacier ice behaves, particularly in terms of how it flows. This necessitates some consideration of a glacier's thermal regime, the nature and distribution of meltwater, the mechanics of glacier flow, internal deformation, sliding at the glacier base and the deformation of basal sediment.

The melting point of ice reduces with increasing temperature and/or pressure. Cold ice is below the pressure melting point and so remains frozen with no movement except for brittle fracture. Warm ice is at the pressure melting point and so, as well as ice crystals undergoing brittle fracture, they can also plastically deform and rotate. Each of these processes involves friction, which produces some melting, with the water produced acting as a lubricant to enhance movement. The result of literally millions of these actions is the slow creep movement of the ice either down slope due to gravity, or out from areas of thicker ice, resulting in greater internal pressures between ice crystals and greater pressure at the base of the glacier. As we move from lower temperatures in the ice, at around -25°C up to -10°C, the rate of deformation of ice increases by up to five times. This is especially important in cold-based glaciers where the base is frozen with no movement, but the upper layers are warmer and undergo slow creep processes.

Temperate glaciers, such as the European Alps and those in Norway, have warm ice with the surface layers undergoing seasonal warming and cooling fluctuations. The ice is warmer than cold-based, polar glaciers and so internal deformation by fracture and creep processes operates faster. Further, as the glacier is not frozen at the bed, water is present either via the glaciohydrological system (see *Glacier hydrology* on p117) or as a result of basal movements. In either case, the presence of water, especially under pressure, reduces bed-to-ice friction and increases basal sliding. This is often the main control over the rate of glacier movement. This basal sliding is also controlled by friction at the bed from the underlying micro topography, and from any sediment along this ice-to-bed interface. The presence of topographic highs can also locally lead to ice deformation. Regelation is where especially small obstacles cause high pressure against the ice, resulting in melting. Water flows around the obstacle and refreezes as the pressure causing the melting has been released. Enhanced basal creep is where increased pressure against large obstacles leads to higher rates of ice deformation than normal.

The deformation of basal sediment is where tectonic fractures and flows of basal sediment carry the ice mass along with it. However, where this sediment-laden ice is moving more slowly than the higher portions of the glacier, shearing can take place. This is well demonstrated by the Austerdalsbreen glacier and can be seen in figure 5.6 on p117. This contrasts strongly with the situation at the glacier surface where brittle fracture takes place due to the lower pressures experienced with a lack of ice overburden. This produces crevasse patterns which can be seen in figure 5.7 on p117.

Figure 5.6:
Basal shear plane in the Austerdalsbreen glacier with ice moving faster above than below along with crevasse patterns in the same glacier

See accompanying CD-Rom

Glacier flow.ppt

Figure 5.7:
Crevasse patterns in the Gorner glacier, Switzerland, and Tuftebreen glacier, Norway

See accompanying CD-Rom

Glacier flow.ppt

Glacier flow velocities clearly depend on the thermal regime of the glacier, especially the glacier bed, the effect of gravity with regard to underlying slope, the friction produced by the glacier-to-bed geometry, and the mass balance of the glacier. Normal flow ranges fall between 10 and 100m yr^{-1}, with the fastest ones achieving from 100 to 1,000m yr^{-1}. The fastest flowing glacier in the world is Jakobshavn Isbrae in western Greenland at 7,000m yr^{-1}. Warm-based glaciers have occasionally been known to advance very rapidly. This phenomenon is known as 'surging'. As these events are isolated occurrences, the causes are probably specific glacier related, most likely to do with glacier drainage and the amounts of meltwater present under the ice, possibly mixed with subglacial sediment. These glacier surges usually show periodicity between active phases. Some surges, like the 65m per day of the Variegated Glacier, Alaska, during 1982 and 1983, have been linked to the increased released of ice from the accumulation zone. Again [☞], we see the inverse relationship between the magnitude of an event and its frequency – a recurring theme in the study of geomorphological process.

MAKING THE LINKS

See ch 2, Rivers (p45).

Glacier hydrology

Water, or to be more specific, meltwater, is an extremely important component within the glacier system. As we have already seen, it has a range of roles to play in glacier flow mechanics, but it is also an important contributor to understanding the sediment budget of a glacier, and is the main ablation product of glacial melting. A typical temperate glacier hydrological system is shown in figure 5.8. Water is produced both from within the ice mass and from outside, with internal sources usually being by far the most important. The greatest water source, especially in valley and outlet glaciers, is from surface melting, especially during the summer, when approaching 90% of meltwater can be produced. This process can be seen clearly in the discharge monitoring shown in figure 5.9. This is supplemented by the relatively minor discharge from basal melting, due to friction and pressure melting from glacier flow, as well as slight heating from the geothermal heat flux. Other sources of water [☞] entering the glacier are from direct rainfall, or from streams and other surface sources of subaerial run-off, again normally seasonal [☞] in a glacial environment.

See ch 2, Rivers (p43).

See ch 2, Rivers (p42).

Figure 5.8:
A typical temperate glacier hydrological system

See accompanying CD-Rom

Glacier hydrology.ppt

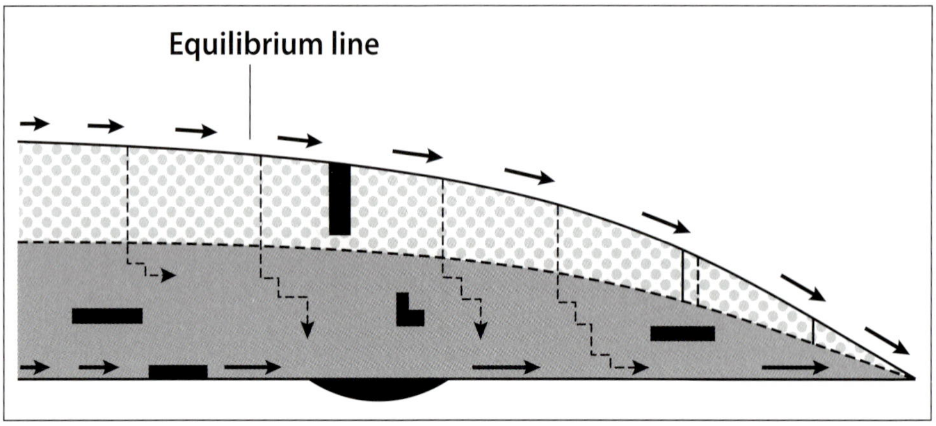

Source: adapted from Sugden and John, 1976.

Figure 5.9:
Monitoring of the river flow in the Lodalsbreen meltwater stream, Norway

See accompanying CD-Rom

Glacier hydrology.ppt

In the accumulation zone, surface melting percolates through the snow and may freeze, aiding ice formation. Alternatively, it may infiltrate slowly downwards saturating the firn layer or moving into the ice mass, especially if structural pathways such as fractures or crevasses exist. A third option is for the meltwater to travel as throughflow to emerge at the snowline as surface run-off. Run-off only forms channels when surface ablation is greater than water infiltration or absorption into the glacier. These supra-glacial channels are sometimes structurally controlled and sometimes cut across structures and can be seen meandering (see figure 5.10 on p119). Such a stream network displays a dendritic pattern until the main streams disappear into the glacier via crevasses or other structural weaknesses, often forming vertical tubes (moulins) as shown in figure 5.11 on p119. The surface pattern developed tends to be restructured annually, with only the most significant channels surviving from one ablation season to the next.

Figure 5.10: Views of superglacial streams on the Gornergletscher in the Swiss Alps

See accompanying CD-Rom

Glacier hydrology.ppt

Figure 5.11: Moulins on Austerdalsbreen, Norway

See accompanying CD-Rom

Glacier hydrology.ppt

Once inside the glacier, the nature of the englacial channels depends on their relationship to the glacial water table as shown in figure 5.12 on p120. As we can see in the photograph of the snout of Lodalsbreen, a classic cylindrical englacial tube is starting to develop a keyhole aspect as the water table drops. These moulins, and other englacial channels, are kept open by a combination of flow friction and water density (roughly 10% denser than glacier ice). Water can also be stored in small pockets and sheets for short periods, before being evacuated elsewhere. We can also see the nature of the bedload that can be carried by such a stream in the photographs of meltwater draining from Austerdalsbreen and Bergsetbreen (see figure 5.13 on p120).

Figure 5.12:
The glacial water table – englacial channel at the snout of Lodalsbreen, Norway

See accompanying CD-Rom

Glacier hydrology.ppt

Figure 5.13:
Austerdalsbreen and Bergsetbreen meltwater streams and bedload transport, Norway

See accompanying CD-Rom

Glacier hydrology.ppt

The englacial water makes its way down to the glacier bed, where there are a number of possible flow patterns. Under large ice masses in cold environments where little surface melt is present, water arriving at the glacier bed tends to be under high pressure, and moves as sheetflow. From the evidence of dye-tracing experiments and glacial outburst floods (jökulhlaup), backed up by small-scale morphometric and radar studies, it is apparent that subglacial channelised flow occurs, sometimes incised up into the glacier (Röthlisberger channels), and sometimes into the underlying bedrock (Nye channels) (see figure 5.14 on p121). These channels may be part of a linked subglacial cavity system, or of a more braided style system, especially if they are cutting through potential glacial sediments. Emerging meltwater streams (see figure 5.15 on p121) usually appear as a single (portal) stream channel, often quite turbid in nature because of the high suspended sediment load from subglacial erosion processes. These channels may feed a fluvioglacial or a proglacial lake location, or may calve into the sea (see figure 5.15 on p121).

Figure 5.14: Bedrock incision showing Nye channel, Mull, Scotland

See accompanying CD-Rom

Glacier hydrology.ppt

Figure 5.15: Portal stream from Nigardsbreen, entering Nigardsvatn, Norway

See accompanying CD-Rom

Glacier hydrology.ppt

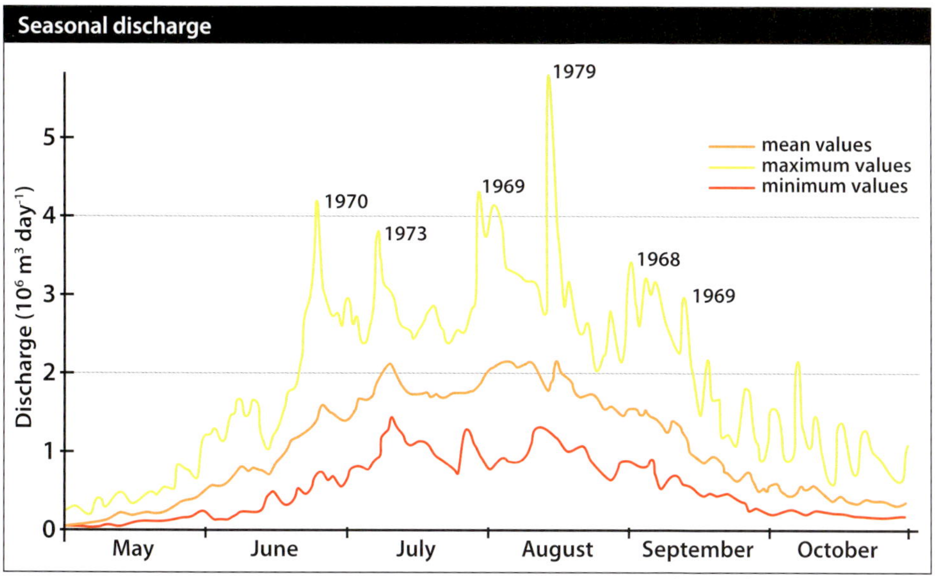

Source: based on NVE data.

In terms of the discharge of glacial meltwater, we can discern both seasonal and diurnal influences, as well as a flashier component related to storm rainfall events or unusually rapid melt. The discharge curve for Nigardsvatn (see figure 5.15 on p121) has demonstrated the seasonal nature of meltwater discharge, with approaching 90% of the total discharge occurring between mid-June and early September. The Matter-Vispa River in the Valais canton in the Swiss Alps clearly shows the nature of the diurnal variations in discharge (figure 5.16), whereas the rating curve for Strupvatnet (figure 5.17) shows a jökulhlaup (glacier flood event) lasting some 12 hours. Extremes of flow, and how this effects a marked increase in the suspended sediment yield, can be seen in figure 5.18 on p123 representing examples from the Bergsetbreen portal stream in the Jostedal region of Norway.

Figure 5.16: High and low flow stages of the headwaters of the Matter-Vispa River, Valais, Switzerland

See accompanying CD-Rom

Glacier hydrology.ppt

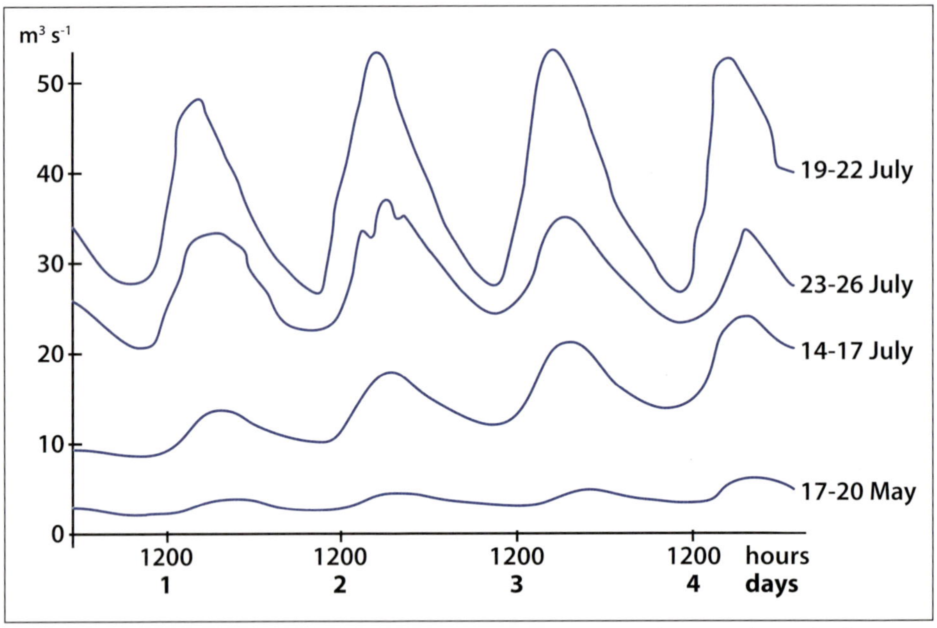

Source: adapted from Sugden and John, 1976.

Figure 5.17: Rating curve for Strupvatnet, Norway, showing 12-hour jökulhlaup event

See accompanying CD-Rom

Glacier hydrology.ppt

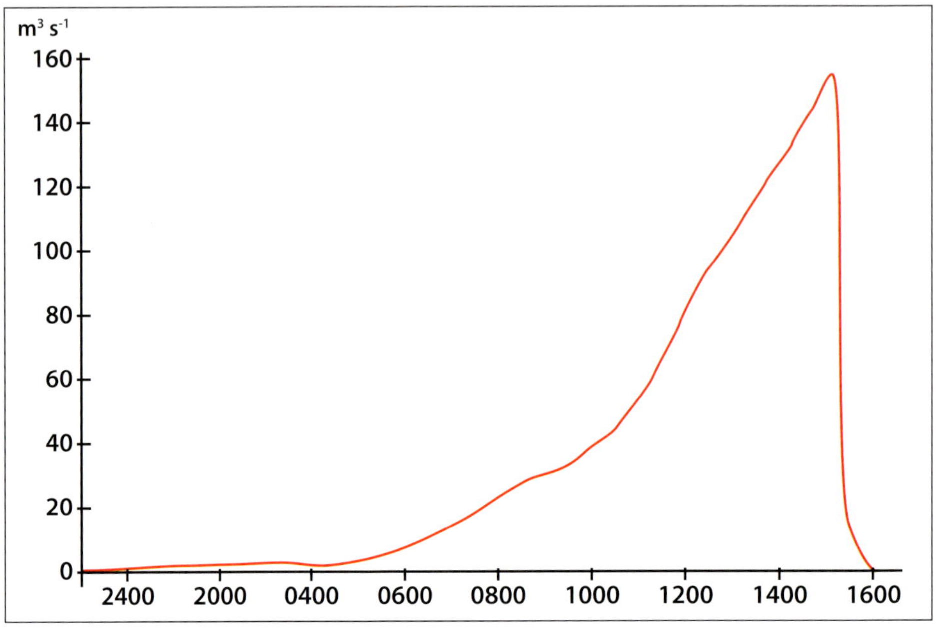

Source: adapted from Sugden and John, 1976.

Figure 5.18: Suspended sediment discharge in Bergsetbreen portal stream, Norway

See accompanying CD-Rom

See Glacier hydrology.ppt

The glacier-sediment system

In this section, we are going to be looking at production, transportation and deposition of sediment within the glacier system. We shall look at processes of glacial erosion, then sediment, transport locations and pathways, and finally the nature of depositional materials and processes.

Processes and products of glacial erosion

Glacial erosion can be considered as the production of glacial sediments by glacial processes. However, if we stop to consider a valley glacier system for a moment, we will see that this is a simplistic and somewhat erroneous view. In a valley glacier system the glacier may originate as an outlet or corrie glacier that flows down a valley, usually one carved by multiple phases of glaciation, and so, for much of its life, it may only occupy part of the valley. There is only a limited area being directly affected by glacial erosion processes. Sediment production and arrival into the glacier system is also occurring from the valley sides above, as indeed it would be from nunataks (isolated peaks surrounded by glaciers) in an ice-cap or ice-sheet location. Thus, there are two sources for glacially transported sediment. Where the glacier is advancing, the sediment over which it is moving has been prepared by previous processes, possibly both glacial and non-glacial in origin. Again, the character of this material may not be entirely of glacial origin, depending on the degree to which further weathering by glacial processes has occurred. Erosion rates in terms of material produced are usually by far the highest in the initial stages of glacial coverage of an area. As ice builds up, pre-weathered rock and sediment produced by non-glacial processes is used up, the ice thickens and moves above the valley and mountain tops, and so we move into a phase of erosion being by glacial processes alone. When the maximum glaciation has passed and the ice is in long-term retreat, with minor re-advances, the landscape returns to a multi-source scenario once again.

This discussion has demonstrated that there is a sequence building up to full glacial erosion before returning, eventually, to non-glacial processes. Similar sequencing can be identified with aspects of glacial deposition (see *Nature and deposition of glacial debris* on p127). Here we shall briefly concentrate on glacial, or more properly, subglacial erosion processes, so that we have the basis to understand the material and landforms produced.

Processes of subglacial erosion are generally rather poorly understood, due largely to the inaccessibility of the sites where they take place. It is possible to identify four main sets of processes that might operate. Firstly, there is the possibility of crushing by the weight of overlying ice, especially where there are repeated loading and unloading cycles as ice thickness fluctuates. Figure 5.19 shows such blocks exposed by the recent retreat of the Lodalsbreen glacier. Such crushing would be most effective on already weakened rock, for example with a close jointing pattern, or along a fault zone, and would produce fairly large angular boulder fragments. As ice slides across the underlying surface, so fragments frozen in the basal ice will gouge against this surface, taking off chips (chatter marks and concave-shaped crescentric gouges, shown in figure 5.19) and producing scratches (striations, also visible in figure 5.19). This second process requires the basal ice fragments to be harder than the bedrock, and to be angular or pointed in order to stick and gouge along the surface. In this case, replenishment of this basal material is required, along with removal of the small angular rock chips produced in order to enable contacts to be maintained and the abrasion processes to continue. The third process that develops in such situations is where fragments of bed material, perhaps loosened by freeze-thaw action along cracks or fractures, are frozen to the basal ice by regelation processes of ice melting under pressure, and then refreezing as the pressure is released (see *Glacier ice character and flow dynamics* on p116).

Figure 5.19: Microerosion features

See accompanying CD-Rom

Glacial erosion.ppt

Nigardsbreen glacier, Norway

Fabergstolsbreen glacier, Norway

The final group of glacial erosion processes are those produced by the subglacial meltwater system. Erosion is by chemical corrosion activity, mechanical corrasion and cavitation, where hydraulic pressure vortices, set up by turbulent flow in the water, suck at the rock putting it under high pressure locally and resulting in the loosening of fragments. This is similar to what happens in normal streams [☞], but with the high pressure, velocity and sediment load, these processes can be extremely efficient locally, producing smoothed bedrock, channels and potholes (see figure 5.20 on p125, showing the nature of such erosion from the recently exposed bedrock in the Stordalen valley, and figure 5.14 on p121, showing the smooth cross profile of a Nye channel). Subglacial meltwater also allows chemical erosion processes [☞] to take place, such as carbonation and hydrolysis. These processes are often enhanced by the influx of fresh acidic rainwater and fresh rock surfaces (the product of other forms of glacial erosion), and by the higher solubility of carbon dioxide (CO_2) in cold water, which will enhance the carbonation process.

MAKING THE LINKS

See ch 2, Rivers (p45).

See ch 1, Restless Earth (p29).

Material produced by all the erosion processes discussed above is modified at the base of the glacier as it becomes crushed, abraded and undergoes meltwater erosion. In this manner, the material contrasts even more with the largely unaltered, angular fragments produced at the surface. It is more rounded, chipped, striated and often shows breakage marks, as well as producing an abundance of very fine material, known as rock flour. As a result, there is a very wide range of sizes and shapes of material making up the total glacier sediment yield. With increasing distance of transport, more and more eroded material is reduced to smaller sizes, but this material is supplemented by fresher, less travelled material as we move out from ice centres towards the dynamic ice margins. In this way, the wide textural range is increased, as is the range of rock types as the ice advances over greater and greater areas. Rock fragments are called erratics when they are transported beyond the source area for their lithology (figure 5.21) and the matching of the range of rock types in a glacial deposit back to their sources is a useful tool in identifying glacier flow directions.

Figure 5.20: Smoothed nature of subglacial meltwater features in the Stordalen valley, Norway

See accompanying CD-Rom

Glacial erosion.ppt

Figure 5.21: Examples of glacial erratics

See accompanying CD-Rom

Glacial erosion.ppt

Dean Brook, Lancashire

Hest Bank, Lancashire

Glacial erratics and human responses

The presence of large 'alien' rocks has triggered a range of interesting responses from the societies within which they are located. Figure 5.22a on p126 shows The Big Stone (Great Stone of Four Stones) above Bentham in Yorkshire, which has become a tourist attraction with a carved staircase to allow the visitor to climb onto the stone. Perhaps even more intriguingly, the large glacial erratic found in the River Elbe during dredging for river traffic in Hamburg (figure 5.22b) has been placed on the bank of the river and was used in publicity material as 'Hamburg's oldest immigrant' during a campaign to enhance cultural diversity and reduce hostility to more recent 'immigrants'.

Figure 5.22: Glacial erratics and human responses

See accompanying CD-Rom

Erratics.ppt

a. The Big Stone (Great Stone of Four Stones) above Bentham in Yorkshire

PHOTO: CHARLES RAWDING

b. Hamburg stone

PHOTO: MARGARETA RADLOFF

Transport paths of glacial material

Once entrained by the glacier, eroded material can be transported in four locations (figure 5.23). The eroded material may be transported passively, as supraglacial debris with minimal ongoing weathering, until the surface topography starts to vary, with ice melting, and it becomes the subject of meltwater or gravity transport processes. Similarly, if the material is buried in the accumulation zone, or if it falls or is washed down crevasses or other fractures, then it may be transported passively, possibly frozen in an englacial position, again with minimal weathering. Meltwater processes actively transport debris as bedload and suspension load, and also carry the products of chemical weathering processes in solution. During this transport, the sediment will undergo increased abrasion, rounding and sorting, as in any other fluvial environment [☞]. The subglacial load is also highly modified during transport, as erosion processes continue to reduce the size and alter other characteristics of the material (see *Processes and products of glacial erosion* on p123). As a result of these four transport pathways, we have a set of glacial sediments with an increasingly diverse character. The wide textural variety is a hallmark of glacial deposits.

MAKING THE LINKS

See ch 2, Rivers (p45).

Figure 5.23: Transport locations of glacial debris

See accompanying CD-Rom

Glacial transport.ppt

Englacial till, Gornergletscher, Switzerland

Bergsetbreen supraglacial, Norway

Subglacial meltout, Bergsetbreen, Norway

Flowage, Austerdalsbreen, Norway

Nature and deposition of glacial debris

Traditionally, glacial deposits are regarded as the product of glacial erosion and transportation, but as we have already seen, these products are in fact more varied. Non-glacial processes operate alongside glacial ones. The situation with regard to glacial deposition is no different. Glacial deposits are normally classified in a generic manner in terms of their process of deposition. Initially, it is possible to distinguish between till, sediment deposited directly from a glacier, outwash deposits, and deposits transported and sorted to some extent by glacial meltwater. Till deposits cover some 70 to 80% of mid-latitude regions, with glacial outwash deposits being found slightly beyond these maximum ice margins. Four main types of till are commonly identified: lodgement, meltout, flow and deformation. Lodgement till is deposited where frictional drag between eroded particles and the glacier bed causes the larger fragments, often boulders, to stick to the bed and form clusters, entrapping a wider range of fragments. This action increases topographic variations at the bed, leading to higher friction and more deposition, thereby producing layer upon layer of lodgement till. The nature of the sediment-rich basal ice layers, and of typical lodgement till, can be seen in figure 5.24 using examples from Tuftebreen, Nigardsbreen, Bergsetbreen and the Isle of Man. As a result of the nature of these accretionary layering processes, lodgement till tends to be over-consolidated and composed of a wide range of sediment sizes transported at the ice-bed interface, with little being removed by meltwater. Lodgement tills are therefore typically poorly sorted with abundant fine calibre materials in the matrix.

Figure 5.24: Basal lodgement till examples from Tuftebreen, Nigardsbreen, Bergsetbreen and the Isle of Man

See accompanying CD-Rom

Glacial deposits.ppt

Meltout till occurs when ice enclosing debris melts releasing the debris. This may occur at the base, surface or other margins of a glacier. At the base of the glacier, as debris melts out of the ice, the finer material is often carried away in the meltwater. Because of this, subglacial meltout tills often consist of only the coarser material from the basal ice; the fines are missing. As this debris is deposited beneath a glacier mass, it

Figure 5.25: Examples of meltout till from Austerdalsbreen, Norway, and the Isle of Man

See accompanying CD-Rom

Glacial deposits.ppt

is often well consolidated but does not exhibit the crude layering and presence of very fine sediment as a matrix to bind the coarser fragments together as with lodgement tills. Figure 5.25 shows subglacial meltout till in examples from Norway and the Isle of Man. Release of debris by meltout at the glacier surface and margins produces sediment and water in a gravity-influenced setting: some material is removed by meltwater flow, and the rest is affected by mass movement and flowage processes over the existing glacier's surface and marginal ice slopes.

Austerdalen

Isle of Man

These flow tills (figure 5.26) show an extremely wide range of textures and internal flow structures. They form in a continuum from gravity-induced sliding to liquid mud flows, and operate on an ever-changing topography as the ice surfaces continue to melt. However, such tills can inhibit the melting process as they build up in thickness. Rock is a poor conductor of heat, hence its use as house insulation, and so, when more than a few centimetres deep, it will protect ice from melting. This can be seen in figure 5.27 on p129, which shows the topography of the ice core of a medial moraine protected by debris, along with similar protection afforded by the localised build-up of sediment, producing a dirt cone and a glacial table where a large block of material is protecting the underlying ice from melting. These latter two are ephemeral supraglacial features and often don't survive more than a few years at most, usually just a single season.

Figure 5.26: Examples of flow till formation Austerdalsbreen, Norway

See accompanying CD-Rom

Glacial deposits.ppt

Austerdalsbreen margin

Austerdalsbreen surface

Figure 5.27: Medial moraine, dirt cone and table protecting underlying ice from melting

See accompanying CD-Rom

Glacial deposits.ppt

'Deformation till' is the name given to subglacial deposits that are deformed by subsequent glacier flow processes. As this soft sediment is deposited, changes in ice flow rates and thicknesses can exert varied pressures on the sediment leading to folding, faulting and squeezing of the material. This process can result in a variety of structures and disturbances of the material after initial formation; some examples can be seen in figure 5.28.

Figure 5.28: Deformation till examples

See accompanying CD-Rom

Glacial deposits.ppt

Outwash deposits are the result of deposition by flowing water, or via processes related to deposition in larger water bodies such as pro-glacial lakes or fjords, or in the sea from ice shelves. Increasingly, as we move into these environments, we see a reducing glacial and an increasing non-glacial component to the deposits. The key element is an increase in the sorting of the sediment from the poorly sorted sediments melting out from the ice, to the much better sorted sand and gravel deposits of the braided outwash streams and the rhythmic suspension deposits (varves) of glacier-fed lakes (see figure 5.29 on p130).

Figure 5.29: Braided stream and glacier lake deposits, Austerdalen, Norway

See accompanying CD-Rom

Glacial deposits.ppt

Glacial landscapes

In this section, we are going to look at the landscape elements produced from the removal of material by glacial erosion, and at the landscapes formed when this material is deposited, building new formations out of glacial and related sediments. By the nature of the contrasting processes of erosion and deposition, there is a tendency to get areas dominated by landforms of glacial erosion, and other areas where only glacial depositional landforms can be observed. Between these two types of landforms are found valley floors, valley sides, or entire regions, where ice margins have fluctuated and where it is possible to identify elements of both erosion and deposition. Such features are most common in valley glacier environments, both modern and ancient. These are also the areas where we can see the importance of paraglacial processes and forms, which are those non-glacial processes, such as frost action and increased avalanche and mass movement phenomena, that operate close to an active glacier. These processes can be viewed in terms of a continuum related to proximity to glaciers, with non-glacial processes coming to dominate as glaciers, and their associated glacial processes, retreat. If we think of the number of separate phases of glaciation during the current Ice Age, it becomes apparent that glacial landscapes are polycyclic phenomena built up by many phases of glacial and non-glacial processes in most of the mid latitudes. Britain, for example (see figure 5.4 on p115), has had at least two major glacial periods, the Anglian and Devensian, each with multiple advances and retreats, such as the Early, Mid and Late Devensian maxima and the subsequent Younger Dryas valley glacier-style advance. Each of these periods, and the intervening interglacial periods, has resulted in a range of varying effects on the landscape, culminating in the landscapes of today.

Geomorphology of glacial erosion

The geomorphology of glacial erosion typically includes regions of either aerially scoured surfaces produced by major ice sheet movement, or of increasing dissection of landscapes by valley glaciers, producing much more varied topography. These differences can be seen when we contrast the cnoc and lochan terrain found on the Western Isles with the fjords and pyramidal peaks of Norway and the Alps (see figure 5.30 on p131). Specific morphological features occur at a variety of scales, from millimetre and centimetre-scale striae, chattermarks and crescentric gouges (see figure 5.19 on p124 and *Processes and products of glacial erosion* on p123) to tens and hundreds of metre-scale stoss and lee forms, corries, truncated spurs and hanging valleys (see figure 5.31 on p131) and to major arêtes, pyramidal peaks (or horns) and U-shaped valleys (see figure 5.30 on p131). As we can see from the striations on the corrie lip of Cwm Alasdair in the Black

Cuillins of Skye (figure 5.31), in most of these cases small-scale marks are superimposed on larger-scale features. With each subsequent glacial advance over an area, the smaller-scale features are removed as the larger-scale ones become enhanced, a new generation of small-scale elements forming on their surfaces.

Figure 5.30: Landscapes of glacial erosion, areal scouring producing cnoc and lochan in the Western Isles and Alpine style pyramidal peaks and deep glaciated valleys in the Alps and Norway

See accompanying CD-Rom

Glacial landscapes.ppt

Figure 5.31: Large-scale feature of erosion with small-scale features superimposed, Isle of Skye, Scotland

See accompanying CD-Rom

Glacial landscapes.ppt

Geomorphology of glacial deposition

Areas of glacial deposition usually offer more subdued relief than those of erosion. They include features produced from the different till types (see figure 5.32 on p132) along with fluvioglacial and other proglacial elements (see figure 5.33 on p132). Typical forms include hummocky ground moraine formed from subglacial meltout and lodgement tills as ice retreats, push moraines from minor advances often producing deformation tills, and terminal and lateral moraines produced largely by meltout and flow tills. Drumlins and other streamlined depositional forms are produced in a subglacial location, from lodgement and other subglacial materials modified either by subglacial meltwater erosion or by streamlining due to variations in local flow rates bringing about further erosion, transport and deposition of existing subglacial materials. Other elements can be produced by dry calving of ice creating dead ice blocks and ridges; subsequent slow melting leads to water-filled kettle holes and kames (dumped fluvioglacial material), which are deposited in positions controlled by the dead ice topography. Such landscapes are termed 'kame' and 'kettle' topography. Features related to fluvioglacial and other outwash processes include subglacial and ice-marginal eskers and kames, proglacial braidplain (sandur) stream deposits and proglacial lake shorelines and kame deltas.

Figure 5.32: Examples of glacial till types forming landforms

See accompanying CD-Rom

Glacial landscapes.ppt

Figure 5.33: Example of fluvioglacial deposition producing landforms, Fabergstolsgrandane, Stordalen, Norway

See accompanying CD-Rom

Glacial landscapes.ppt

The paraglacial environment

During ice retreat, and around the margins of glaciers, the landscape is one of a very marginal nature in terms of the processes operating. Glacial processes operate where ice cover exists, but associated with this we have seen the influence of meltwater, and of gravity, and as we move away from the glacier margin these processes, along with aeolian processes, become all the more important. Also, we have seen the short-term fluctuations that can affect glacier margins (see *Glacier fluctuations* on p113, including figure 5.2). This is clearly an environment that is often subjected to changes in geomorphological processes as systems switch from glacial to non-glacial and back again. Two examples will serve to illustrate this point.

In the Fabergstolsdalen valley on the eastern margin of the Jostedalsbreen ice cap, we have a retreating valley glacier outlet. This is in an east-west oriented valley and has left bare rock slopes on the south side with thick accumulations of glacial debris on the north side (figure 5.34). A model of paraglacial slope development here has been proposed by Ballantyne and Benn (1994). They suggest that the initial lateral moraines, which were produced as a series of sub-parallel valley side ridges, started to become destabilised by snow avalanches and gully development, and that this has eventually cut right through the moraine and back to the bare rock sidewall. The material removed by these run-off and mass movement processes has been deposited as alluvial fans at a much lower slope angle in the bottom of the valley on the floor where the toes of the overlapping fans are being removed by the current meltwater stream. The features of this can be seen in figure 5.35.

Figure 5.34: View westwards along the Fabergstolsdalen valley, Norway, showing erosion and redistribution of lateral moraine material

See accompanying CD-Rom

Paraglacial.ppt

At the south end of the Jostedalsbreen ice cap, the Austerdalen and Langedalen valleys join at the small summer community of Nystolen. Sited here because of the flat valley floor and abundant aggregate from the adjacent alluvial fan, this is also the source of fresh water from snowmelt. Although outside the area of the Little Ice Age maximum advance, this fan is still not an equilibrium landform, and suffers from periodic changes in discharge and sediment production, because the source of most of the water forming it is the edge of the Jostedalsbreen ice cap above the valley. Figure 5.35 shows the nature of part of the Nystolen alluvial fan. In the same area, we can also see the pulses of past fan development, and the results of one of the more serious avalanche events. Although these valleys provide summer pasture, they are still clearly in an unstable geomorphic state and are thus a hazard [☞].

MAKING THE LINKS

See ch 6, Geohazards (p162) and ch 7 Globalisation (p172).

Figure 5.35: Views of Nystolen, Norway, and its alluvial fan

See accompanying CD-Rom

Paraglacial.ppt

Glacial environments and humans

Glaciers affect humans, both directly and indirectly, in a number of ways, hence, as with all major Earth surface processes, we can see benefits (resources) and detrimental effects (hazards). Present glacial processes, materials and landforms affect only a small proportion of people directly. By contrast, a larger proportion of the population is affected in terms of current glacial meltwater and materials, while much of the world's population is affected by the direct and indirect effects of past glaciations. For example, much of Great Britain has been glaciated; the entire set of islands has been affected by cooler climates associated with glaciation, and the entire coastline has been altered by glacially driven eustatic and isostatic sea-level changes. The resulting landforms and materials provide much of the character of our country, especially the uplands and the glacial-depositional lowlands, and so a case can be made for the need to consider the effects of past glaciations in the study of any part of the physical geography of the British Isles.

Teaching idea 5.3

With respect to your local area or a different study area chosen from elsewhere in the UK, ask students to use an Ordnance Survey 1:50,000 scale map to identify the main landform elements present. Identify which of these are directly attributable to glacial processes (for example, drumlin, corrie, U-shaped valley) and which are due to more indirect events (for example, over-steepened valley side collapse, marshy surfaces due to poor drainage through clay-rich glacial sediments). Ask them to assess the percentage of the landscape affected by each set of processes and landforms.

The nature of glacier materials and processes as hazards or resources is often purely a matter of human perception. High meltwater discharges can produce floods and severe erosion – a problem for bridges and roads near to meltwater streams – but can be a boon to the production of hydroelectric power and even to water supply for many people. Glacier walking and skiing are becoming ever more popular, a good tourist asset, but such activities also put people at risk from avalanches and unseen crevasses. The effective prediction of glacier hazards and the use of glacial meltwater and sediments are based on an understanding of the glacial system, both present and past. We shall now consider a few of the aspects of the glacial system that can be viewed as hazards, resources or both.

Avalanches

Snow and ice avalanches are frequent hazards in glaciated mountain and valley areas. These hazards can be a great risk to individuals. For example, in the Swiss Alps, between 1901 and 1983, 124 people were killed. In one event, 88 hydroelectric power site construction workers were killed by an icefall from the Allalingletscher glacier in Switzerland in 1965. Again in Switzerland, an entire village was buried beneath an icefall near the Simplon Pass in 1957. Probably the best known ice avalanches are the two from Peru's highest peak, Nevado Huascarán. Avalanches in 1962 and 1970 were both generated by earthquakes, and triggered glacier ice to cascade down the mountain, mixing with snow and rock debris to form a liquid slurry as the snow and ice melted. The 1962 event travelled some 16km in eight minutes, reaching speeds above

100km h^{-1} and producing some 4,000 victims. The avalanche buried nine villages in an icy mudflow up to 20m thick. The 1970 event travelled further, to include the town of Yungay, and claimed some 18,000 victims. Despite these globally newsworthy events, it is the more frequent small event, often overlooked, that has a great impact on the lives of people. For example, figure 5.36 shows the results of a typical small snow and ice avalanche at Nystolen (see *The paraglacial environment* and figure 5.35 on p132-133). Such events are a frequent winter occurrence in locations like this.

Figure 5.36: Results of avalanche at Nystolen, Norway

See accompanying CD-Rom

Glacial humans.ppt

Teaching idea 5.4

Are your students aware of any avalanche-prone areas? What reasons can they suggest for these avalanches. With the aid of the Ordnance Survey 1:50,000 maps of one or more selected upland areas, and the associated Google Earth image(s), ask your students to identify potential avalanche-prone sites. What can they say about the areas they are found in? What criteria did they use to choose the sites?

Glacier floods

Glacier floods can be locally devastating. They are caused by rapid snowmelt, the combination of snowmelt and rainfall, or by the sudden release of glacier-stored or dammed water. These rapid glacier floods are termed 'jökulhlaups'. Such floods usually involve water, ice and sediment, with the erosive power of the water and the deposition of the sediment being the main long-term hazards. The Jostedola River in Norway (see figure 5.37 on p136) shows how societies can respond to such events. Here a combination of bank protection with levées and control of headwater discharge by dam and reservoir construction (see *Water resources* on p136) has been undertaken. Despite these measures, flooding again occurred in this area in September 2009.

Figure 5.37: The Jostedola River, Norway, site of glacier flooding

See accompanying CD-Rom

Glacial humans.ppt

Teaching idea 5.5

Use Ordnance Survey 1:50,000 maps of one or more selected upland areas in the UK and the associated Google Earth image(s) to get your students to identify glacial valley sites of habitation. Are these potential flood sites today? Use Google Earth images alone of areas such as the Swiss or French Alps or the Jostedal area of Norway (alternatively you might use appropriate Ordnance Survey-style maps, atlas or road map resources) and ask your students to identify inhabited valleys that are fed by glaciers. Are these flood sites today? What would make them more hazardous? How do they compare to the UK sites?

Glacier advances

Over longer timescales, glacier advances pose the threat of overriding the landscape and then of producing higher meltwater discharges as they retreat. The Little Ice Age advance of Nigardsbreen, Norway in the 18th century destroyed nine farmsteads, while the recent 1990 to 2000 short advance and rapid retreat has led to increased avalanche activity and minor flooding in the same region (see *Glacier fluctuations* on p113).

Water resources

Glacial meltwater sources many of the world's major rivers. This results in rivers having peak flows from late spring through the summer months. As such, the water is often provided at times of greatest need in many locations. This can be seen clearly with many of the rivers that flow into the Mediterranean from the Alps during periods when rainfall is at a minimum.

Teaching idea 5.6

Supply your students with atlases and set them the task of identifying areas of mountain glaciers that feed river systems. Get them to trace the river systems down to the sea and make assessments of the use or potential use of these for water supply and transport with respect to population centres found downstream. Ask them to consider the potential for spring flooding in such a river regime. Alternatively, ask them to investigate a specific river system that experiences significant inputs from glacier and snowmelt, such as the River Rhone, flowing out of the Swiss Alps, through France into the Mediterranean. What are the effects of the river having an ice and snow-fed system on its regime and the people living in its valley?

One of the main uses of water is for hydroelectric [☞] power generation (HEP). Norway provides all of its own electricity from HEP and exports to other countries in Europe, notably Germany, at peak demand periods. Many of the HEP schemes in Norway are multipurpose, the Jostedal scheme begun in 1984 being an excellent example. Here the lakes of Austdalsvatnet and Styggevatnet were enlarged into one new Styggevatnet lake. This lake was also fed by pipeline from the adjacent lake of Kupevatnet. These water sources are at the head of the Sprongdalen arm of the Jostedal valley, and the dam is designed to look like a scree slope in order to blend in with the surroundings. More than 60,000m of tunnel was excavated between here and the tailrace at Gaupne, where the Jostedal valley joins the Gaupnefjorden arm of Sognefjord. The power generation plant is located some 1,300m into the mountainside at Myklemyr, where the head of water has some 1,200m vertical fall. The scheme started producing electricity in 1989 with final completion in 1990. The benefits of the scheme are 887GWh of electricity per year, reduced flood risk by storing run-off in the upper catchment, increased bank protection works, and improved road access to the mountain areas for a range of outdoor tourist and leisure activities such as walking, riding, glacier lake canoeing, glacier walking and ice climbing. Figure 5.38 shows some elements of this scheme.

MAKING THE LINKS

See Volume 3: Environmental Geography, ch 4, Energy (p95).

Figure 5.38: The Styggevatnet HEP and flood control scheme dam and lake in the Jostedal valley, Norway

See accompanying CD-Rom

Glacial humans.ppt

Glacial materials

See Volume 3: Environmental Geography, ch 4, Energy, figure 5.8.

Sand and gravel are major products of glacial and fluvioglacial activity. The British construction industry [☞] typically uses some 300 million tonnes of such materials per year. These deposits are largely landform-related with glacial outwash deposits being more graded, and hence needing less processing, than direct glacial deposits. Not only do glacial deposits provide building materials, they also provide an entirely new land surface, one characterised by a wide variety of landforms and deposits. The glacial processes leading to the production of certain types of till and outwash sediments also produce characteristic landforms, and hence landform sediment associations, which allow us to use visible landforms as indicator of sediment type and, therefore, sediment properties. Subglacial lodgement tills are very consolidated having been deposited under the overlying pressure of active flowing ice; they are clay rich and so relatively impermeable and have a strong fabric and fissility which affects their shear strength. As such, these deposits have good strength bearing properties and stability, but are more difficult to excavate.

Teaching idea 5.7

Ask your students to use the local area or one chosen from an appropriate Ordnance Survey map. Firstly, ask them to map the glacial and/or fluvioglacial depositional landforms. Then ask them to assess the nature and approximate volumes (by calculating surface area and estimating approximate depths, such as 2 or 3m) of sediment in these landforms. To what uses could these materials (aggregates) be put? Would demand for these uses be local or would a lot of transport be needed? What costs might this transport incur and what processing of the aggregates might increase their value? If there is already evidence of mineral working, can your students identify transport infrastructure?

Summary

Glaciers have affected many of our landscapes, and left us with a strong heritage in terms of distinctive landforms and materials, while currently glaciated areas provide both resource and hazard scenarios for human populations. These landscapes are one of the most varied geomorphological process-landform-material associations in the environment, and have had, and are still having, many direct and indirect impacts on the lives and livelihoods of human populations.

Endnotes

1. Measured in kg m^{-3} = kilograms per cubic metre.

2. 10^6 m^{-3} = 1 million cubic metres.

Useful websites

For glacier fluctuations: *www.energimerking.org/FileArchive/79/Glacier%20length%20change%201982-08_int.pdf*

World Glacier Monitoring Service website: *www.geo.unizh.ch/wgms*

List of glaciers in Norway: *http://en.wikipedia.org/wiki/List_of_glaciers_in_Norway*

Useful background to the Jostedal region: *www.jostedal.com/*

The website of the RGS-IBG *www.discoveringthearctic.org.uk* contains a wide range of useful teaching resources. See also *www.discoveringantarctica.org.uk*

Google Earth can be used for examining glaciers: *http://earth.google.com*

Further reading

Ballantyne, CK and Benn, DI (1994) 'Paraglacial slope adjustment and resedimentation following glacier retreat, Fabergstolsdalen, Norway'. *Arctic & Alpine Research*, 26, 255-269.

Holden, J (Ed) (2008) *An Introduction to Physical Geography and the Environment (2nd Ed).* Pearson, England.

Knight, PG (1999) *Glaciers*. Stanley Thornes (Publishers) Ltd, UK.

Smithson, P, Addison, K and Atkinson, K (2008) *Fundamentals of the Physical Environment* (4th Ed). Routledge, Oxford, England.

6

Geohazards

Introduction

In studying the concept of geohazards, this chapter aims to demonstrate how aspects of the natural environment interact with society. Closely associated with this relationship is the concept of 'risk', that is to say, the likelihood and impact of certain results from a particular geohazard event. Geohazards, therefore, incorporate the study of the causal agents of natural hazards, and the likelihood or probability of a natural hazard event occurring. The impact and magnitude of a particular event on our society needs to be considered, along with the socio-economic, political, spatial and temporal contexts of the event. It is the concept of 'threat', to people and their livelihood, that makes this an important topic for study. The concept of risk relates to looking at the specific 'threats' to individuals or societies at a particular time and place, along with the measurement of our vulnerability to these threats.

The distinction between the ideas of hazard and risk is extremely important, as it shows different perspectives about how risks to people's way of life are perceived and assessed, rather than focusing on the identification and attempted management of the geohazards that produce the risks in the first place. We are not including 'technological' hazards directly here. These are socio-economically or politically constructed hazards, which are the products of our society. Rather, the chapter focuses on the natural environment, and its production of extreme geophysical events; that is to say, the study of low-frequency, but high-magnitude, aspects of natural processes. It is clearly the interaction of people with natural processes, in particular places at particular times, that converts these natural processes into potential geohazards, and subsequently into specific risks.

After a consideration of the timing and incidence of geohazards, this chapter will look at a range of different hazard scenarios, including their risk factors, and the potential management responses employed in attempting to reduce the human and environmental impacts. We shall look at the nature of the causal agents and then focus on specific geohazard types and events: their location in time and space, the types of people that might be under threat from these hazards, the risks that might be posed and how these risks may be responded to. Finally, the chapter investigates specific examples of the relationship between geohazards and human society.

Geohazards in space and time

Geographic location, scale and geological timing are important in understanding the distribution and impacts of geohazards. The complex nature of the processes and settings that produce a geohazard, along with associated political and socio-economic responses, increase as we move from the local to the regional, and then on to the global scale. For instance, it is simpler to identify the specific causal agents and impacts of an individual slope failure at a local level, than to understand the range and scale of the impacts of an earthquake causing a tsunami.

Some geohazards have multiple causal agents. For example, river flooding (figure 6.1) may result from snowmelt, glacial lake outbursts, excessively heavy, prolonged or intense rainfall. Also, flooding will produce different hazards and risks for populations within different political, socio-economic and even historical settings. In Keswick, where the River Greta and the River Derwent join in the Lake District, entirely different conditions occur compared to those at Chandpur on the Ganges-Brahmaputra River in Bangladesh. Environment, infrastructure and history have all produced different perceptions and responses to past flood events. Furthermore, some causal agents produce multiple hazard and risk scenarios rather than single impacts. For instance, the eruption of Mount Saint Helens produced a sonic blast, knocking down trees and buildings, a major landslide, a series of lahars removing sediment, vegetation, animals, houses, cars and bridges, and dust and ash clouds descending over a variety of surfaces. Because of this link, between the event itself and the location and timing of its impacts, we need to re-evaluate potential risk continuously, as the nature of human occupancy on the Earth's surface changes in time and space. In such changing scenarios, it is reasonable to discuss what the impact of any of these events would have been in these or similar locations 500, 2,500 or even 5,000 years ago.

Figure 6.1: River Severn, flooding fields near Shrewsbury

See accompanying CD-Rom

Space time.ppt

Teaching idea 6.1

Ask students to investigate a recent major geohazard event and then ask them to consider how the main impacts of this event might have differed 50 years ago, or 500 years ago or how the impacts might be different 25 or 50 years into the future.

With our appreciation of time and space we, as geographers and geoscientists, have an effective training to afford us a valuable perspective on geohazards. This training and focus helps us to appreciate the differences in the timing and location of different hazards, from the sudden event of slope failure to the slow increase in aridity leading to the long-term impacts of drought; or from the low magnitude and incidence of earthquake hazard in Britain to the high magnitude and incidence of earthquakes along the west coast of Chile. This understanding of the variability in the temporal and spatial patterns of geohazard events is central to our appreciation of the character and range of impacts of different hazards.

Figure 6.2: River Severn being held by flood embankments in Ludlow

See accompanying CD-Rom

Space time.ppt

The monitoring of potential geohazards

As observations on the temporal and spatial aspects of geohazards are crucial to our understanding of their risks, geohazard/environmental monitoring programmes are essential for effective data collection at all scales. The Global Environmental Monitoring System (GEMS – *www.gemswater.org*) is an example of essential cross-boundary monitoring and sharing of information on water, since rainfall, river floods or tsunamis don't recognise national boundaries. In terms of many geohazards such baseline monitoring is needed to provide information at the regional and global level, for example the United Nations Environmental Programme [☞] (*www.unep.org*) relies on such a scheme. One of the foremost hazard research institutes in the world is based in the UK, the Aon Benfield UCL Hazard Research Centre (*www.abuhrc.org/Pages/index.aspx*).

MAKING THE LINKS

See Volume 3: Environmental Geography, ch 1, Ecosystems and ch 7, Environmental management.

Once effective monitoring of the physical processes operating in our environment that might cause potential hazards has been achieved, the next stage in assessing the possibility of these events putting people at risk is to identify the likelihood of any causal agents operating at a magnitude that will bring about an extreme event. Usually, this would be done by looking at the recurrence interval of a particular event, such as river discharge, and plotting these values against each other as a line graph on which we can superimpose various discharge levels chosen to depict specific flood or near flood events (see figure 6.3 on p144).

It is essential that we identify the nature of the potential hazard(s) itself, in a specific place at a particular time, as the environmental parameters producing any hazard are very dynamic. For example, if a potentially flood-inducing rainfall occurs, and trees are full of leaves to intercept some of the rain, and the soil is relatively dry so soil moisture storage can accommodate more of the rain, then a flood may not occur. If, however, it were early spring and the trees were still largely bare, while previous rainfall events had left the soil waterlogged, then a flood probably would result.

The whole human environment – land use, buildings, communications and the political structure of the location – contains dynamic factors that change as the result

Figure 6.3: Recurrent interval graph

See accompanying CD-Rom

Space time.ppt

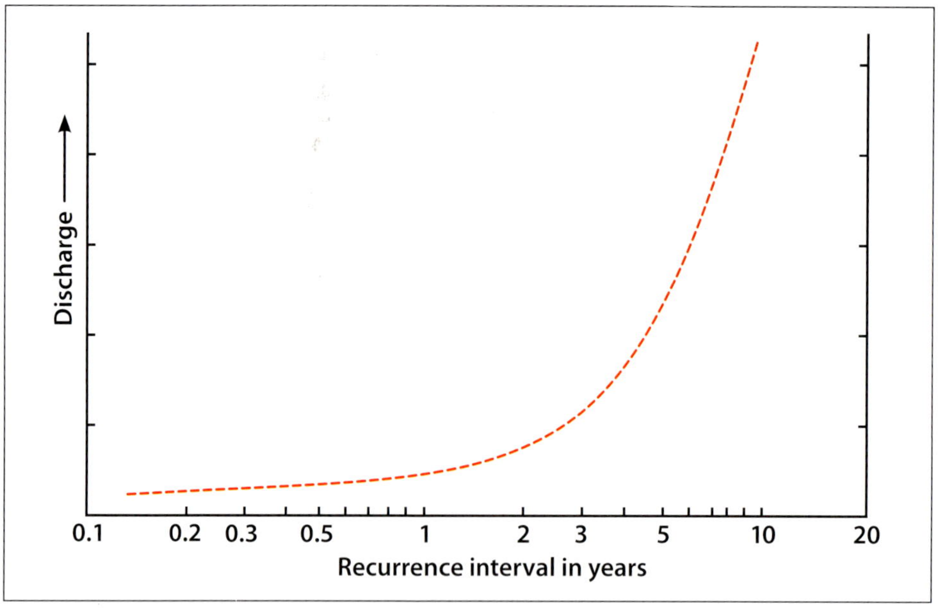

Source: Cooke, JC and Doornkamp, J, 1974.

of people's experience, education, social and political evolution. These changing elements will govern both what and where it is deemed necessary to monitor the physical environment, and also how this data may then be interpreted. Increasingly, mathematical, interactive computer models are being used. For example, general circulation models of atmospheric processes are being used to predict probable consequence of increased global warming. The use of such models is not foolproof. Although they do tend to produce a sense of satisfaction as to knowing what is happening, our knowledge base may be imperfect and our deductions false. The reality may be far different from what is predicted. Models need to be updated and refined as research progresses. They need to be evaluated each time they are used, and the results fed back into the model-building process. Such procedures bring us to the final stage in assessing the specific risk that is likely to occur under a given set of physical and human circumstances.

The perception of risk

Risk perception is largely a product of individual or group history and experiences, personal values and judgements. To illustrate this point, viewpoint on costs and options for flood protection of your house will vary according to whether or not you have experienced a flood while living close to a river. Perception of the risk would differ according to experience, and differ from that of other people with other backgrounds and life experiences. Our own academic geographical viewpoint would clearly colour our judgement in such a scenario when compared, for example, to a civil engineer. We need to be able to appreciate why individuals or groups follow certain actions in response to potential or actual geohazards, to see what they regard as the possible range of responses available to them, and to understand how they can make informed decisions from these.

The information that we need in order to be able to make informed decisions, in terms of risk management and hazard response, would normally include the following:

- the nature of the hazard, and the potential risks it produces in a particular location at a particular time
- the nature of the benefits to society of risk reduction strategy and policies
- the alternative response strategies to reducing the risk and how effective they have been in similar situations elsewhere
- a consideration of any uncertainties surrounding the effectiveness of the responses
- awareness of responsibility for management and monitoring of the hazard and risk reduction and response programme
- the effectiveness of the 'line of command' and the dissemination of information to the general public.

Teaching idea 6.2

Ask students to investigate how they might acquire the knowledge and information needed to be able to identify potential risks to their community and then effectively manage a particular hazard in or near their home. A good starting point for such an enquiry would be a County Emergency Planning Unit, usually accessed via local government websites. For instance, Lancashire's can be found at: *www3.lancashire.gov.uk/corporate/web/view.asp?siteid=3009&pageid=6415&e=e*

Have students experienced a geohazard, such as flooding? If so, how has this experience changed their perception of the issue?

Managers in such positions would need to appreciate that people rarely agree about the potential range and impacts of risks. People generally tend to underestimate the impact of geohazards, especially when they have no direct experience of a particular impact themselves. They often fail to fully appreciate the accounts of experienced witnesses, and there is a tendency to simplify the nature and impacts of potential geohazard events, and similarly the risks they can produce. Also, people tend to forget the detail of their past experiences over time, forming an opinion and retaining it no matter how the potential responses to a hazard might have developed. Public education about potential geohazards, and the risks they pose, is thus central to any effective management scenario.

This perception stage is often viewed as the establishment of a 'dose-effect' relationship. Here, we are looking at the nature and magnitude of the impacts of risks to people or the environment – for example, whether low doses or impacts of a particular risk can be tolerated or not. We might consider the likelihood of a minor flood episode, which might affect the garden or part of the garage of a typical home in the UK, to be acceptable, if it only has a limited impact. This then asks the question, at what magnitude of risk to our property, livelihood or to ourselves does this impact become significant, or does it do so immediately the hazard occurs, no matter what its magnitude or location (see figure 6.4 on p146)? Such responses are not static, and must be continually updated in terms of the perceptions and experiences of the changing socio-economic make-up of any society.

Figure 6.4: Comparison of properties at risk from flooding in Ludlow to a flooded open farmland area from Northumberland

See accompanying CD-Rom

Hazard perception.ppt

Once there is a working knowledge of the extent and severity of a particular geohazard and its potential risks, we can move on to see how to use this information in formulating appropriate responses, before and after an event occurs. Here the scale and urgency of the risk need to be considered. A flood is obviously imminent when the water level reaches bankfull stage. However, it is the frequency of such occurrences in the future, and our responses in terms of accommodating future environmental change, that need to be considered here. The potential impacts of climate change due to global warming need evaluating. Is the frequency of storm events going to increase, for example, so that rainfall events become more frequent and intense and so increase their impacts? How urgent is a particular risk scenario? Risk assessments will always be controversial; there are always different views of risk between the 'experts', the 'policy-makers' and the 'public'. There is always an 'uncertainty' element to any risk and response scenario.

Risk assessment

The essential element of assessing risk is to identify the frequency and magnitude of the particular geohazard event in order to identify the probable risk under a given set of environmental, socio-economic and political circumstances. This is termed vulnerability analysis and is needed in order to identify how we may respond to the impacts of specific hazardous events. Information such as where a particular flood hazard has occurred in the past, how frequently flooding has occurred here, and so how likely it is to occur here again in the future, might well lead to a decision to avoid the area entirely if the probability of a reoccurrence is high. Alternatively, the location may be zoned for certain land uses if flooding is only expected to be infrequent. Other responses, alongside avoidance and land-use zoning, include various planning strategies, the use of engineering structures, and ways of distributing any losses that might occur. Alternatively, for some geohazards, we might be able to reduce the severity or even the occurrence of the hazard itself. For example, land use planning might be more effective in the upland areas of a catchment in reducing the amount of surface run-off (quickflow) and so reducing the peak river discharge, rather than in controlling the uses of the floodplain in the flood susceptible area.

Although we still need the traditional monitoring of environmental phenomena, and to know the why, the where, the when, and the magnitude of a geohazard and its attendant risks, we must also be aware that the cultural, historical, socio-economic and political status of the people at risk is just as important in understanding how the risks are responded to. The same geohazard produces different risks and different responses in different people at different times in different places.

Global geohazard settings

This section will consider some of our more common and better documented geohazards. These hazards include seismic and volcanic hazards, hydrological hazards and slope stability issues. All hazards have specific locations in which they occur, and others in which they do not, or are less likely to occur. The easiest hazards to see are those associated with the global plate tectonic settings that govern seismicity, volcanicity and the distribution of the world's major mountain belts [☞]. Most active earthquake and volcano sites occur at constructive or destructive plate boundaries, or above hot spot locations, and so are easy to locate at a general level.

See ch 1, Restless Earth (p8).

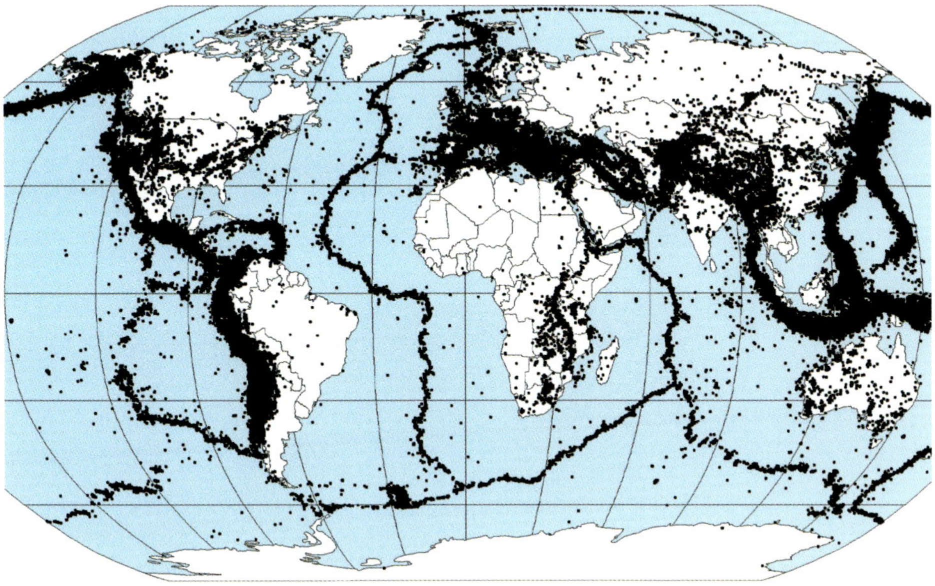

Figure 6.5: Plate tectonic activity focusing on location of earthquake activity

See accompanying CD-Rom

Global setting.ppt

Note: Useful background information can be found at the USGS (United States Geological Survey) website, This Dynamic Planet section: *http://pubs.usgs.gov/gip/dynamic/dynamic.html*

Figure 6.5 shows clearly the location of the major earthquake zones around the Earth, the densest clusters showing the most recently formed mountain belts associated with the circum-Pacific and Alpine-Himalayan subduction zones, areas still highly active. The older belts, such as the Appalachians in the USA and the Scandes in north-west Europe, were the products of similar historical boundaries [☞]. These mountain belts, along with the input from ocean circulation patterns, which are themselves partly controlled by the current continental disposition, affect global atmospheric circulation patterns, and so the location of monsoons and hurricane-generating weather systems, as well as snowfall and rainfall patterns, which can then lead to flood-producing run-off. The mountain belts, and especially those associated with ocean-to-continental crust subduction zones, also produce many of the world's steep coastlines, which, in turn, are major sites of slope instability, especially in association with volcanic peaks and earthquake zones.

See ch 7, Globalisation (p172).

The previous paragraph illustrates that many of the instances of geohazard events around the globe can be explained by the unifying concept of the plate tectonic cycle [☞]. It is no surprise that it is along plate boundaries that some of the most hazardous places in the world, such as South-east Asia, can be found. The most hazardous area lies in a triangle formed by the islands of the Philippines and Indonesia,

See ch 1, Restless Earth (p8).

both of which are bordered by active subduction zones, and are home to notable active volcanoes such as Krakatau, Tambora and Pinatubo. The region is also within monsoon and hurricane territory, has many steep mountain peaks, and is one of the least economically developed regions of the Earth, with relatively poor communications and other aspects of socio-economic infrastructure.

Seismic hazard

Earthquakes

Although earthquakes can occur in a wide variety of settings, most major seismic hazards have been located in proximity to plate boundaries. For instance, the 1906 San Francisco earthquake was sited along a conservative plate boundary, the San Andreas Fault zone. The 2004 Sumatran tsunami was the result of movements along the Java Trench subduction zone. The 2010 Chile earthquake occurred where the Nazca Plate descends under the South American Plate to form the Peru-Chile Trench.

Teaching idea 6.3

Ask students to use either the British Geological survey (*www.bgs.ac.uk*) or the US Geological Survey (*http://earthquake.usgs.gov*) websites to collect data to plot earthquakes on a world map to see how closely they follow plate boundaries. Where are the majority of events? How can the distribution be explained? This activity could then be repeated for volcanic eruptions and a comparison made between the two.

The main product of an earthquake is the vibration of the Earth's crust set up by the pressure waves produced when crustal blocks move past each other as they overcome friction. Initially, stresses build up in the Earth's crust as blocks of rock are pushed or pulled in opposing directions, and the rocks respond by starting to deform. If sufficient force is applied to these rocks, they fracture in a brittle manner, and movement ensues (the strain) to release the built-up stresses. Once movement has taken place, the fault plane produced is locked by friction, until forces build up again to overcome this, and further movement takes place reactivating the fault. Plate boundaries are such zones of stress and movement and this is where earthquakes are generated.

The focus is the term for the point/zone of rupture; the deeper this is beneath the ground surface, the more the energy will be absorbed by the intervening rocks, and the less will be the amplitude of the vibrations reaching the epicentre on the Earth's surface directly above. The magnitude of the energy released is usually measured according to the logarithmic Richter scale (named after the American seismologist who proposed it in 1935): 2 is 10 times greater than 1, 4 is 1,000 times greater than 1 and so on. This makes the magnitude 9.5 event, the largest ever recorded, in Chile on 22 May 1960, over 100,000,000 times greater than 1. These magnitudes can be related to the amount of ground movement that takes place at the Earth's surface. A magnitude 4 event has 10^4 microns of amplified maximum ground motion, equivalent to a movement of 1cm.

Teaching idea 6.4

Ask students to extract the Richter magnitude data for the earthquakes they mapped in teaching idea 6.3 and to plot these magnitudes on a global map. Can they identify any pattern and, if so, how do they explain the different magnitudes in different places. Are higher- or lower-magnitude events more frequent?

Although the Richter scale is appropriate for measuring the energy released and can be related to ground motion or tonnes of explosive equivalent, it doesn't always give an easy visualisation of the actual damage done. To this end, earthquake intensity scales have been developed. Although the Modified Mercalli (MM) scale is used in many places, including the USA, in Britain, the similar European Macroseismic Scale (EMS or EMS-98, as it was proposed in 1998) is in use. The EMS, like the MM scale, goes from 1 to 12. A scale 1 event is not felt, even under favourable conditions; 3 is weak, felt by a few people, especially those at rest; 5 is strong and felt by most people indoors, with objects such as lights and doors swinging and glasses and pots clinking together. When we move on to 6, we start to get clear visible damage, such as cracks in plaster and small objects falling and breaking (see figure 6.6 on p150). At 9 notable destruction starts, monuments collapse, ordinary buildings might partially collapse, a few weaker structures completely. By intensity 11, devastation occurs, with most ordinary buildings collapsing, while 12 sees practically all structures, both above and below ground level, being heavily damaged or destroyed. This type of scale gives us damage scenarios that can be related to, and is far more meaningful in terms of planning for future events.

Teaching idea 6.5

Ask students to imagine the effects of an earthquake of EMS intensity 6 and then a 9 or 10 in their local area. Ask them to identify the likely risks/impacts: what types of possible response scenarios would be required in these instances?

The intensity of the earthquake damage around any location is governed by a range of both natural and anthropogenic elements. The magnitude of the earthquake is extremely important as it governs the amount of energy released, and hence the scale of the vibrations produced. The depth of the focus of the earthquake is a modifying factor in this instance; the deeper the focus the more potential area above on the Earth's surface to be damaged, but the greater the volume of rock present to absorb the vibrations. Linked to this depth, we can see that the longer the direct line distance from the focus, the less impact that is likely to be felt at the surface. The local geomorphological ground conditions relate to how surface and near-surface materials react to the vibrations. Solid bedrock may remain strong, whereas unconsolidated sediments and soils with high water content will liquefy, with the water moving to the surface, the strength of the material reducing and buildings and other structures sinking into the ground. The build quality of structures is an obvious element in impacts: the poorer the building standards, the greater the likelihood of higher levels of damage. There are clear consequences to be drawn here from the differing standards of construction to be found across the world, something that can be largely equated with the wealth of the countries concerned.

Figure 6.6: Examples of earthquake damage during the Loma Prieta earthquake, California, 1979 (6.9 on the Richter scale)

See accompanying CD-Rom

Seismic hazard.ppt

Source: courtesy of the US Geological Survey *http://pubs.usgs.gov/dds/dds-29/screens/*
Link to useful information and images of the Loma Prieta event *http://pubs.usgs.gov/dds/dds-29/*

A final group of related facilities to consider are the utilities and communications networks that govern fresh water, sanitation and transportation both for the arrival of aid and for victims being evacuated. These facilities all relate to the effectiveness of the response effort. These are all elements that change from one event to the next, and so make the risk and vulnerability different each time; every event is in part unique.

We shall now consider three past events to demonstrate both the uniqueness of seismic events and also their similarities. The 1985 earthquake in Mexico City registered 8.1 on the Richter scale with aftershocks reaching 7.5. As the epicentre was located off the coast of Mexico, and the main event only lasted just over two minutes, the effects in Mexico City itself should have been relatively mild. However, Mexico City is situated on an old lake bed, on reclaimed but still water-saturated lake sediments, so when the vibrations arrived the sediment started to liquefy and turn to mud. The building standards were poor, with little regulation or inspection, and the buildings started to move in rhythm with the ground vibrations. This is termed 'resonance' and it increases the effects of the earthquake vibrations on structures, causing more than 800 buildings to collapse, many pancaking floor by floor. The result was approximately 20,000 deaths, 40,000 injured and 100,000 homes destroyed. The main hazards had been the liquefaction of the ground and the resonance of the buildings shaking because of the poor building standards.

In Niigata, Japan, in 1964, a magnitude 7.5 event occurred. Buildings were built on reclaimed but relatively waterlogged soil, the structure of which started to break down with water moving upwards and causing liquefaction. Here building foundations subsided and whole buildings sank and partly toppled but remained intact and relatively undamaged internally due to high building standards and the nature of the reinforced concrete multi-storey blocks. This considerably reduced the potential casualty figures. Some of these blocks were even jacked up and repaired after the event.

The 1906 San Francisco event also demonstrates that buildings on sediments, especially reclaimed wet materials, suffer more than those on bedrock areas. Here many of the buildings were wooden, and fractured gas pipes were ignited and set fire to many parts of the city. The fires continued out of control for four days, many of them having started in the aftermath of the earthquake itself. In this instance, again, the building standards were a major contributor to the amount of damage done. A good source of information about this event can be found at the University of California, Berkeley, Earthquake Engineering Research Centre (*http://seismo.berkeley.edu/seismo/hayward/seismicity.hist_1906.html*).

In terms of response and hazard management, a range of elements can be identified. Seismic hazard maps can be produced based on past events, the nature of surface conditions and the style of occupancy. Advance warning systems linked to the monitoring of precursor events such as changes recorded by creep, strain and tilt meters and magnetometers can be used. Similarly, gas monitors are able to show changes in the ground as stress opens minute cracks, which alters the electromagnetic properties of the material and allows traces of gases such as radon to escape. From the cases above, we can clearly see the need for building design and construction regulations, which need to extend to utilities and communications networks as well. Education and communication with the public are necessary so that people know what to do if an emergency is called or an event takes place; everyone needs to understand what to do in an effective disaster plan. Japan, for example, has disaster response practice days for the public as well as the authorities.

Tsunamis

Linked to earthquakes are the specific problems that arise from submarine events, where displacement of the Earth's crust occurs below the water surface. This displacement is transmitted to the overlying water, which drops down, then surges upwards, moving out in all directions as a low-height, long-wavelength and high-speed (up to 700km/h) tsunami wave. These tsunami waves do little damage in open water, but as they approach a shoreline, like all waves, they become shorter and steeper (heights of 25 to 30m have been observed) and, as they slow down (to about 5 to 10km/h), they break against the shore. Breaking at an oblique angle they do only moderate damage, but if they are near to, or perpendicular to, the shoreline then the damage can be extensive, especially on a low-lying coastline. Factors such as the state of the tide (if low) and the presence of offshore shoals can help to reduce the impacts.

In 1964, at Anchorage in Alaska, a magnitude 8.6 earthquake occurred offshore. The subsequent tsunami wave produced drowned 15 people and resulted in damage to buildings and infrastructure over $400km^2$, with the ground surface displacement being -2m on the landward side and up to +8m on the seaward side. The 1992 Nicaraguan tsunami began as an earthquake some 56km offshore, and produced a 9m-high wave along a 240km stretch of the Nicaraguan coastline, spreading as far inland as 0.8km, and resulting in 81 deaths, 101 missing and 3,700 homeless. It is events like the Anchorage one, and ones affecting Hawaii and Japan, especially around the Pacific, that led to the setting up of the Pacific Tsunami Warning System. A similar scheme is now in operation in the Indian Ocean after the Boxing Day event of 2004. (For information on the Boxing Day tsunami see *www.thebcom.org/ourwork/reliefwork/96-the-boxing-day-tsunami-facts-and-figures.html*; For an overview on tsunamis see the NOAA Centre for Tsunami Research *http://nctr.pmel.noaa.gov*).

Volcanic hazard

As with earthquakes, the major volcanic hazards are located at plate boundaries or at hot spot locations [☞]. Most active volcanoes are situated around the Pacific Ring of Fire, along the almost continuous subduction boundaries here, with others volcanoes found along the Mediterranean and Caribbean subduction zones. Another group is to be found at constructive or incipient plate boundaries, such as the East African Rift Valley or, like Iceland and the relatively new island of Surtsey to the south, on a mid-ocean ridge. The final main group are those related to hot spots, where large pulses of magma periodically move to the surface to produce notable volcanic centres such as the Hawaiian chain. These sites of magma, rising to the surface and erupting as lava or pyroclastics, and sometimes producing blast waves from explosions and gas emissions, produce both new landscape features such as volcanic mountains [☞], extensive lava plains and wide craters and calderas, and also a range of specific geohazards with associated risks to the people living nearby. Along the mid-ocean ridges, the myriad volcanic outpourings of lava and the associated dyke sheet intrusions produce our new ocean floor crust [☞].

See ch 1, Restless Earth (p20).
See ch 7, Globalisation (p172).
See ch 1, Restless Earth (p26).

The nature and style of any volcanic eruption depends initially on the nature of the magma rising to the surface. Magma may be derived from a range of locations within the Earth's mantle, each with its own different chemical composition. This may range, for example, from the melting of subducted oceanic crust, its chemical composition depending on the exact nature of this area of crust and of the sea floor sediments accumulated on it, to the deep mantle-derived hot spot magma with little contamination. Magma derived from the mantle is more basic and rich in iron and magnesium (termed 'mafic rich'). That derived from subduction is still mafic but with some more silica (often termed 'basic magma' [☞]), and that contaminated by existing crustal material tends to be the most silica rich and least mafic of all (termed 'acid magma'). The more acid the magma, and therefore the lava produced at the surface, the more viscous or sticky it will be (note the change from the term 'magma' – intrusive or beneath the surface – to 'lava' – at or above the surface). The initial magma chemistry and its subsequent development history are the main governing factors in the type of eruption event and hence the range of potential geohazards likely to occur.

See ch 1, Restless Earth (p27).

We can identify five main types of volcano on the Earth's land surface (see figure 6.7 on p154). Firstly, flood or plateau basalts are very liquid lavas produced mainly by fissure eruptions without the build-up of a specific volcanic cone. The Deccan Traps are an excellent example of this type of effusive eruption building up a major landscape element in India. Closer to home, the plateau basalts of the Isle of Staffa (part of the British Tertiary Volcanic Province), which were formed as the northern part of the Atlantic Ocean was opening some 60 to 65Ma ago, are a similar feature (see figures 6.7a and 6.7b). Where liquid lava builds up to form a cone around a central vent, a shield volcano such as Mauna Kea in the Hawaiian chain of islands results (figure 6.7c). Cinder cones show more explosive activity and generally produce small cones, often in swarms linked by fractures to the underlying magma chamber, as shown by the lower flanks of the volcanic island of Tenerife (figure 6.7d). Composite or stratovolcanoes, such as Mount Teide on Tenerife (figure 6.7e) are a mixture of layers of lavas and pyroclastics debris, showing repetitive changes in the nature of the volcanicity over time. The eruption of Mount Saint Helens, in 1980, showed one of the more eruptive phases of such a volcano, whereas the current lava dome, forming inside the crater produced, is an excellent example of the viscous lava activity often associated with composite volcanoes. Calderas are the collapsed remnants of large composite volcanoes after a period of either magma chamber subsidence or of extreme explosive activity. Mount Teide in Tenerife sits inside such a caldera, the Cañadas volcano (figure 6.7f). It is worth noting here that the Spanish word *caldera* was first used to denote such features by Leopold von Buch, a German geologist, when he visited Tenerife in 1815. One of the best known calderas is that in which sits Yellowstone National Park in the USA, produced by supervolcano activity in the past. A variety of other volcanic features can be seen in figures 6.7g to 6.7l.

In terms of potential hazards from any volcanic eruption, it is necessary initially to consider the materials involved. Hot molten lava is a product of many eruptions, especially effusive vulcanicity, and it flows over the surface, covering it in molten rock and setting light to surface structures and natural vegetation. Pyroclastic material results from more explosive behaviour, and includes ash (less than 4mm), lapilli (4 to 32mm) and blocks and bombs (more than 32mm) and, once produced, these volcaniclastic sediments can be reworked by later eruptions or other physical processes. The larger bombs are a direct missile hazard, with the finer materials settling over surfaces to bury material. The fine ash causes respiratory problems, clogs engines and can mix with water to produce mudflows (lahars). If hot or incandescent, this ash-like material can produce a nuee ardent (glowing cloud) travelling at tens of kilometres per hour, which will engulf and burn anything in its path. This was the case with the famous 79AD eruption of Vesuvius that engulfed Pompeii.

The gases produced by these eruptions are dominated by steam, with carbon dioxide and carbon monoxide, although a range of sulphurous gases are possible as well. These gases produce acid fogs and mists (termed 'vog') and a hydrochloric acid mist where lava flows enter open water and chemically react with the water (called 'laze'). They may also combine with water droplets in the atmosphere producing acid mists and rain, which can be deposited over the land surface, and may acidify lakes and other surface waters. The gases may also produce a shock wave in more explosive eruptions, as demonstrated by that of Mount Saint Helens in the 1980 eruption, and they can

a. Columnar basalt, Staffa

b. Columns in basalt flow, Staffa

c. Mauna Kea, Hawaii

d. Cinder cones, Tenerife

e. Mount Teide, Tenerife

f. Las Cañadas caldera, Tenerife

g. Blocky lava, Kilauea

h. Haleakala volcanic cones, Maui, Hawaii

l. Plateau lavas, Iceland

j. Lava entering sea, Kilauea

k. Lava tube, Mount Teide

i. Volcanic scenery, Andes

PHOTOS: C, G, H, I, J, L GERRY LUCAS; A, B, D, E, F, K STEVE SUGGITT

Figure 6.7: Evidence of volcanic activity, past and present

See accompanying CD-Rom

Volcanoes.ppt

PHOTOS: (TOP) GERRY LUCAS; (BOTTOM) STEVE SUGGITT

Figure 6.8: Volcanic eruption products

See accompanying CD-Rom

Volcanoes.ppt

asphyxiate as they are heavy gases that tend to move across the surface. Although not often thought of as a hazardous material, we should also include the shallow-depth, high-level intrusions of the magma plumbing system. These raise rock temperatures, produce steam and, by putting pressure on near-surface rocks, generate moderate earthquakes. Figure 6.8 shows some of these products.

These main products of eruptions – lava, pyroclastics and gases – and the way they are ejected produce the most obvious hazards, but in particular settings lahars may be produced from the reactivation of unconsolidated ashes by later high rainfall events, as has been the case around Mount Pinatubo in recent years. Associated with the melting of snow or ice, major floods (jökulhlaups) can occur, one of the most documented being associated with the 1996 eruption of Grimsvotn volcano in Iceland.

Landslides are further phenomena that can be triggered by volcanic eruptions, such as the lateral collapse of Mount Saint Helens, or the formation of the Orotava valley below Mount Teide in Tenerife. Here a large submarine deposit below Orotava has been interpreted as a major landslide deposit due to isostatic adjustments and high elevations and slope angles acting on the composite lava and pyroclastics of the stratovolcano. In this instance, as the mass movement was into the sea, it is probable that a tsunami was produced. It is likely that this hazard may be generated again within the Canary Islands.

Tenerife and the Canary Islands as a whole form an excellent case study of the varying nature of volcanic eruptions, and the materials they produce over time. They are located off the coast of Morocco and the Western Sahara, sitting on top of a volcanic hot spot, well away from any plate boundaries. This chain of islands is roughly linear with an approximate decrease in age of the volcanism from east to west. This progression in age does not appear to be as simple and regular as that found in other hot spot volcanic island chains such as the Hawaiian chain, the Society Islands or the Marquesas in the Pacific Ocean. The islands are thought to have started to form some 30Ma, building up from the Atlantic seabed to form individual shield volcano islands around 8.5Ma. From here until 3.3Ma, basalt lavas and pyroclastics occurred. Erosion was dominant until

1.9Ma when a large composite cone, the Cañadas volcano was produced. This volcano collapsed about 0.17Ma to form the large caldera noted above, and led to widespread basalt eruptions, largely from small parasite scoria cones on the lower flanks, probably exploiting fissures due to their alignment. Activity since then has seen the current composite stratovolcano, Mount Teide, form as a result of explosive Strombolian and Plinian eruptions, with the most recent activity in 1909 being from the small Pico Viejo on the lower flanks of Teide (figure 6.9).

Figure 6.9: View of Pico Viejo and Mount Teide, Tenerife

See accompanying CD-Rom

Volcanoes.ppt

Note: A good starting point for information about the Canary Islands volcanoes is *http://vulcan.wr.usgs.gov/Volcanoes/CanaryIslands/framework.html* and *www.volcano.si.edu/world/region.cfm?rnum=1803*

The style of an eruption, and its potential damage, is described by the Volcanic Explosivity Index (VEI), a scale from 0 to 8, though events above 5 (for example, the Mount Saint Helens 1980 eruption) are very rare. The rating of this scale is made up of several elements, the most important of which are the rate of the eruption; the eruption column height; its tropospheric and stratospheric injection and its duration; the volume of material ejected; and how explosive it is (figure 6.10). The higher the VEI the more dangerous is the eruption event.

Figure 6.10: Factors contributing to the Volcanic Explosivity Index (VEI)

See accompanying CD-Rom

Volcanoes.ppt

0 to 8 scale, related to many factors including:

- **rate of eruption**
- **eruption column height, tropospheric and stratospheric injection**
- **duration of eruption**
- **volume of ejecta**
- **explosivity related to magma type, from gentle to terrific (Hawaiian to Ultraplinian).**

Warning of the increased possibility of an impending eruption can be shown by certain precursor events. Upward-moving magma can cause the ground surface to become raised and tilt (tumescence), and will raise the temperature of surface rocks. Such movement also produces earthquakes, and the precise location of these earthquakes offers a good indicator of where the magma is moving at a particular time, as does the change in the style of gas emissions from steam and water vapour to sulphur compounds, as the lava approaches the surface.

The mitigation of volcanic hazards is largely based around the principles of evacuation and safety training. Once an explosive eruption sequence has started, it is often too late to evacuate as lavas, pyroclastics and lahars may rapidly block transport routes. Walls, ridges and trenches can be constructed to try to control potential lava flows. Explosives and cooling the lava to control its movement have had some success with fluid basalt flows. For instance, this has been successfully used on the island of Heimaey in south-west Iceland by the pumping of seawater to solidify and so divert a lava flow. On the other hand, nothing can be done to control ash fall deposits and gas emissions. In essence, volcanic hazards can only really be mitigated by the 'be elsewhere' principle.

Teaching idea 6.6

Ask students to use the USGS Volcanic Hazards Program website (*http://volcanoes.usgs.gov*) to research volcanic ash as a hazard and identify measures that could be used to protect people from this hazard during an eruption. Ask students to model a range of scenarios based on a volcanic eruption according to different conditions and wind directions from ash outfall. This could be carried out as part of an exercise in emergency planning. Alternatively, ask students to use Google Earth to identify the location of a hazard and then map a sequence of possible scenarios.

The eruption of the Eyjafjallajökull volcano, Iceland, April 2010

The eruption of volcanoes in Iceland is a frequent occurrence. However, the recent eruption of the Eyjafjallajökull volcano in southern Iceland has been newsworthy for the effects of its volcanic ash on the travel patterns of northern Europe.

Initially, the eruption caused extensive local flooding where ice from the Eyjafjallajökull glacier melted, washing away roads and causing the evacuation of about 800 people. Large areas of farmland were also washed away. However, it was the combination of large quantities of ash with north-westerly winds (unlike the more usual westerly and south-westerly winds) that caused chaos for airlines, with flights being cancelled over much of Europe as a result of the ash being blown further south than is usually the case (figure 6.11). The consequences of these cancellations indicated both the wide-ranging uses for air travel and how dependent on it some sectors of the economy are (see figure 6.12 on p158).

Figure 6.11: The distribution of ash from Eyjafjallajökull volcano

See accompanying CD-Rom

Volcanic ash.ppt

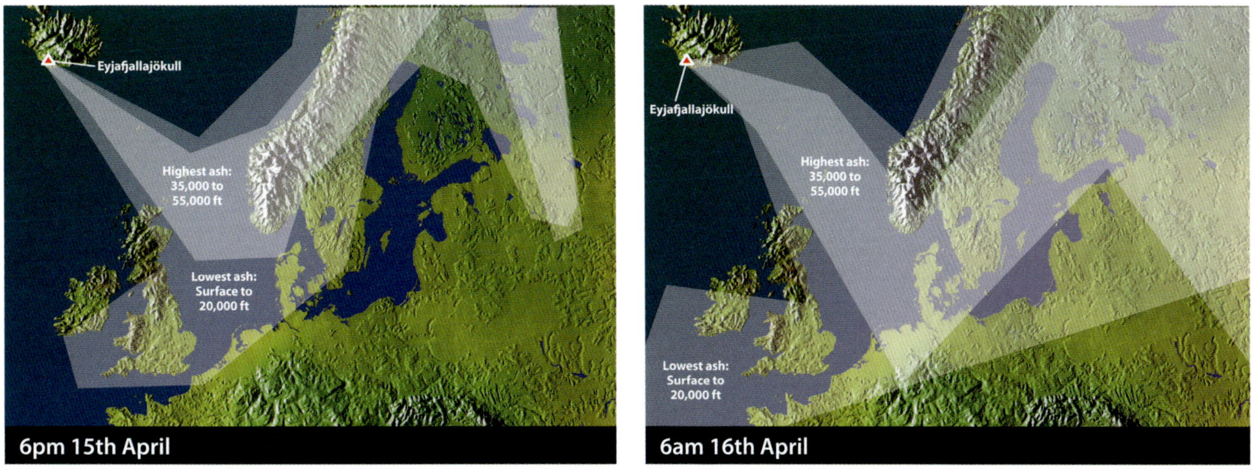

Source: adapted from Metoffice, Euro control.
For a view of the changing distribution of the ash clouds see: *www.guardian.co.uk/uk/interactive/2010/apr/15/volcano-airport-disruption-iceland*

Figure 6.12: The impacts of airspace closure

See accompanying CD-Rom

Airspace closure.doc

Musicians stranded due to volcanic ash	How an Icelandic volcano helped spark the French Revolution
That volcano could also mess up satellite communications	Volcanic eruption leaves holiday plans in ashes
Icelandic volcano: are you enjoying the clear skies?	Non-flying circus: John Cleese's £3,300 taxi fare
How the volcano took out our fruit salad	Iceland volcano shuts all UK airports
Icelandic volcano: is this the start of the 'traincation'?	More UK gigs hit by volcanic flight ban
BBC's volcano coverage attracts record 5.5m users in one day	New volcanic ash cloud threatens to cloud UK airspace again
Iceland volcano: imagine a world without planes	European flight paralysis exacts high price on the Kenyan flower trade
Schools in chaos after teachers and pupils stranded	Icelandic volcano causes fall in carbon emissions as eruption grounds aircraft

(All headlines taken from *The Guardian*, 15-20 April 2010)

See Volume 3: Environmental Geography, ch 5, Food supply (p119).

Teaching idea 6.7

Ask students to select two or three of the headlines in figure 6.12. How did the eruption of the Eyjafjallajökull volcano trigger their chosen news stories? Ask them to imagine that they are being affected by the event – how would they have reacted to being prevented from using air travel? What alternatives could they consider?

Flood hazard

River flooding

Riverine flooding is one of the most ubiquitous of geohazards. River valleys have always been popular sites for occupancy and transportation routes. They have flat land, fertile soils and a readily available water supply for drinking, irrigation, manufacturing and waste disposal. On the other hand, they are also the sites of river flooding, especially where anthropogenic changes have exacerbated the natural flood regime. Floods are natural events that occur when river flow exceeds bankfull discharge and spills onto the adjacent flood plain (figure 6.13). The reason for the term 'flood plain' is literally because flooding has produced it in the first place, and will continue to modify it with each subsequent flood event.

See ch 2, Rivers (p45).

Figure 6.13: Flood levels, River Till, Northumberland

See accompanying CD-Rom

Flooding.ppt

The most common cause of a natural river flood is intense or prolonged rainfall; again these are high-magnitude but low-frequency geomorphological events. Other major causes include spring snowmelt and the high-rainfall, high-tide estuarine situation. In each case, climatic or weather conditions are key constituents. Other, non-climatic river floods may be caused by landslides blocking a valley, or the failure of water control structures such as dams or levées. Climate-induced river floods are the single most important and frequent flood occurrence, but we cannot assume that excessively heavy or prolonged rainfall will cause a similar flood, or even a flood at all, either in adjacent drainage basins or in the same basin every time. It is important to consider the specific physical setting on each occasion, along with the drainage basin characteristics, the channel network style and the channel itself. These factors are viewed as the flood-intensifying conditions, which govern whether or not a flood will occur when discharges are around bankfull, and also the duration and severity of a flood when bankfull is exceeded.

Each drainage basin will have some stable characteristics, such as area, shape, altitudinal fall and slope angles, which only change extremely slowly. But a basin will also have some more dynamic variables, such as the interactions between climate, geology, soils, vegetation and anthropogenic influences. These variables may change much more rapidly. These variables affect the storage capacity of the soil and bedrock, the infiltration rate into the soil, and the transmission rate of water through the soil, bedrock or over the surface. All these factors are controls on quickflow, and hence how much water enters the channel within a given period of time.

Similarly, the channel network contains relatively stable factors, such as the basic drainage pattern that has developed over time, and more dynamic aspects, like the total length of channel, the amount of surface water storage and whether there is any artificial channel drainage, surface furrows or field drainage system to enhance surface flow (figure 6.14).

Figure 6.14: Run-off along furrows and from field adjacent to River Till, Northumberland

See accompanying CD-Rom

Flooding.ppt

Channel characteristics themselves also have stable and variable elements. Surface slope and any existing hard engineering flood control, river regulation or channel stabilisation works are all relatively static elements. Variable characteristics would include shape and hence storage capacity of the channel itself, and channel roughness and load, which will affect speed of flow.

As we have seen, the relationships between rainfall and run-off can be established, with variables added for changes in basin characteristics. As a result of monitoring such variables, flood alert warnings are given when necessary in Britain as with most other MEDCs. This is often not the case in LEDCs, due to the cost of instrumentation for monitoring and the often limited communications networks.

Coastal flooding

Coastal flooding is caused by extreme climatic events and some geophysical agencies. Estuarine situations, as noted above (p159), are a hybrid between high freshwater discharge levels from land and high tide levels from the sea. Estuaries are funnel shaped and become shallower inland, and so the tidal range in them is naturally increased – for example, a tidal range of 1m in the North Sea rises to 5m near Hull in the Humber estuary. The risk of inundation to the city of Hull resulted in the construction of a barrage on the River Hull at the point where it enters the Humber (figure 6.15). Thus, the danger times for estuarine flooding are when spring tides coincide with high river discharges.

Figure 6.15: The tidal barrage, Kingston upon Hull

See accompanying CD-Rom

Hull barrage.ppt

Note: Detailed information on flood management for Hull is available at: *www.hullcc.gov.uk*

In non-estuarine coastal areas, flooding is normally due to severe meteorological conditions, such as extreme low pressure causing high sea levels, especially if these coincide with spring tides giving a storm surge. This is, in essence, the difference between the predicted and the observed tide level. This inflated tidal level can be exacerbated by strong onshore winds, which are often associated with deep depressions, and these can produce high waves, which act at an increased height along the coastline. The well documented[1] 1953 floods along the east coast of England and the entire coast of the Netherlands are an excellent example of a storm surge event caused by meteorological phenomena.

Coastal flooding can also result from tsunamis caused by earthquakes or volcanic eruptions (see *Seismic hazard* on p148). The 2004 Boxing Day tsunami in the Indian Ocean was due to a magnitude 9.1 earthquake, which occurred 255km south south-east of Banda Aceh, Northern Sumatra, at 10km depth, leading to a fracture on the seabed roughly 100km long, with a maximum vertical displacement of 20m. The resulting set of tsunami waves travelled between 300 and 500km/h. Due to the 160km-wide, shallow continental shelf off Bangladesh, the waves were slowed down and their energy dissipated, whereas Sri Lanka, with a deep ocean floor to the east, had over 29,000 casualties. This tsunami-induced storm surge also affected Thailand, coasts around the Bay of Bengal and the distant East African coastline. Some 150,000 people died in total.

Flooding in the UK

Urban flooding is becoming an ever increasing problem; some 80,000 properties are at risk in the UK in areas where storm run-off systems are no longer able to cope with the amount of artificial quickflow being generated from buildings and roads. As with other geohazards, flooding is an entirely natural occurrence and only produces hazards and risks to people in areas of residential, industrial or agricultural developments or along transport routes (figure 6.16).

Figure 6.16: Flooding in Much Wenlock

See accompanying CD-Rom

Flooding.ppt

PHOTOS: PAUL WEEDEN

Teaching idea 6.8

Ask your students to use the Environment Agency pages on flood risk to find out about flood hazard around their home. Get them to identify how far away the nearest flood-prone areas are, and why. (*www.environment-agency.gov.uk/homeandleisure/floods/default.aspx*)

See accompanying CD-Rom

Much Wenlock flooding.doc provides a detailed case study of the current situation in Much Wenlock.

In the UK, there are currently some 2 million properties potentially at risk from flooding; in England and Wales alone, properties exceeding a total of £200bn and over 4 million people are at risk. Flooding and flood management cost the UK over £2.2bn per year; some £800m being spent on hard engineered flood defences. We sustain, on average, £1,400m of flood damage each year. Although the level of spending is steady, the cost of flood damage is sporadic and can be extremely high when a major flood occurs.

The type of flood damage sustained can be classified, as with other geohazards, according to the type of land use affected (residential, industrial, agricultural, recreational, etc) or, more usually, according to the type of damage sustained. This damage can be further subdivided into tangible and intangible impacts on people. Tangible impacts can be quantified in monetary terms and may be direct, such as physical damage to buildings or contents, which can readily be valued by the cost of restoration or replacement; or they may be indirect, such as industrial production losses. Intangible impacts cannot be directly measured in monetary terms, but would include physiological experiences such as the increase in hospital attendances due to the effects of damp properties, or psychological effects such as the stress and anxiety of how restoration is going to be paid for, or how to get to work if transport routes are closed.

In terms of managing flood hazard, most places have traditionally used engineering works such as flood embankments or relief channels. This usage is a reflection of the dominant role of the engineering profession in traditional flood hazard management. In reality, there are a number of alternatives to flood alleviation and hazard management, and four main groups of adjustment can be identified. The likelihood of flooding can be reduced by using engineering works such as embankments, relief channels, flood retention reservoirs, flood flow temporary storage areas or by watershed management to reduce quickflow, such as the planting of woodland. Alternatively, attempts to reduce the likelihood of the flood damage can be initiated. Such measures include land use control to limit residential development on flood plains, flood proofing of vulnerable properties to make them more water resistant, or introducing or improving flood warning schemes to increase the time people have to move valuables from ground floor locations and move to safer locations. The burden of flood damage that does occur can be eased by the operation of flood insurance schemes, or by the setting up of disaster relief funds in flood-susceptible locations. The final option is to do nothing, a surprisingly common response as people often underestimate the likelihood or the nature of the impact of potential flooding, and adopt the attitude that someone else will put things right.

Slope failure hazard

Slope failures are often grouped under the generic term of landslides, and encompass all mass movements of soil, sediment and rock down slope under the influence of gravity, often with aid from water. These movements occur when gravitational forces overcome the friction and shear strength of the slope material. They include events such as block fall, rotational slip rock slides, debris and mud flows and turf tearing (see figure 6.17 on p163) The rate of movement can vary from rapid to very slow, and can be initiated suddenly or build up slowly over a long period of time.

Figure 6.17: Examples of slope movements

PHOTOS: (TOP, BOTTOM RIGHT) STEVE SUGGITT; (BOTTOM LEFT) CHARLES RAWDING

See accompanying CD-Rom

Slopes.ppt

Factors that help keep slopes stable include the inherent strength and cohesion of the slope material, including the internal friction between grains in unconsolidated slope materials, the water content of the material, and the binding effect of vegetation cover and its ability to help control the water content. Factors that help gravity to bring about slope failure may act gradually or rapidly. Gradual factors include increases in slope angle as material undergoes natural weathering and transport processes, increases in the water content of the slope materials, removal of vegetation, or removal of the base of the slope by fluvial or marine erosion. Rapid factors are causal agents such as earthquake vibrations, volcanic eruptions or torrential downpours. Anthropogenic influences can have a major effect on slope stability, particularly through construction works and land use changes.

Once a slope failure has occurred, the area in question is more susceptible to further failures as some of the inherent strength of the material has been reduced around the failure plane. Mam Tor, on National Trust land some 2km north-west of Castleton in Derbyshire, is an excellent example of repeated slope movements causing the eventual closure of a major road, the then A625 main route from Manchester to Sheffield. It is easily accessible and is a well-developed landslide feature that provides an excellent example of an active landslip. The road was first repaired below Mam Tor due to the sliding of water-saturated, weathered surface and subsurface materials along an existing failure plane in 1909, some three years after Derbyshire County Council became responsible for the road's maintenance and repair. The materials in question are the Carboniferous age Edale Shales (grey laminated marine shale with clay and pyrite rich bands), which are highly susceptible to chemical weathering processes that leach out pyrite and carbonate cement from the rocks, increasing porosity and permeability and decreasing rock strength [☞]. Between 1912 and 1942 it was repaired a further 11 times because of repeated sliding. In 1946 a major realignment of the road took place, but between 1948 and 1955 it needed repair for further movements on four occasions. In 1965 it was closed, repaired and reopened. In 1977 it closed and, after more repairs, was opened to single-file traffic in 1978. In 1979 it failed again and was permanently closed. Figure 6.18 on p164 demonstrates the nature of the failed material and the effects of the movement.

See ch 1, Restless Earth (p29-30).

Figure 6.18: Road disruption at Mam Tor in Derbyshire

PHOTOS: A, B, E, F, H CHARLES RAWDING; D, E, G STEVE SUGGITT

See accompanying CD-Rom

Slopes.ppt

The largest historic landslide in the world occurred during the eruption of Mount Saint Helens in 1980 (see *Volcanic hazard* on p152) when some 2.8 cubic kilometres of material failed. The most expensive landslide was just down valley from the town of Thistle in Utah. Here rapid snowmelt led to a saturated slope failing and blocking the Spanish Fork River which produced a temporary lake, completely flooding the town. Controlled draining of the lake, repairs to properties, loss of earnings, and realignment of a road and construction of a railway tunnel was estimated at US$200m (1984). The most deadly event is the 31 May landslide in Peru in 1970. An earthquake linked to the Peru-Chile Trench caused the collapse of the summit ice cap on Mount Huascarán, leading to a large debris flow of pulverised ice, rock, sediment

Figure 6.19: Slope protection and stabilisation methods – examples from A55, North Wales, Uig, Isle of Skye, Scotland and Estellenchs, Mallorca

See accompanying CD-Rom

Slopes.ppt

and meltwater containing blocks in excess of 15m^{-3}. This debris flow moved rapidly down slope at speeds over 320km/h, devastating the town of Yungay, which is now buried beneath the material, leaving approximately 25,000 victims.

Mass movements can often be anticipated. It is possible to review a region's past history of slope failure, both from historical sources and in terms of characteristic slope failure landforms. Strain gauges and movement detectors can be installed, along with water level and moisture content meters. Such instrumentation can be used to assess changes in slope parameters and indicate the approach of potential failure events.

As with flood hazard, there are a number of preventative and remedial measures that can be employed to help stabilise failed or potentially dangerous slopes. A range of hard engineering methods employed are shown in figure 6.19 on p165 including rock bolting, the use of gabions and netting above Uig on the Isle of Skye, and the use of containment netting and crash nets to catch falling material at Estellenchs in Mallorca. Methods to reduce the frequency or magnitude of the event include land use controls, water content control and the use of geomembranes to help establish vegetation and reduce erosion. Passive measures include a range of options to reduce the potential damage and loss, for example by land-use planning zonation, building regulations, and planning responses such as evacuation procedures. Other passive measures include planning for or spreading the losses by subsidised insurance or public relief funds.

Decisions by individual communities to remain in areas of risk may appear bewildering to outsiders (see *Why take the risk?* on p167). Figures 6.20 and 6.21 (p167) provide information relating to slope failure in the case of the community of La Conchita, California.

Figure 6.20: La Conchita, Ventura County, California

See accompanying CD-Rom

La Conchita.doc

'In 1995 the hill behind La Conchita failed and buried 9 homes but no lives were lost. Ventura County immediately declared the whole community a Geological Hazard Area. This essentially stole the soul of our community. They placed building restrictions on the community so no new construction could take place. It was years before any new families moved into town and just recently we once again felt like a community. On January 10, 2005 the hill failed again only this time it killed 10 residents and destroyed 18 homes. The remainder of the community (171 homes) is – according to Ventura County – in peril from any additional heavy rain. This situation must be corrected for our community to survive.

1995, a geological firm and an engineering firm, together developed a hillside remediation plan. This plan calls for terracing of the hill and stated that when the remediation plan was completed, the community could use all property within the community without restriction and essentially remove the Geological Hazard designation from the entire community. Since the 2005 slide, the community has been working diligently towards a plan that will get the hill fixed. We have contacted Ventura County for their support. The County is afraid to say or do anything for fear of litigation. This fear stopped them from doing anything for our community in 1995. We will not let them do nothing again!

In 1995 as in 2005, just prior to the hill failure mudflows came down the canyon just North of La Conchita closing the 101 Coast Highway and the Union Pacific railroad tracks. The 101 Coast Highway (the major artery between Southern and Northern California) as well as the railroad were closed for at least one week. According to news press releases the coast highway closure cost the State of California 10 million dollars a day and un-disclosed cost to the railroad. The hill behind La Conchita and the canyon to the North are not just a La Conchita problem, but a State and Federal issue. It is in the best interest of all that this issue be addressed by Local, State and Federal officials immediately.'

Source: *www.laconchita.net/mudslide.htm*

Teaching idea 6.9

Ask students to look at the extract from the La Conchita website (figure 6.20 on p166) and figure 6.21. What are their first impressions of the tone of writing on the community website? How would they feel if they were residents? What would their reaction be if they lived elsewhere in Ventura County?

PHOTOS: ROB MALONE

Source: *www.laconchita.net/mudslide.htm*

Figure 6.21: La Conchita mudslide

See accompanying CD-Rom

La Conchita.ppt

Why take the risk?

Whenever natural disasters are covered in the media, questions are asked about why people live in such seemingly dangerous places. In many cases, there are perfectly sensible reasons for human habitation. For instance, Bam, a city of more than 200,000 people in Iran, was hit by an earthquake of magnitude 6.6 in December 2003. As a result, over 43,000 people were killed, 20,000 injured, and 60,000 left homeless. Much of the city was destroyed. In fact, the city had been deliberately located on a fault line (which triggered the earthquake), as the geology of this location results in water being available; effectively the location is an oasis in an area of desert.

Rapid population growth in many areas of the world also means that more people are now exposed to earthquake risks. Again in Iran, the city of Tehran, with 13 million people, sits on an active fault. While we know about more disasters as the result of better reporting, changes in classification mean that they are in fact more numerous and population growth has led to more people being affected by them. However, death tolls are actually reducing. Equally, it is almost certain that Istanbul, Turkey (population: 10 million), will be hit by a major earthquake in the next 30 years.

Changing lifestyle aspirations in wealthier nations are also resulting in people moving to more risky locations. In the case of the United States, large numbers of people are moving to hazard zones – away from the rust belt cities of the north and east of the country, towards possible hurricanes on the Gulf Coast, or earthquakes in California. A desire to live in coastal locations has also resulted in new communities being located on the coast rather than in traditional, and safer, locations slightly inland.

Summary

All geohazards are a result of the high magnitude of a natural process producing risks to the wellbeing of people. There is no hazard or risk without people being affected. This means that a large part of the world where extreme events occur would not be classed as hazardous unless we started to occupy and use it. Without human occupancy or use of the area affected by a high magnitude natural event then the natural process or event is simply that, a natural process, no matter what its intensity or frequency, and it will therefore have no impact on people or their livelihood at all. We have looked at the nature of geohazards in general, and at some specific hazard types in order to demonstrate some of the variability in the nature of, and responses to, specific causal agents. Everywhere in the world is at risk in one way or another from a geohazard.

In many ways, the study of geohazards presents an excellent case for integrated approaches to geography. While an understanding of the processes that trigger such hazards clearly lies in the realm of physical geography, an understanding of the impacts of these hazards is only possible through a full appreciation of human and environmental geographies. As we have seen, the size of a disaster related to geohazards is often associated with the level of development of the community in which it occurs. While there are clearly exceptions, as with Hurricane Katrina in New Orleans in 2005 and the Boxing Day tsunami of 2004, in general terms, the richer a country, the more able it is to both prepare for and cope with disasters. During a single six-month period in 2007/8, Cyclone Sidr in Bangladesh (15 November 2007), Cyclone Nargis in Burma (2 May 2008) and the Wenchuan earthquake in China (12 May 2008) resulted in an estimated 90,000 deaths and about 25 million people being displaced from their homes (Collins, 2009).

Endnote

1. For information on the 1953 floods see: *www.metoffice.gov.uk/corporate/library/dws/east_coast_floods_31_January_1953.pdf* and looking back at its anniversary on the 31 January (2010) *www.bbc.co.uk/weather/features/understanding/1953_flood.shtml*

Useful websites

ESRI provides online bitesize podcasts, which include lesson plans and ideas relating to plate tectonics and hurricanes: *www.esriuk.com/schools*

Global Environmental Monitoring System: *www.gemswater.org*

Aon Benfield UCL Hazard Research Centre: *www.abuhrc.org/Pages/index.aspx*

Drinking water quality United Utilities: *www.unitedutilities.com/Annualsummaries.htm*

A good source of river discharge data in the UK:
www.nwl.ac.uk/ih/nrfa/river_flow_data/river_flow_data_download.htm
(Annual tables of daily flow data for around 200 gauging stations throughout the UK are available for downloading.)

This site contains a compilation of monthly mean river discharge data for over 3,500 sites worldwide: *www.sage.wisc.edu/riverdata*

For a general flood link go to:
www.environment-agency.gov.uk/homeandleisure/floods/default.aspx

NOAA Tsunami Research Centre: *http://nctr.pmel.noaa.gov*

Both of the following have much information on hazards and afford excellent starting points and links to elsewhere on the web: British Geological survey: *www.bgs.ac.uk* and US Geological Survey: *http://earthquake.usgs.gov*

The British Geological Survey also runs the schools seismology project: *www.bgs.ac.uk/schoolseismology* and has an exercise based on the 1997 eruption of the Montserrat volcano.

A good starting point for finding out more about flood hazard and coastal protection in the UK is via the Defra and Environment Agency flood and coastal defence research programme: *www.river-conveyance.net/1_CES_UserGuide.pdf*

Further reading

Coch, NK (1995) *Geohazards, Natural and Human*. Prentice Hall, New Jersey.

Collins, A (2009) *Disaster and development*. Abingdon, Routledge.

Department of Environment (1994) *Landsliding in Great Britain*. HMSO, London.

7

Globalisation

Introduction

It has been demonstrated in earlier chapters that a variety of processes have operated on different materials, with different intensities, to produce the present landforms of the globe. We shall now present a series of discussions to try to draw out some of the similarities and differences we can see in landform types and processes around the Earth. As such, this chapter will adopt a geomorphodynamic style of approach, where we consider the major elements of our global morphological system – materials, landforms and processes – to link together as a whole, in what is often viewed as a systems approach to the subject. A change in any one element has effects on the others. Initially, we can see this because of the role major global morphological patterns and global climatic parameters play in the development of regional landscapes, but also because this systems approach allows us to feed in other factors that are of importance, for example, lithology in limestone environments. No matter what approach is adopted, the ideas of landforms evolving through time, their polycyclic nature, and their subjection to a range of climates as they change will all be part of the discussion, as will the balance between magnitude and frequency of operation of the processes under consideration. The increasing importance of anthropogenic effects on our landscapes will also be considered, along with the impact of geophysical processes on a globalising world. To illustrate this point, somewhat anecdotally, the 2004 Boxing Day tsunami [☞] in South-east Asia, was Sweden's highest recorded death toll from a natural disaster.

See ch 6, Geohazards (p151).

The approach, outlined above, to viewing global patterns and looking at the similarities and differences between landscapes in one place and another is not uncommon. However, trying to tie all the threads together as part of the unified evolution of the planet is not always sufficiently appreciated. Since the advent of plate tectonic theory and the development of an increasingly detailed and reliable chronology of the evolution of our planet throughout geological time, it has been possible to appreciate modern process studies in a more effective context. The landscape, at any one particular time, anywhere on the Earth, can be seen as a snapshot in evolution, a unique element in a continuum of change. This is an important concept: landscapes do not suddenly appear, they depend on the rocks and landforms that have been produced in past environments by past processes acting on the products of weathering and erosion of even earlier phases of landscape production. These processes that have operated in the past may be quite different from the processes operating under current climate systems and so will have been modifying materials and producing landforms in different ways. Our current processes, in turn, are altering the basic landscape elements of today, and will continue to do so in the future. Most landforms, and the landscapes they are part of, form quasi-equilibrium elements in our changing world. The main reason for this is that, especially at the present time, we are in a geological phase of quite marked climatic fluctuations with the advance and retreat of glaciers globally. The last main glacial pulse peaked between 18,000 and 20,000 years ago, and we only started to get our modern climatic distributions settling down somewhat at the start of the Holocene, 10,000 years ago. Modern geomorphological systems are still largely operating on landforms and with materials largely produced by other processes, glacial in much of Britain, pluvial in much of northern Africa.

The growth of a global mass media has resulted in the increasing integration of society throughout the world. For instance, it is possible to turn on a news programme and it is global in its coverage, watch a natural history programme and it could be about anywhere in the world. The increasing presence of international organisations and the almost instant access to knowledge about places anywhere on the planet via the World Wide Web and search engines such as Google, or through the pages of Wikipedia, brings home the truth that we all live on the same planet. This leads to the fostering of a global approach to the study of landscape evolution, to being able to appreciate that understanding about one place or feature can lead to appreciation about other places and features, elsewhere in the world. This chapter will link this focus on the landforms, materials and processes at a global level with some thoughts on the hazards they produce, the resources they provide, and the sustainability of the environment as it undergoes increasing anthropogenic influences at different scales.

See ch 5, Ice, figure 5.27.

There is a certain 'wow' factor in studying our global environments, in looking at some of the natural wonders of our world; there are many amazing places to see and discover. To illustrate this point, think of some of the world's most well-known mountain peaks, Mount Everest, Eiger or Matterhorn areas [☞], or of Mauna Loa rising some 10,000m from the floor of the Pacific Ocean, or at the national scale, our own Ben Nevis in Scotland. There is a good feeling about trying to understand and appreciate how landform features like these were produced and continue to evolve.

Mountain environments

Without doubt, mountains are among some of the most breathtaking and awe-inspiring of natural environments. Mountain peaks, hidden valleys, rushing rivers and windswept glaciers have caught the imagination of many people throughout human history (see figure 7.1 on p173). Mountains are visually dominant landscape elements, but remain fragile for all of their majesty. They often qualify as marginal landscapes with great sensitivity to environmental change. The sensitivity of mountain landscapes came to the notice of the United Nations Environment Programme (UNEP) in 2003 because of their susceptibility to landslides, soil erosion and high sediment yields, flooding and reduction in biodiversity. Mountains are global in their distribution and show a direct link to current and past plate tectonic processes.

There have been many attempts at classifying mountains based on aspects such as pure elevation, tectonic setting or spatial scale of individual and group elements. No matter what classification is used, it is important to note that some 25% of the Earth's land surface is covered by mountain environments. All mountain areas are characterised to some extent by high altitude summits and steep slopes and/or high plateaux. Further characteristics include high precipitation and low temperatures, with the result that snow and ice are at least seasonally present. In addition, high-magnitude but low-frequency episodes of geomorphic activity are found. All mountain landscapes have distinct vegetation and climate zones. Mountains can be seen to fall into a number of

Figure 7.1: Mountain environments

See accompanying CD-Rom

Mountains.ppt

main groups. Alpine types have been conditioned by intense glacial activity and the formation of specific features such as arêtes, pyramidal peaks, cirques and glacial troughs with later periglacial and paraglacial elements [☞] of scree slopes and debris fans. Volcanic, often cone-shaped, mountains have unique morphological elements based on the nature and materials involved in their creation, along with the more climatically driven geomorphological processes operating on these forms and materials.

See ch 5, Ice (p132).

The evolution of mountain systems is linked to plate tectonic movements throughout geological time. An example of these is shown in figure 7.2 on p174 in relation to their plate boundary and interior settings [☞]. Historically, three major mountain-building episodes of continental collision are responsible for many of our current mountain areas. The Caledonian orogeny occurred in the Lower Palaeozoic, when the three large continental orogens of Gondwana, Laurasia and Baltica came together. The Variscan orogeny occurred in the Upper Palaeozoic, when North Africa collided with Europe and, most recently, the Alpine orogeny was associated with Late Mesozoic and Cenozoic subduction boundaries, which produced the Alpine-Himalayan and Circum-Pacific mountain belts. From this sequence, we can see that the spread of terrestrial mountains due to plate tectonic processes is indeed global in pattern. The first two of these orogenic episodes are long finished, but their products still resist the forces of erosion. The latter episode is still current and it is these fresh mountain areas that are the most studied today, both in terms of their evolution and the processes operating on them.

See ch 1, Restless Earth, figure 1.9.

An alternative way of studying mountains, and one evolving mainly in these young Alpine mountain belts, is through a more functional approach, looking at the processes operating and the variations in their spatial and temporal rates of operation. Uplift and erosion values are at their maximum in these areas, and so altitudinal fall, along with overall elevation and slope angle, help us define a range of overlapping process systems at work here. The glacial system generally operates at the highest elevations, though it is possible for glaciers to reach the sea, as in the case of Patagonia.

Figure 7.2: Plate tectonic settings of mountain environments

See accompanying CD-Rom

Mountains.ppt

Plate setting	Types	Examples
Converging plates – destructive margins	Ocean to ocean	Japanese Alps; Aleutian Arc
	Ocean to continent	South Island, New Zealand; Cascades Range north-west USA
	Continent to continent	Himalayas
Diverging plates – constructive margins	Oceanic spreading	Iceland
	Intercontinental rifting	Sinai Peninsula; East African Rift valley
Transform plates – conservative margins	Ridge past ridge	California coast ranges
	Trench past trench	Anatolia, Turkey
	Ridge past trench	Pakistan-Afghanistan
Plate interiors	Hot spots	Hawaii; Yellowstone National Park, USA

Figure 7.3: Processes reworking sediment in Austerdalen, Norway

See accompanying CD-Rom

Mountains.ppt

See ch 5, Ice (p113).

As we have seen in chapter 5 [☞], the glacial system is one of the most variable in terms of the processes operating, and in terms of its location in time and space. Glacier catchments are characterised by glacial, frost, fluvioglacial, paraglacial and some mass wasting processes as shown in figure 7.3. In such situations, sediment production and temporary storage is at a maximum, and fluctuations in climate are continually challenging where and when these process systems operate. For example, as glaciers retreat they leave behind unconsolidated till and fluvioglacial sediments that are readily eroded by gravity, rainfall and streamflow. The same is true of periglacial deposits, such as frost-shattered scree.

Teaching idea 7.1

Provide your students with maps, photographs and Google Earth images of a study area such as the Lake District (see figure 7.4 on p175) or Snowdonia (see figure 7.5 on p175). Ask them to identify the main mountain features and how they were formed. Ask them to try to identify the sequence of events that led to these features being produced and identify the different processes that operated at different times to try to engender a perspective of landscape evolution.

PHOTOS: CHARLES RAWDING

Figure 7.4: The Lake District – a mountain environment

See accompanying CD-Rom

The Lake District.ppt.

Figure 7.5: Snowdonia – a mountain environment

See accompanying CD-Rom

Snowdonia. ppt.

Sediment systems in mountains

Sediment systems in mountain areas can be dominated by either coarse sediments, largely derived from glacial and frost processes, or by fine sediments from glacial processes and chemical weathering. The coarse-grained sediment system is dominated by mechanical weathering and mass movement. It may operate as a feeder into valley glacier systems or on its own. Avalanches, rockfalls, landslides and debris flows are common mass-movement phenomena producing landforms, such as scree slopes, alluvial fans and feeding braiding gravel bed streams (figure 7.6). These processes and landforms are initially controlled by lithology, but climatic regimes and, of course, past climate fluctuations are all part of the equation to be solved. These systems are easily altered by human impacts, such as deforestation (for example, in the Canadian Rockies) or the construction of routeways (for example, in Japan), which reactivate stable slopes and alter run-off regimes. It has been estimated that this system needs eight years to recover from road construction and up to 20 years from logging activities.

Figure 7.6: Scree in Borrowdale, Cumbria and Nant Ffrancon, North Wales

See accompanying CD-Rom

Mountains.ppt

The fine-grained sediment system is dominated by locally derived weathering products of soil and unconsolidated sediments (see figure 7.7 on p177) suggestive of longer-term processes, with a higher impact from chemical weathering. Such a system can also be affected by windblown loess and coversand materials from past, and present, glacial and cold desert activity, and from the lack of vegetation in some mountain areas. Fluvial processes come into their own here, transporting materials to sites of temporary deposition on slopes and floodplains and within channels themselves (see figure 7.8 on p177). Although the total amount of sediment being transported may be greater in this zone, the specific yield of sediment per unit area will probably decrease because of this temporary storage aspect.

The geochemical system is generally subsidiary to that of mechanical weathering in mountain areas, due to the lower temperatures, which retard chemical reactions. However, where run-off is lower, because of the presence of snow or ice, then mechanical weathering will have produced more fine material to provide greater surface areas for chemical processes to operate on. Though chemical erosion rates have been shown to be quite high in some Alpine glacierised catchments, this does not happen in all instances where ice is present. For instance, the metasediments of the European Alps may produce high rates of chemical weathering, but the more acid metamorphic rocks of Norway do not. Solution loads in these glacier-fed catchments are negligible in many cases.

Figure 7.7:
River Derwent, Cumbria, transporting slope and glacial materials

See accompanying CD-Rom

Mountains.ppt

Figure 7.8:
Austerdola River, Austerdalen, Norway

See accompanying CD-Rom

Mountains.ppt

Some hazards either only, or largely, occur in mountain environments, for example, snow avalanche or most rock slides. Other hazards, such as debris flows, flash floods, and most glacier hazards, are mainly but not exclusively found in mountain regions throughout the world. Mountains are seen as extreme geomorphic environments. In this context, we can categorise, for example, intermontane basins of high aridity, locations of fire-susceptible mountain forests, areas of extremely steep slopes with little vegetation, and areas of explosive volcanicity. These extremes are generally regarded as the reasons for mountains being perceived as especially hazardous places. Having

See ch 6, Geohazards (p164).

said this, hazards in mountain areas are often under-represented as they are frequently triggered by non-mountain causal agents. An example here might be the Mount Huascarán avalanche [☞]. In this context, the linking of factors creating hazardous conditions needs to be stressed. Most volcanic eruptions and earthquakes occur at plate boundaries, as do mountain areas. At the same time, the mountainous areas are also where high intensity rainfall storms often happen. These agents account for more than half of all mountain hazard event triggers. Gravitational, glacial, fluvial or aeolian forces do the main damage, with mass movement events being the most powerful.

The vast majority of major earthquake disasters have taken place in the still-forming Alpine mountain belts, and account for over one-third of all mountain geohazards. Clearly the key link here is between plate boundary and mountain belt formation, with earthquake and surface processes then taking over, and being directly responsible for the impacts and casualties. A survey by Hewitt (2004) of the 242 largest earthquake disasters in the 1950 to 1990 period identified that 95% of the earthquakes occurred entirely or significantly in mountain areas. Where mechanisms for damage were cited, geomorphic processes were the direct cause in over 50%, and the largest cause of death in over 30%. In general, in mountain areas, potential damage locations are related to slope steepness, composition (solid rock, unconsolidated material, water content), vegetation type and cover, and to anthropogenic landscape modifications. Patterns of damage are related directly to geomorphologically unfavourable locations. With this in mind, land use and construction controls then become fundamental in any mountain setting.

Traditional mountain societies have developed risk-aversion practices with respect to land use and settlement. They avoid either sites or seasons of high incidence of hazard events and so minimise their risks. In Norway, many rural mountain communities have animals in summer pasture (the traditional transhumance system), and stay for periods in small communities of huts to look after them. The photographs of Nystolen and Tungestolen in the Jostedal area demonstrate this (figure 7.9). These practices illustrate the point that risk is as much about perception and adaptation as it is about the extreme events themselves. Such adaptations are fine in traditional societies that have a historical background in this lifestyle, but as mountain areas are increasingly coming under pressure from people inexperienced in this way of life, then levels of risk are likely to increase, as unsound environmental practices are developed. The usage of mountain environments is increasing. This increase can be related to demands for resource exploitation, water supply, hydroelectric power generation, and for recreational activities such as skiing and snowboarding. Such scenarios result in more people, more inexperience, and hence increased risk in such environments when hazard events occur.

Figure 7.9: Nystolen and Tungestolen, at the meeting of Langedalen and Austerdalen, Norway

See accompanying CD-Rom

Mountains.ppt

The Jostdal Valley in Norway is a good example of the increasing use of a mountain area for resource and recreation. In the late 1980s, a joint hydroelectric power (HEP) and flood control scheme was started at Styggevatn in the north-west extremity of the valley. This scheme involved a major dam project to join two lakes together in order to provide water supply for the HEP scheme and to control one of the two main glacier-fed tributaries to the Jostedal Valley [☞] (figure 7.10). The increased size of the lake, due to dam construction, has produced a water body directly fed from the Austdalsbreen glacier. As well as affording control to meltwater discharges and reducing flood hazard in the area below the dam, this has introduced the possibility of sieches (tsunami waves generated in lakes by rock or ice falls as well as earthquakes) occurring in the lake. A suitable safety margin between the water height and the top of the dam has been designed to allow for this rare possibility. The dam is sensitively blended into the landscape as a scree-covered feature and the water abstraction and HEP plant are all carved out of tunnels and chambers underneath the mountains. The mined rock was used in the dam construction and access road maintenance. Although the access roads are no longer fully maintained, they have increased access to the mountains and led to a number of walking routes being established. The reduced flood risk, as a result of the engineering works protecting and improving road access, along with the provision of state grants, has increased levels of local camping and pensionjat (guest house) provision, and resulted in facilities being upgraded. In the last three to four years, this has resulted in an increase in visitor numbers, and has resulted in activities such as glacier guiding, ice walking, mountain guiding and glacier lake rafting enterprises becoming established. This development can be seen as a success story in terms of the increased use of natural landscape resources, but also highlights the potential for greater vulnerability of visitors, because of the higher-risk activities being undertaken.

MAKING THE LINKS

See ch 5, Ice (p113) and ch 6, Geohazards (p158).

Figure 7.10: The Jostdal Valley in Norway

Teaching idea 7.2

Ask students to produce a recreation-themed holiday advertisement and/or guide to the Jostedal region. Students might use Google Earth images, local websites such as *www.jostedal.com* and the photos supplied in figure 7.10.

See accompanying CD-Rom

Mountains.ppt

Natural and anthropogenic process change

Anthropogenic activities tend to affect the environment and the processes operating therein to a greater or lesser extent. This means that, although we may consider physical processes responsible for the development of our modern environment, this increasingly has to be modified, as we begin to appreciate the impact of humans on these processes, both today and in the past.

A case study of West Lancashire

The influence of humankind on the landscape can be seen everywhere. For instance, if we look at the area from the West Pennine Moors across the south-west Lancashire Plain to the Irish Sea, we have a landscape that appears to be composed of natural elements with little evidence of the influence of people much before Roman times. However, place name evidence from the Roman period onwards, such as Ribchester and Ormskirk, suggests a greater human impact. Medieval buildings such as Rufford Old Hall provide evidence of settlement, while industrialisation and urbanisation in the 19th and 20th centuries have increased the level of human impact. Transport landscapes can be added to the previous layers of settlement, as with the modern motorway landscape. All this evidence shows the continuance of human impact for more than 2,000 years. If, however, we look a little deeper, we can find evidence of Bronze Age on the moors, as at Round Loaf barrow, and a plethora of flint arrow heads and other artefacts in the blanket peat (see figure 7.11 on p181). Moving towards the coast, examples of flint arrow heads have been located in the River Douglas floodplain. Other indicators of prehistoric impacts on the landscape include spherical carbon particles (SCPs), indicative of high-temperature burning for charcoal production and indicators of woodland reduction to a more open habitat (probably woodland clearance), which have been identified in the pollen record at Mere Sands Wood LNR (Local Nature Reserve) near Rufford. On the coast at Formby, there are Neolithic human and animal footprints found in estuarine silt beds, which are exposed when the current sandy beach is combed down. Such evidence puts back the story of human influence in the landscape several thousand years. It also helps to explain the reduction in trees underneath the blanket peat of the moorlands, if we think of people living at the coast moving inland as continued post-glacial sea-level rise flooded their habitats. As people were forced to move inland, population densities would increase, lifestyles would change and local resources would be put under pressure. Initially, this impact would be on woodland. Subsequently, the cultivation of crops would have a major impact on vegetation and, through this, surface processes. Humans have been affecting the landscape for a long time.

Teaching idea 7.3

Ask students to investigate within their local area: place names, archaeological sites, medieval field systems or any other evidence of human impacts. Ask them to compile this evidence and then make an assessment of the impacts of people on the landscape over time? What does the evidence tell us about the effects of natural processes alone?

Figure 7.11: West Lancashire

See accompanying CD-Rom

West Lancashire.ppt

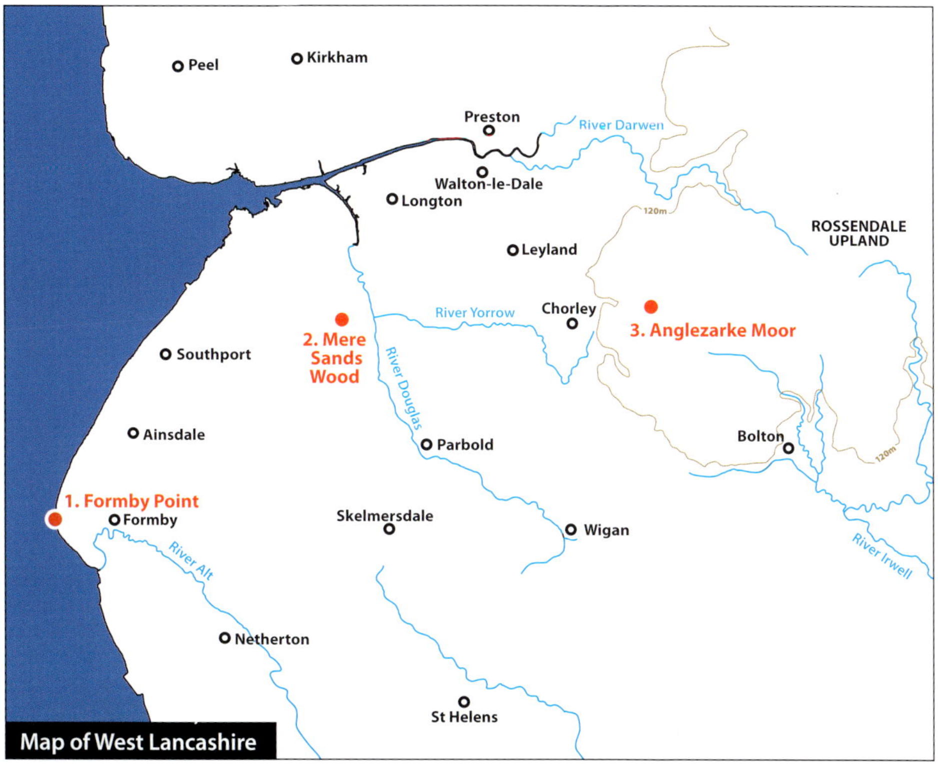

Map of West Lancashire

Anglezarke Moor

Anglezarke Moor

Mere Sands Wood section

Formby footprints

Travelling further back in time, we start to move through the early Holocene into the Post Glacial and then the Late Glacial. The last main glacial advance in Britain was the Late Devensian maximum around 18,600BP (before present). At that time, ice covered an area from the Pennines across part of the Irish Sea and down towards Birmingham. As this ice started to melt, so the glacial processes changed from active ice producing subglacial lodgement and meltwater processes, to those associated with ice decay, such as terminal moraine and kettle hole features. In turn, these features would

See ch 5, Ice (p132).

be modified by fluvioglacial elements, such as the main drainage channels dissecting moraines and drumlins to the north and east of Chorley, which are now used as a major reservoir complex (figure 7.12). As ice retreated further, so slope failure would take place on unvegetated slopes under the paraglacial environment [☞]. Elsewhere, the fluvioglacial and glacial deposits would be affected by wind activity, producing loess and coversand deposits like the quartz-rich Shirdley Hill Sand of the south-west Lancashire Plain. Climatic change resulting in an increase in temperature and moisture moves us into the Holocene, where we begin to establish a cool, temperate climate and the geomorphological processes with which we are more familiar today.

Figure 7.12: Landscape to west of Anglezarke

See accompanying CD-Rom

West Lancashire.ppt

See ch 6, Geohazards (p141).

As we can see, the current development of a landscape anywhere is but a quasi-equilibrium stage; one that is increasingly seen as an interaction between natural and anthropogenic influences. This can provide hazards, such as flooding by rivers [☞] in extreme rainfall events, which can be exacerbated by human aspects, such as the building of bridges or the occupancy of floodplain areas, but can also produce useful resources. The Shirdley Hill Sands, for example, being over 99% quartz rich, were the reason for the development of the glass industry in southern Lancashire, especially around the town of St Helens. The glass industry is now much reduced in scale, and the sand comes from mainland Europe, most of the workable Shirdley Hill sand having been covered by urban and industrial developments in the region.

See Volume 3: Environmental Geography, particularly ch 7, Environmental management.

The previous example has illustrated how the current landscape is the product of past landforms, materials and processes being modified all the time, as natural processes operate and change, but with an increasing direct and indirect influence from the activities of people. This increasing impact of people on natural systems needs a global perspective to appreciate it fully. There are plenty of examples of modifications and damage to ecosystems [☞] – rainforest clearances, oceans (overfishing, oil pollution), water supply, salination, atmosphere, increases in greenhouse gases – and of damage to surface processes – for instance, land use changes and construction, which often increase slope instability and erosion. Examples of such developments can be found all round the globe. It was increasing evidence of these effects that led to the United Nations Conference on Environment and Development [☞] in 1992, the Rio Earth Summit. This was probably the first time that there was a full appreciation, at governmental level, of the need to view the evolution and continued wellbeing of our planet as a global issue, and that it would need the cooperation of countries everywhere to eventually reach an acceptable level of sustainability. The conference produced five key outcomes: the conventions on climate change and biodiversity, the statements of principle on sustainable forest products, the right of countries to their own natural resources, and an obligation not to damage the environment of other countries, along with the Agenda 21 [☞] action plan, which was seen as a blueprint for action on environment and development. The Rio Summit marked the beginning of a sequence of international gatherings, which have managed to focus attention on the continuing human impact on natural processes around the world and how our planet operates.

See Volume 3: Environmental Geography, ch 6, Sustainability (p186-187).

See Volume 3: Environmental Geography, Ch 6, Sustainability (p153).

The increasing concern about the state of the natural environment, at national and global levels, has led to greater use of modern technologies for monitoring our environment. Global standards have become more common in the collection, analysis, interpretation and presentation of environmental data. Global statistics can now be more meaningfully assembled and disseminated. Remote sensing, computer simulation modelling and the use of geographical information systems (GIS) have seen great advances in these areas. Many elements are now monitored regularly by satellite, from the short-term movement of weather patterns and storm tracks, to the longer-term spread of deserts and the fluctuations in glacier ice coverage. Monitoring such as this is particularly useful in helping us to construct and appreciate a more detailed understanding of how our global environment works, and how it is being affected by human activities.

The adoption of a more global perspective on surface processes and human influences has allowed us to appreciate just how widespread some environmental problems are, and that there is often a knock-on effect from one place to another when we affect natural processes, and when we try to manage them effectively. Our knowledge of the workings of the environment is not yet good enough to see all the linkages, but it is improving.

Managing natural processes

The River Nile

The River Nile (see figure 7.13 on p184) can be used here as an example to illustrate some of these linkages, and to see how benefits can be achieved from environmental management, but also how problems can develop. The Nile is the longest river in the world at 6,700km, and drains roughly 10% of Africa, some 4.5 million square kilometres. The Nile is sourced from the Ethiopian Highlands (the Blue Nile) and the East African Plateau (the White Nile), and flows across the Sudan and the eastern Sahara desert in Egypt on its way to the Mediterranean. Some 95% of the population of Egypt live along the banks of the Nile or on its delta. Regular flooding has produced a nutrient-rich, moist floodplain, which has been occupied for millennia. In the past 5,000 years the climate has been drier, and the desertification of the Sahara has increased, with the result that people have relied more and more on the river for their water supply.

Figure 7.13: Map of the River Nile

See accompanying CD-Rom

Nile.ppt

The Nile has an annual late-summer flood regime, and gravity-fed irrigation systems have been used along it for over 6,000 years. In the 1840s, small dams were constructed on the Nile Delta to store water, allowing for year-round irrigation to supply an increasing population. With the increasing demand for water, annual flow variations from flood to drought conditions increased in importance, as did the need to coordinate the increasingly disparate and uncoordinated local water management initiatives.

A number of coordinated schemes took place between 1900 and 1960. The main element was the construction of the Aswan Dam. First built in 1902 and with its level raised in 1912 and 1934, ultimately standing some 190m high and storing 5.7km^3 of water for controlled irrigation, the dam was modified for hydroelectric power (HEP) generation in 1960. Between 1960 and 1969, the Aswan High Dam (see figure 7.14 on p185) was built some 6km upstream from the original dam, with the purpose of reducing drought and offering flood protection, providing water for irrigation to support increased agricultural demand, and to produce HEP for Egypt's increasing industrial base. The High Dam is 111m high and nearly 4,000m across the top, and has created Lake Nasser, some 480km long and up to 16km wide, which has a capacity of 160km^3 of water (roughly two years' average flow of the Nile). It houses 12 HEP turbines.

Figure 7.14: Aswan High Dam

See accompanying CD-Rom

Nile.ppt

The scheme has been successful in terms of flood and drought control. It has allowed irrigation to increase agricultural production from an original cropping pattern of one crop following the annual flood, into a system where triple cropping has become possible. As a result of the scheme, nearly 4,000km^2 of adjacent desert has been converted into agricultural land. The electricity generated by the scheme is a renewable and sustainable resource, providing some 7,000kWh of energy per year.

In terms of its initial design, the scheme is undoubtedly a success, but there have been a number of detrimental impacts from the scheme. At a human level, the construction of Lake Nasser resulted in the displacement of 100,000 people, with many being forced to leave their homes. Meanwhile, a range of physical processes have had significant impacts on human livelihoods and activities. Water losses from seepage into the sandstone underneath Lake Nasser and from the unlined canal network delivering irrigation water to the fields, as well as high evaporation rates of the reservoir water, have reduced the irrigation supply to approximately 50% of the expected quantities. The seepage has raised groundwater levels, and some groundwater can now be abstracted, but this water evaporates as it nears the surface resulting in increases in salinity. Now that the annual flood no longer happens, there is no annual removal of these salts precipitated at the surface from groundwater evaporation. At the same time, the evaporation rates from the reservoir and the canal systems produce water over 10% more saline than that of the former Nile. Increased salinity levels have begun to have an impact on crop yields – salt crystallisation damages root hairs, and so plants are less able to acquire nutrients and water from the soil moisture. The dam is an effective sediment trap, and collects roughly 100 million tonnes of sediment per year. Even at this rate, the life expectancy of the reservoir is over 500 years, an extra 25% capacity having been built into the original design in anticipation of this eventuality.

Beyond the river itself, the Nile is a major source of water and water-born nutrients for the south-east Mediterranean, and is the sediment supply for the Nile Delta. Both of these areas are now experiencing significantly reduced levels of nutrients. The Nile Delta is increasingly unable to combat coastal erosion, as a result of its reduced sediment supply, and so agricultural lands are becoming vulnerable. Natural nutrient supply is much reduced now that flooding is controlled, with the result that large quantities of expensive commercial fertilisers have to be used.

In terms of direct human impacts, the knock-on effect of reduced nutrients is felt by the fishing industry in the south-eastern Mediterranean, with the Egyptian fishing industry losing an estimated 3,000 jobs, while specific catches, such as sardines, have fallen by up to 95%. The incidence of the water-transmitted disease schistosomiasis (bilharzia) has increased. The disease, which is painful and debilitating and can be fatal, is carried by snails living in shallow water along the river. The population of these snails has grown as they are no longer being culled by the annual flooding of the Nile.

The Aswan Dam is a successful scheme in many ways, but it also illustrates the problems of not understanding the process systems operating at the Earth's surface and how they interlink. It clearly shows how much people depend on the natural environment and its resources, and that the development of sustainable management of the environment is very difficult to achieve. It will be interesting to reflect in 40 years' time on the effectiveness of environmental management strategies relating to the more recent Three Gorges Project in China (figure 7.15).

Figure 7.15: Three Gorges Dam

See accompanying CD-Rom

Nile.ppt

Currently, there are some interesting similarities between the two schemes. The main part of the Three Gorges Project is situated some 38km from the associated Gezhouba Dam completed in 1988, and consists of three major elements – dam, HEP generation and ship locks – and aims to provide flood control for the middle and lower reaches of the Yangtze River. The HEP element has 26 generators of 700,000kW each and an annual output of some 84.7bn kWh. Power was first generated on 10 July 2003. The ship locks can accommodate vessels up to 10,000 tonnes, with a single 3,000-tonne capacity vertical lift, and the rise in water level above the dam will improve navigation for 660km in Sichuan Province. The locks came into operation on 26 June 2003.

Teaching idea 7.4

Ask students to undertake a research exercise to investigate the Three Gorges Project and then try to identify the potential benefits and contrast those with potential drawbacks. A debate/role-play might be instigated, with students taking the position of different groups that either benefited or suffered as a result of the scheme. A useful starting point would be: *http://en.wikipedia.org/wiki/Three_Gorges_Dam* along with *www.internationalrivers.org/node/356*

Global process variations

One of the inevitable consequences of our current global warming [☞] scenario will be a rise in sea level. These sea-level rises are brought about by global eustatic sea-level fluctuations, which represent changes in the level of the world's oceans with respect to the land surfaces. Such changes usually relate to global glacio-eustatic or tectono-eustatic causes, or are a result of regional or local isostatic and tectonic changes (see chapter 1 [☞]). If temperatures rise, the oceans heat up and so expand, glacier and subsurface ice melts and returns cold water to the oceans, which reduces their heating for a time, but adds more volume to them. Surface ice melt unloads the land and can trigger local isostatic or tectonic movements. Overall, this is a complex situation which can only be resolved at a local level with any accuracy. Sea level will rise by different amounts in different places (see figure 7.16 on p188 for variations in this isostatic rebound around the British Isles).

See Volume 3: Environmental Geography, ch 3, Climate change.

See ch 1, Restless Earth (p25).

Given that some global rise in sea level is inevitable, it is appropriate to consider the impacts of such a rise. In a general sense, a rise in sea level might be expected to cause increased coastal erosion and coastal flooding. This would remove many of the present buffer regions of wetlands or dunes, and so storm surges and tsunami could be expected to become more effective because of the increased exposure of the coast. This higher sea level would also exacerbate the impact of any elevation in the sea surface level due to low atmospheric pressure. Most of our understanding about sea-level rise is related to the glacial-interglacial fluctuations throughout the Quaternary [☞], where the basic premise of sea-level drop as ice builds up, and sea-level rise as it melts, is greatly affected by changes in the shape of the globe. These changes are a result of changes in the loading of the crust on the underlying mantle, the effects of local tectonic activity triggered by these changes, the rate of any adjustments, and the worldwide ongoing suite of plate tectonic movements.

See ch 1, Restless Earth (p11).

Dating of changes over the late Quaternary from around the globe enable us to make out some general trends in sea-level behaviour. There are periods of relatively stable sea levels, periods of sea-level rise, periods of sea-level fall and periods of rapid, sometimes rather catastrophic change (see figure 7.17 on p189). Rapid sea-level rises have occurred at the ends of glacial stages. For example, between 140 and 128kBP (thousands of years before present) sea level rose from -130 to 0m as ice masses melted and water returned to the oceans. Between 18 and 7kBP, at the end of our most recent glacial phase, sea level rose from -125 to +5m, with a major impact on the location of coastlines and the flooding of continental shelf areas as well as on the long profile and erosion and deposition within river channels [☞].

See ch 2, Rivers (p55-56) and ch 3, Coasts, figure 3.24.

Figure 7.16: Isostatic readjustments around the British Isles

See accompanying CD-Rom

Global.ppt

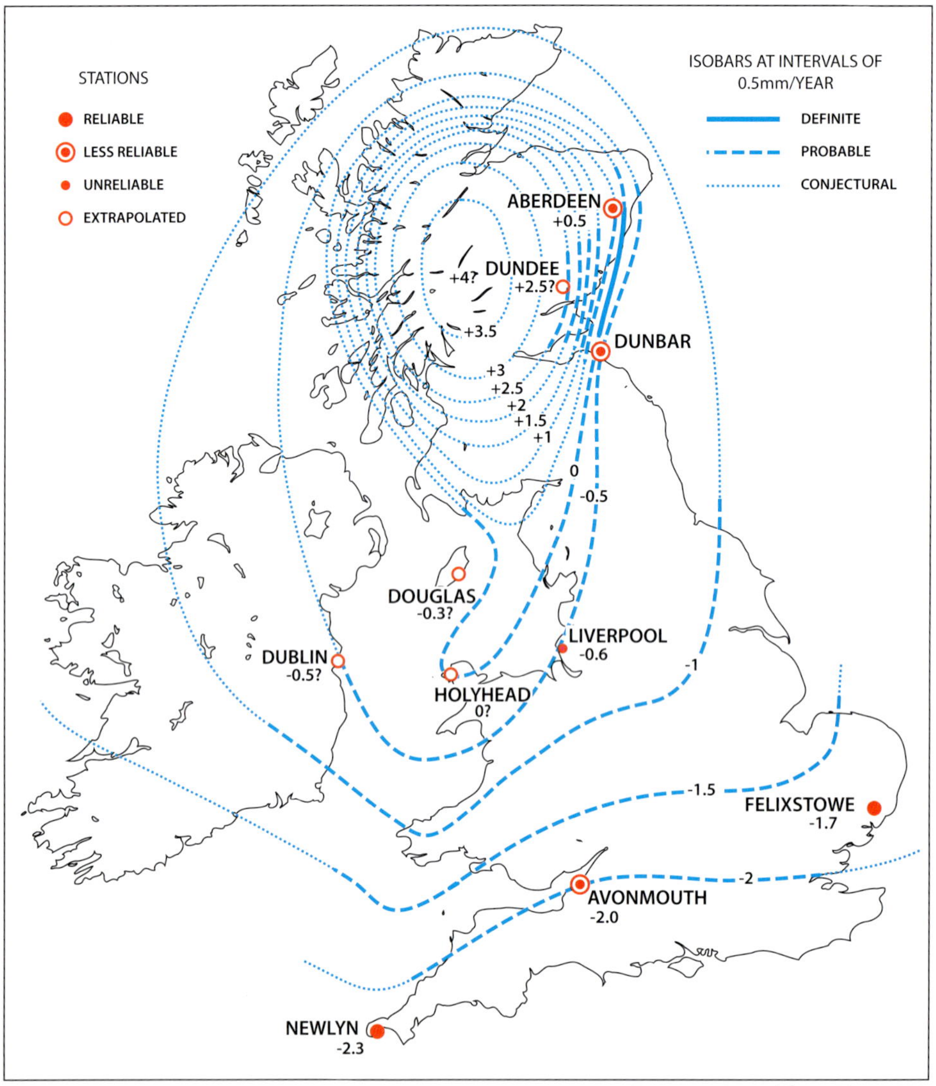

Source: adapted from King 1972.

We have had stable sea levels during warm interglacial phases between distinct glacial episodes, such as that from 128 to 115kBP and also during interstadials (short warm periods within a cold phase) and during one stadial (short glacial episode) from 70 to 60kBP. There have been sharp step-like falls within glacial periods, such as the last main glacial period (late Devensian) when, between 29 and 18kBP, sea level fell from -75 to -120m below its current level. Sea-level behaviour after the peak of this last major ice advance at around 18kBP is dated by the drowning and growth of coral reefs in the Caribbean and Atlantic regions. Here, also, we see that time-averaged curves are misleading. Despite an average of 10mm per year for the period as a whole, the record shows a series of step-like episodes with a 13.5m rise at 14.2kBP, a 7.5m rise at 11.5kBP and a 6.5m rise at 7.6kBP. This suggests slower rates or even stability for parts of this late and post-glacial period and indicates that so far our knowledge on the exact nature of sea-level changes is incomplete at best. The 11.5kBP rise is at the end of the Younger Dryas cold phase, when changing snow accumulation and airborne dust rates indicate a global climate change over a 20 to 50-year time period. Catastrophic megaflood events of meltwater lakes emptying could account for some of these rapid changes. For example, the discharge of Lake Agassiz in North

Time kBP	Movement	Nature of movement	Type of period
4.8 to now	Slowing to 1.25mm	Rise	Post-glacial
7.0 to 4.8	5.45mm per year	Rise	Post-glacial
7.6	6.5m	Rapid rise	Post-glacial
11.5	7.5m	Rapid rise	Post-glacial, cold
14.2	13.5m	Rapid rise	Post-glacial
18 to 7	-125 to +5m	Rise	Late to post-glacial
29 to 18	-75 to -120m	Fall	Glacial
40 to 36		Stable	Interstadial
60 to 58		Stable	Interstadial
70 to 60		Stable	Stadial
72 to 70	-50 to -80m	Fall	Glacial
80 to 74	-27 to -60	Fall	Glacial
82 to 80		Stable	Interstadial
95.5 to 94		Stable	Interstadial
105 to 100		Stable	Interstadial
115 to 110	-8 to -50	Fall	Glacial
128 to 115		Stable	Interglacial
140 to 128	-130 to 0	Rise	Late to post-glacial

Figure 7.17: The nature of recent sea-level changes

See accompanying CD-Rom

Global.ppt

America about 8,000 years ago is estimated as being responsible for a eustatic sea-level rise of between 20 and 42cm and would also have had a marked effect on global ocean temperatures and ocean circulation patterns and, through these, atmospheric temperatures as well. These dramatic events put a different complexion on the nature of climate and sea-level changes. The later Holocene has seen the rate of sea-level rise slowing to an average of 5.45mm per year between 7,000 and 4,800 years ago and since then slowing to an annual rate of 1.25mm by today.

There are many difficulties in trying to map this natural level of sea-level rise, and correlating this rise with anthropogenically induced rises. At a local level, the coastlines themselves may be changing due to local tectonic movements, sediment compaction and the removal of groundwater. These factors may be causing land subsidence, for example, independent of global ocean volume increase. Only when natural local changes are accounted for can we try to extract any anthropogenically induced changes. A number of attempts have been made, but the accuracy of these is still being questioned. Overall, sea level is rising, but this may almost entirely be due to the natural factors of thermal expansion of sea water, growth and decay of glaciers and small ice caps, continued melting of the Greenland Ice Sheet, and mass balance changes in the Antarctic Ice Sheet. Projected sea-level rise predictions are continually being modified.

Teaching idea 7.5

Ask students to select a stretch of coastline. Produce a map of the area and its main infrastructure. Ask them to estimate what would happen in the event of a 10cm and a 50cm rise over the next 25 and 100 years respectively. Ask them to discuss possible management scenarios to mitigate the effects of such rises in sea level.

Summary

In this section of the volume, we have presented some ideas on the similarity of processes around the globe, and on the global linkage of landscape elements. At the same time, we have considered the plate tectonic paradigm. The linkage of natural landscape-modifying processes to those anthropogenically produced has been identified. This linkage has been discussed in terms of the problems associated with the sustainable management of our world. We have seen how, with issues such as global warming, it is so difficult to identify clearly the causal agents, and to determine how we may manage our human impacts, and perhaps try to mitigate against natural ones. To return to the introduction to this section, there is a certain 'wow' factor in studying our global environments, in looking at some of the natural wonders of our world; there are many amazing places to see and discover. Despite an increasing focus on environmental problems, our world is an amazing place and we need to inspire our students to appreciate it.

Useful websites

For the Aswan Dam: *http://en.wikipedia.org/wiki/Aswan_Dam http://en.wikipedia.org/wiki/*

For the Three Gorges Dam: *http://en.wikipedia.org/wiki/Three_Gorges_Dam*

A useful website for many rivers: *www.internationalrivers.org/node/356*

Further reading

Owens, PN and Slaymaker, O (Eds) (2004) *Mountain Geomorphology*. Arnold, London.

References

Ballantyne, CK and Benn, DI, 'Paraglacial slope adjustment and resedimentation following glacier retreat, Fabergstolsdalen, Norway' in *Arctic and Alpine Research*, 26 (1994) 255-269.

Brown, GC and Mussett, AE (1981) *The Inaccessible Earth*. London, Allen & Unwin.

Charlton, R (2008) *Fundamentals of Fluvial Geomorphology*. Oxford, Routledge.

Coch, NK (1995) *Geohazards, Natural and Human*. Prentice-Hall, New Jersey.

Collins, A (2009) *Disaster and development*. Abingdon, Routledge.

Cooke, JC and Doornkamp, J (1974) *Geomorphology in Environmental Management* (1st Ed). Oxford, Clarendon Press.

Department of Environment (1994) *Landsliding in Great Britain*. HMSO, London.

Department for Environment, Food and Rural Affairs (2006) *Working with the grain of nature – taking it forward: Volume I. Full report on progress under the England Biodiversity Strategy 2002-2006*. Bristol, Defra. http://publications.environment-agency.gov.uk/pdf/GEH00508BOAH-E-E.pdf

Dury, GH (1981) *An Introduction to Environmental Systems*. London, Heinemann.

European Environment Agency (2006) *The Changing faces of Europe's coastal areas*. Copenhagen, EEA. www.eea.europa.eu/publications/eea_report_2006_6

Eurosion (2004a) *Living with coastal erosion in Europe: Sediment and Space for Sustainability PART I – Major findings and Policy Recommendations of the EUROSION project*. www.eurosion.org/reports-online/part1.pdf

Eurosion (2004b) *Living with coastal erosion in Europe: Sediment and Space for Sustainability PART II – Maps and statistics*. www.eurosion.org/reports-online/part2.pdf

Goudie, A and Wilkinson, J (1977) *The warm desert environment*. Cambridge, Cambridge University Press.

Heezen, BC and Tharp, M (1977) *World Ocean Floor*. US Navy, Office of Naval Research.

Hewitt, K, 'Geomorphic hazards in mountain environments' in Owens, PN and Slaymaker, O (Eds) (2004) *Mountain Geomorphology*, pp.187-218. London, Arnold.

Holden, J (Ed) (2008) *An Introduction to Physical Geography and the Environment* (2nd Ed). Essex, Pearson.

Intergovernmental Panel on Climate Change (IPCC). www.ipcc.ch/publications_and_data/publications_and_data_reports.htm#1

Isacks, B, Oliver, J and Sykes, LR, 'Seismology and the new global tectonics' in *Journal of Geophysical Research*, 73 (1968) 5855-5899.

King, CAM (1972) *Beaches and Coasts* (2nd Ed). London, Edward Arnold.

King, CAM (1984) *Aspects of Geography – Glaciation*. Macmillan.

Knight, PG (1999) *Glaciers*. UK, Stanley Thornes (Publishers) Ltd.

McKenzie, DP and Parker, RL, 'The North Pacific: an example of tectonics on a sphere' in *Nature*, 216 (1967) 1276-80.

Nicholls, RJ and Lowe, JA, 'Benefits of mitigation of climate change for coastal areas' in *Global Environmental Change*, Volume 14, Issue 3 (2004) pp229-244.

Owens, PN and Slaymaker, O (Eds) (2004) *Mountain Geomorphology*. London, Arnold.

Pethick, J (1984) *An Introduction to Coastal Geomorphology*. London, Arnold.

Safecoast (2007) *Quick scan climate change adaptation with a focus on coastal defence policies in five North Sea countries*. http://safecoast.org/editor/databank/File/Quick_scan_climate_change_adaptation_SC_template.pdf

Smith, AG, 'Continental Drift' in Gass, IG, Smith, PJ and Wilson, RCL (1972) Understanding the Earth (Ch 15). Open University Press – Artemis.

Smithson, P, Addison, K and Atkinson, K (4th Ed) (2008) *Fundamentals of the Physical Environment*. Oxford, Routledge.

Stehr, N and Storch, HV, 'Introduction to papers on mitigation and adaptation strategies for climate change: protecting nature from society or protecting society from nature?' *Environmental Science and Policy*, 8 (2005) 537-540.

Stern, N (2005) *Stern Review final report*. HM Treasury.

Stern, N (2007) *The Economics of Climate Change: The Stern Review*. Cambridge, Cambridge University Press.

Strahler, AN, 'Quantitative Analysis of Watershed Geomorphology' in *Transactions of the American Geophysical Union*, 38 (1957) 913-20.

Sugden, DE and John, BS (1976) *Glaciers and landscape*. London, Arnold.

Vine, FJ and Matthews, DH, 'Magnetic anomalies over ocean ridges' in *Nature*, 199 (1963) 947-949.

Vine, FJ, Tuzo Wilson, J, 'Magnetic anomalies over a young oceanic ridge off Vancouver Island' in *Science*, 150 (3695) October 1965, 485-489.

Willows, RI and Connell, RK (Eds) (2003) *Climate adaptation: Risk, uncertainty and decision-making*. UKCIP Technical Report. Oxford, UKCIP.

Wolman, MG and Miller, JP, 'Magnitude and frequency of forces in geomorphic professes', in Journal of *Geology*, 68 (1960) 54-74.

Examination specification references

	AS/ A2 Specifications			GCSE Specifications					
	AQA	Edexcel	OCR	AQA A	AQA B	Edexcel A	Edexcel B	OCR A	OCR B
Restless Earth									
Earth model				✔			✔		
The theory of plate tectonics	✔	✔		✔	✔	✔	✔		✔
Tectonic and structural landscapes	✔	✔		✔	✔	✔	✔		✔
Land and sea-level changes	✔			✔			✔		
Rock types and materials	✔			✔					
Landscape change over time	✔			✔					
Landscape geodiversity				✔					
Rivers									
Inputs to river systems	✔		✔	✔		✔	✔		✔
Flood events	✔		✔	✔		✔	✔		✔
River channels	✔		✔	✔		✔	✔		✔
River system response to environmental change	✔		✔	✔		✔	✔		✔
River response to anthropogenic influences	✔		✔	✔		✔	✔		✔
River channel management	✔		✔	✔		✔	✔		✔
Coasts									
Coastal zone and sea-level change	✔		✔	✔	✔	✔	✔		✔
Coastal systems	✔	✔	✔	✔	✔	✔	✔		✔
Coastal classification	✔	✔	✔	✔	✔	✔	✔		✔
Waves, currents and tides	✔	✔	✔	✔	✔	✔	✔		✔
Hard rock coastlines	✔	✔	✔	✔	✔	✔	✔		✔
Coasts and management	✔	✔	✔	✔	✔	✔	✔		✔
Deserts									
What makes a desert?	✔		✔	✔	✔		✔		
Why this aridity?	✔		✔	✔	✔		✔		
Effects of past climate change	✔		✔		✔				
Weathering processes	✔		✔		✔				
Morphological environments of hot dry deserts	✔		✔		✔		✔		

	AS/ A2 Specifications			GCSE Specifications					
	AQA	Edexcel	OCR	AQA A	AQA B	Edexcel A	Edexcel B	OCR A	OCR B
Desertification and environmental change	✔		✔	✔	✔		✔		
Humans and desert environments	✔		✔	✔	✔		✔		
Ice									
Glaciers and glacier dynamics	✔		✔	✔	✔	✔		✔	
Glacier hydrology	✔		✔	✔	✔	✔		✔	
Processes and products of glacial erosion	✔		✔	✔	✔	✔		✔	
Transportation and deposition of glacial debris	✔		✔	✔	✔	✔		✔	
Glacial landscapes	✔		✔	✔	✔	✔		✔	
The paraglacial environment	✔		✔	✔	✔	✔		✔	
Glacial environments and humans	✔		✔	✔	✔	✔	✔	✔	
Avalanches	✔	✔	✔	✔	✔	✔		✔	
Glacier floods	✔		✔	✔	✔	✔		✔	
Water resources	✔		✔	✔	✔	✔		✔	
Glacial materials	✔		✔	✔	✔	✔		✔	
Geohazards									
Geohazards in space and time	✔	✔	✔		✔	✔	✔	✔	✔
The monitoring of potential geohazards	✔	✔	✔	✔	✔	✔	✔	✔	✔
The perception of risk	✔	✔	✔	✔	✔	✔	✔	✔	✔
Earthquake hazards	✔	✔	✔	✔	✔	✔	✔	✔	✔
Volcanic hazards	✔	✔	✔	✔	✔	✔	✔	✔	✔
River flooding	✔	✔	✔	✔		✔	✔	✔	✔
Coastal flooding	✔	✔	✔	✔	✔	✔	✔	✔	✔
Slope failure		✔	✔			✔		✔	✔
Globalisation									
Mountain environments		✔	✔	✔					
Natural and anthropogenic process change			✔	✔			✔		
Managing natural processes (River Nile)			✔	✔			✔		
Global process variations			✔						

Index